SHAKESPEARE AND GENDER

RELATED TITLES

ANTIPODAL SHAKESPEARE: REMEMBERING AND FORGETTING IN BRITAIN, AUSTRALIA AND NEW ZEALAND, 1916–2016
Gordon McMullan, Philip Mead, Ailsa Grant Ferguson, Kate Flaherty and Mark Houlahan
ISBN 9781350126541

IMAGINING CLEOPATRA: PERFORMING GENDER AND POWER IN EARLY MODERN ENGLAND
Yasmin Arshad
ISBN 9781350058965

PERFORMING SHAKESPEARE'S WOMEN: PLAYING DEAD
Paige Martin Reynolds
ISBN 9781350002593

SHAKESFEAR AND HOW TO CURE IT: THE COMPLETE HANDBOOK FOR TEACHING SHAKESPEARE
Ralph Alan Cohen
ISBN 9781474228718

SHAKESPEARE AND FEMINIST THEORY
Marianne Novy
ISBN 9781472567062

SHAKESPEARE AND QUEER THEORY
Melissa E. Sanchez
ISBN 9781474256674

THE SHAKESPEARE HUT: A STORY OF MEMORY, PERFORMANCE AND IDENTITY, 1916–1923
Ailsa Grant Ferguson
ISBN 9781474295840

WOMEN MAKING SHAKESPEARE: TEXT, RECEPTION AND PERFORMANCE
Gordon McMullan, Lena Cowen Orlin and Virginia Mason Vaughan
ISBN 9781408185230

SHAKESPEARE AND GENDER

SEX AND SEXUALITY IN SHAKESPEARE'S DRAMA

Kate Aughterson and Ailsa Grant Ferguson

THE ARDEN SHAKESPEARE
LONDON • NEW YORK • OXFORD • NEW DELHI • SYDNEY

THE ARDEN SHAKESPEARE
Bloomsbury Publishing Plc
50 Bedford Square, London, WC1B 3DP, UK
1385 Broadway, New York, NY 10018, USA

BLOOMSBURY, THE ARDEN SHAKESPEARE and the Arden Shakespeare
logo are trademarks of Bloomsbury Publishing Plc

First published in Great Britain 2020

Copyright © Kate Aughterson and Ailsa Grant Ferguson, 2020

Kate Aughterson and Ailsa Grant Ferguson have asserted their right
under the Copyright, Designs and Patents Act, 1988, to be identified as
the authors of this work.

For legal purposes the Acknowledgements on pp. ix–x constitute an extension
of this copyright page.

Cover design: Charlotte Daniels
Cover image © Ingrid Pollard

All rights reserved. No part of this publication may be reproduced or transmitted in any form or
by any means, electronic or mechanical, including photocopying, recording, or any information
storage or retrieval system, without prior permission
in writing from the publishers.

Bloomsbury Publishing Plc does not have any control over, or responsibility
for, any third-party websites referred to or in this book. All internet addresses
given in this book were correct at the time of going to press. The author and publisher regret any
inconvenience caused if addresses have changed or sites
have ceased to exist, but can accept no responsibility for any such changes.

A catalogue record for this book is available from the British Library.

Library of Congress Cataloging-in-Publication Data
Names: Aughterson, Kate, 1961- author. | Ferguson, Ailsa Grant, author.
Title: Shakespeare and gender : sex and sexuality in Shakespeare's drama /
Kate Aughterson and Ailsa Grant Ferguson.
Description: London ; New York : The Arden Shakespeare, 2020. |
Series: The Arden Shakespeare | Includes bibliographical references and index. | Summary:
"Shakespeare and Gender guides students and teachers through the
complexities of the representation of gender and sexuality in Shakespeare's work. Informed by contemporary
debates and insights into gender and sexuality, including intersectionality, feminist geography,
queer and performance studies and fourth-wave feminism, this book provides a lucid and
lively discussion of how gender and sexual identity are debated, contested and displayed in
Shakespeare's plays and sonnets. Using close textual analysis hand-in-hand with verbal and
visual contextual materials the book offers an accessible and intelligent introduction both to
how gender debates are integral to the plays and poems, and why we continue to read and
perform them with this in mind"–Provided by publisher.
Identifiers: LCCN 2020007253 (print) | LCCN 2020007254 (ebook) |
ISBN 9781474289979 (paperback) | ISBN 9781474289986 (hardback) |
ISBN 9781474289993 (eBook) | ISBN 9781474290005 (ePDF)
Subjects: LCSH: Shakespeare, William, 1564-1616–Criticism and interpretation. |
Sex (Psychology) in literature. | Feminism. | Queer theory.
Classification: LCC PR3069.S45 A94 2020 (print) | LCC PR3069.S45 (ebook) |
DDC 822.3/3–dc23
LC record available at https://lccn.loc.gov/2020007253
LC ebook record available at https://lccn.loc.gov/2020007254

ISBN:	HB:	978-1-4742-8998-6
	PB:	978-1-4742-8997-9
	ePDF:	978-1-4742-9000-5
	eBook:	978-1-4742-8999-3

Typeset by Integra Software Services Pvt. Ltd.

To find out more about our authors and books visit www.bloomsbury.com
and sign up for our newsletters.

For our children and our students

It would be a thousand pities if women wrote like men, or lived like men, or looked like men, for if the two sexes are quite inadequate, considering the vastness and variety of the world, how should we manage with one only? … For we have too much likeness as it is, and if an explorer should come back and bring word of other sexes looking through the branches of other trees at other skies, nothing would be of greater service to humanity.
    Virginia Woolf, A Room of One's Own, *1929*

CONTENTS

List of Illustrations · viii
Acknowledgements · ix

Introduction · 1

1 **The Woman's Voice** · 17

2 **The Male Body, Kingship and the Body Politic** · 39
    Practitioner Perspective: Adjoa Andoh · 65

3 **Testing the Marriage Plot: Form, Violence and Gender** · 73

4 **Cross-Dressing and Gender Transgression(s)** · 97
    Practitioner Perspective: Lucy Phelps · 122

5 **Gendering Madness** · 127

6 **Paternity and Patriarchy** · 153

7 **Sexual Excess: Space, Sex and Gender** · 179

8 **Anxious Masculinity** · 205

9 **Maternal Bodies: Female Powers** · 231

Bibliography · 256
Index · 267

ILLUSTRATIONS

Figures

I.1 'The Poet's Dream Realised', from Charles Sorel (1654) *The Extravagant Shepherd*, London: Thomas Heath, plate facing p. 22   9
1.1 Emma Thompson as Beatrice and Kenneth Branagh as Benedick (4.1), *Much Ado About Nothing* (Kenneth Branagh, 1993)   28
2.1 Nigel Lindsay as Bolingbroke and David Tennant as Richard, *Richard II* (Gregory Doran, Royal Shakespeare Company, 2013)   54
4.1 *The Valorous Acts Perform'd at Gaunt, by the Brave Bonny Lass Mary Ambree* (c. 1674)   116
4.2 Imogen Stubbs as Viola and Stephen Mackintosh as Sebastian, *Twelfth Night* (Trevor Nunn, 1996)   117
4.3 Lucy Phelps as Rosalind, *As You Like It* (Kimberley Sykes, Royal Shakespeare Company, 2019)   122
6.1 Anthony Hopkins as Lear and Emma Thompson as Goneril, *King Lear* (Richard Eyre, 2018)   167
8.1 Seventeenth-century ballad, *The Hen-Peck'd Frigate*   224
9.1 Sophie Okenedo as Margaret of Anjou, *The Hollow Crown: Henry VI Part 2* (Dominic Cook, BBC, 2016)   237
9.2 Alexandra Gilbreath as Hermione, *The Winter's Tale*, (Gregory Doran, Royal Shakespeare Company, 1998)   246
9.3 Unknown artist, portrait probably depicting Anne of Denmark (c. 1605)   248

Tables

7.1 *Twelfth Night*'s Locations   187
7.2 *Antony and Cleopatra*'s Locations   193

ACKNOWLEDGEMENTS

We thank our students of Early Modern Literature and Reviewing Shakespeare for inspiring us to write this book and whose questions and fresh ideas are always a joy.

We are grateful to our colleagues in the Performance and Communities Research and Enterprise Group at the University of Brighton; in particular, for the support of Deborah Philips, Jessica Moriarty, Craig Jordan-Baker and Julie Everton. We would like to thank Emma Bell for her support and dedication and Stephen Maddison for his, as Head of School.

We are extremely grateful to staff of the University of Brighton Falmer Library, particularly Lucy Rowland; the staff at Ringmer House for all their help; our brilliant Falmer Humanities administrative and IT teams, whose expertise and dedication ensures we can balance our teaching, research and writing. In particular, we would like to thank Verity Ford for her patience and support.

We feel incredibly privileged to have worked with practitioners on interviews for this book. Huge gratitude is due to Adjoa Andoh for her illuminating interview, for supporting the use of her image for the cover of this book and for her generosity in sharing her wisdom and time. We would like to thank Lucy Phelps for her brilliant ideas and her time, and for articulating so beautifully the view from the inside of a production.

We would like to include special thanks to Coppélia Kahn, who has been an inspiration in both our careers.

We would like to thank the Royal Shakespeare Company for supporting Lucy Phelps in sharing her ideas with us; the staff at the Shakespeare Birthplace Trust, particularly Nick Walton and Paul Taylor, for their continuing help and support; Victoria Lane at the Globe Archive; and Erin Lee at the National Theatre Archive for sharing their expertise and for welcoming our students into the archives.

We would also like to thank the editorial team at The Arden Shakespeare for their support in bringing this book to print, particularly Margaret Bartley, Mark Dudgeon and Lara Bateman. We also thank all Arden play editors, particularly Ann Thompson, all of whose work has underpinned this book.

Acknowledgements

We are most deeply grateful to our families for their patience and support, without which we would not have been able to write this book at all:

Thanks to my partner Elizabeth, my children Jacob and Molly, and my mother Patricia, for their support and inspiration in writing this book. KA

Thank you to my husband Ian, my children Milo and Eada, and to my parents, Helen and Luath, for their unconditional support and inspiration. AGF

Finally, and most importantly, we would like to acknowledge each other's emotional, scholarly and academic support and inspiration throughout the truly collaborative process of writing this book.

INTRODUCTION

Claims that feminism as a political movement and analytical tool are both exhausted and no longer relevant have proved premature. The seismic global events of the 2008–9 financial crash, the increasingly urgent global climate crisis, the growth of demagogic nationalism, the #MeToo movement, the emergence of a vocal LGBTQ+ movement, and Brexit recall us to the necessity of global political awareness. Current feminist activism, sometimes describing itself as intersectional, sometimes as a 'fourth wave', locates its philosophical roots in the original feminist enterprise of equality of representation and rights on a global level (Chamberlain, 2017; Cochrane, 2013; Rivers, 2017). However, contemporary intersectional feminisms are more alert than their ancestral sisters to the diversity of femininities, female bodies, life journeys, sexualities, classes, divergent abilities and nations, and to the ways masculinities, male bodies, and unsexed bodies should be part of feminism's radical political agenda and have been used as a norm against which women and femininity are measured. This book engages inclusively with Shakespeare's plays as interventions in early modern and contemporary discourses of gender and sexuality. Contemporary performances can challenge the 400-year-old texts, find strange commonalities across the centuries and, through performance, play out both our prejudices and stereotypes of gender and sexuality, inviting us to confront them.

In 2018, the diversity campaigner Danuta Kean wrote an opinion piece for the *Guardian* that neatly articulates the problem of Shakespeare's apparently conservative gender roles and plots and the need to find a contemporary performative response, given Shakespeare's continued role as National Bard: 'So bad is the Bard's treatment of women, it could earn him a whole MeToo hashtag on Twitter …. How can the physical and psychological abuse endured by Katherina at the hands of her suitor Petruccio in *The Taming of the Shrew* be played for laughs, as originally intended?' (Kean, 2018). This book debates Shakespeare's texts within their original historical and political contexts and examines how their performativity can still unsettle and challenge stereotypes of identity despite what many argue is an underlying implicit misogyny (Daileader, 2005; Rackin, 2016). Radical unsettling can be sourced in both early modern contextual material and in the unstable nature of the performed text itself, endlessly rediscovering identity and bodies on stage.

So why gender and sexuality and why now? Four recent publications on Shakespeare and feminism help answer this: the second edition of the canon-forming *A Feminist Companion to Shakespeare* (ed. Dympna Callaghan, 2016); Valerie Traub's *The Oxford Handbook of Shakespeare and Embodiment: Gender, Sexuality and Race* (2016a); Ania Loomba and Melissa Sanchez's *Rethinking Feminism in Early Modern Studies: Gender, Race and Sexuality* (2016); and Marianne Novy's *Shakespeare and Feminist Theory* (2019) severally attest to a revival of active interest and engagement in feminism's confrontation with Shakespeare the historical playwright, Shakespeare the bard of the male canon, Shakespeare as cultural icon and Shakespeare as performed dramatist. This book shares with those four publications a sense that intersectional feminist interventions in these various versions of Shakespeare is timely, in a politicized world where gender and sexuality are still so clearly embedded in political power structures, discursive habits and theatrical practices. Challenges to those practices can come from both within and without the academy and the theatre: from all of us.

Thirty years ago, Joan Scott wrote 'Gender: A Useful Category of Historical Analysis' (1986), problematizing and situating the term 'gender', a conceptualization she has recently revisited:

> 'Gender' opened a whole set of analytic questions about how and under what conditions different roles and functions had been defined for each sex; how the very meanings of the categories 'man' and 'woman' varied according to time, context, and place; how regulatory norms of sexual deportment were created and enforced; how issues of power and rights played into definitions of masculinity and femininity; how symbolic structures affected the lives and practices of ordinary people; how sexual identities were forged within and against social prescriptions. Gender provided a way of investigating the specific forms taken by the social organization of sexual difference; it did not treat them as variations on an unchanging theme of patriarchal domination ...
>
> [G]ender continues to be useful only if it is taken as an invitation to think critically about how the meanings of sexed bodies are produced in relation to one another, how these meanings are deployed and

Introduction

changed. The focus ought to be not on the roles assigned to women and men, but on the construction of sexual difference itself.

(Scott, 2010: 10)

This notion of gender as a critical tool and an object of analysis is apposite in considering early modern and contemporary performed versions of Shakespeare's plays for four intersecting reasons. First, Elizabethan and Jacobean political theory was explicitly formulated through the figure of the father: James I's notion of kingship connected God, the King and the father in a continuum of authority and role, rendering the family a microcosm of the state and both as models of divine origin and organization (see Resource 7.d in Chapter 7, and Chapters 2 and 6). Patriarchy originates in this political and domestic philosophy: notions of the feminine and the masculine were explicitly located within early modern notions of power and hierarchy. Second, early modern notions of bodily identity were expressed through a combined architecture of humours and bodily formation, which together made up a person's physiology (Arikha, 2007). The balance of humours within an individual person could allow different characteristics to dominate, and such humours were often descriptively gendered and sexualized (Chapters 5 and 8). Third, the theatrical nature of Shakespeare's plays entails the performance of bodies on stage, which in movement and representation re(con)figure our engagement with gender through the moving and visible body as actor (Fortier, 2016: 29). Finally, performance itself has been described as a haunting (Carlson, 2001) in which past texts, performances, sets and costumes reframe themselves on the space of the stage in any one performance, summoned by collective memories of actors, audience and directors. By reviving early modern texts we are in dialogue with those past inhabitations of the represented body and, as such, must be attuned to versions of those bodies through and across time, both gendered and sexualized. This book aims to acknowledge that attunement in our engagement with Shakespeare's texts, not as part of a reverential 'heritage Shakespeare', but as an ongoing dialogue between those early modern textual/performative explorations of identity and contemporary re-engagements through performance and conversations about gender and sexuality, representation and inclusion.

Since political feminism was articulated by Mary Wollstonecraft in the late eighteenth century, feminist political action and discourse have engaged with history as a way of insisting on the necessity of political and social change. Perhaps because Shakespeare's texts were then (and now) such an integral part of national and imperial British male culture (Blocksidge, 2005), his texts and performances have often been part of such feminist debates. Shakespeare's work has been used to articulate supposedly fixed notions of power and identity in which women are marginalized and othered. However, theories of gender and sexuality have varied in focus and emphasis through the shifts within feminist debate, and there has been an ongoing fruitful cross-pollination of theories and engagement with Shakespeare's texts both on and off stage. The convention of referring to feminist theory as 'waves' has recently been critiqued (Traub, 2016b: 4), but the wave metaphor can organically connote that what appear to be distinct successive moments of theories actually intersect, roll over and through each other, and are mutually dependent and inter-relative (see Rivers, 2017). We can find first-, second-, third- and fourth-wave feminism implicit in current debates about cross-casting, equality of representation and intersectional identities. Equally, such debates can be found partially articulated by earlier women writers: the early modern poet Aemilia Lanyer, the pamphlet writer Rachel Speght, and the philosophers Mary Astell and Mary Wollstonecraft all destabilized the theological and naturalized bases for patriarchal misogyny.

First-wave feminism – built on the political writings and action of eighteenth- and nineteenth-century women (including Astell and Wollstonecraft) – fought for women's suffrage and argued for equality of representation in the political and cultural arena. In the early twentieth century, actors and suffragists experimented with voices and representations of women in Shakespeare as modes of liberation (Carlson, 2006; Duncan, 2016; Grant Ferguson, 2019). Second-wave feminism (re-invigorated alongside the counter-culture movement in the 1960s and 1970s) argued that both gender and sexuality are constructed by cultural and social norms and prescriptions, that political activism necessitated challenges to such norms. Scholarly engagements with Shakespeare's texts focused on historical re-evaluations of gender in his work (Jardine, 1983; Neely et al., 1980; Woodbridge, 1984), psychoanalytic debates about characterization (Kahn, 1981) and performative versions of the gender oppressions of characterization (see the Royal Shakespeare Company's production of *Taming of the Shrew*, 1978, dir. Bogdanov). Third-wave feminism challenged the Eurocentric, hetero-centric and white nature of second-wave feminism, broadening debates to include challenges to Shakespeare's cultural positioning as a straight male, and problematizing and challenging the plays' colonial and racial constructions of dominant identities as white and hetero-patriarchal (Lamming, 1960; Loomba, 1998; Rose, 1988; Smith, 1995; Traub, 1992; Wayne, 1991). Landmark performances informed by this cultural shift included a number of black South African and Caribbean productions (such as Suzman's 1987 *Othello* in Johannesburg) and in the UK ones such as Jonathan Miller's 1970 RSC production of *The Tempest* (Singh, 2017). Such theoretical arguments enabled discussions over whether the plays deconstructed or reinforced heteronormative and racial identities as gendered and hierarchical, locating arguments in contemporary politics and theory and in material early modern history (Alexander and Wells, 2000; Hall, 1995; Orgel, 1996; Zimmerman, 1992).

Fourth-wave feminism argues that feminist theory and activism should acknowledge the notions of difference as constitutive of identity, that the intersection of multiple oppressions and identities means that gender and sexual identities are complexly constructed and expressed and that gender and sexuality are both performative and culturally specific at different moments in time and history, inflected by bodily, cultural, sexual and racial discourses and experiences (Butler, 1993; Crenshaw et al, 1995; Traub, 2010, 2016). Feminist theory should thus be inclusive and intersectional, acknowledging and incorporating difference as complexly constitutive of identity. The chapters in this book signpost how theoretical positioning can be used to situate and challenge Shakespeare's texts. Our analyses use close linguistic and generic reading within the context of early modern discourses about gender and sexuality (such as cross-dressing); recent debates about queer performativity and intersectional identities (implicating gender, sexuality and race as co-dependent); and discussion of how bodies inform performance. Recent resurgences of feminist politics have situated a new generation of readers, performers and students to respond to articulations of Shakespeare's work as engaging with marginalized voices, identities and characters (Browne and Lim, 2009; Butler, 1993; Sedgwick, 1994; Cartelli, 2019).

The Sonnets: A Pathway to Exploring Shakespeare's Approaches to Gender

Sonnet 20
A woman's face with nature's own hand painted
Hast thou, the master-mistress of my passion;
A woman's gentle heart, but not acquainted
With shifting change as is false women's fashion;
An eye more bright than theirs, less false in rolling,
Gilding the object whereupon it gazeth;

> A man in hue, all hues in his controlling,
> Which steals men's eyes and women's souls amazeth.
> And for a woman wert thou first created,
> Till nature as she wrought thee fell a-doting,
> And by addition me of thee defeated
> By adding one thing to my purpose nothing.
> > But since she pricked thee out for women's pleasure,
> > Mine be thy love and thy love's use their treasure.

Initially Sonnet 20 appears to be addressed to a woman apostrophized directly through her physical appearance ('a woman's face ... nature's ... / thou') but one who is then reframed in the vocative address as a 'master-mistress'. Throughout this sonnet, words garner double and triple meanings: initially we read this compound noun as an intensifier of 'mistress' – his beloved is the principle owner of his love for 'her'. But in choosing the word 'master' and combining that into a hybridized word ('master-mistress') the poet connotes a new kind of being that elides (or, arguably, possesses both) the masculine *and* feminine. In the opening two lines, we read this progressively: first, we see the beloved as a woman, then as a woman who possesses the characteristics of both sexes. This doubleness of identity continues and escalates as the sonnet continues. The third line returns to the beloved's physical and gendered body ('a woman's gentle heart'), but implies that this beloved does not behave as a stereotypical 'false' woman ('not acquainted / With shifting change as is false women's fashion') – although we are unsure whether he is saying all women are false and behave thus, or whether a 'true' woman might behave differently. So far, so straightforward. However, in line seven the beloved becomes 'a man in hue': one with the appearance of a man who 'steals men's eyes and women's souls amazeth'. The figure and body of the beloved attracts attention from both sexes, an object of desire for both, and this extends the notion of the doubly gendered body to the effect of that body on how erotic attraction might overlay, expand and eradicate binary identifications of gender. Such a notion of desire sends the reader back to the poet's 'false women': the beloved, possessing cross-gendered characteristics and evoking non-binary desires effectively becomes by contrast a 'truer' woman. This doubling-back of reading and interpretation is a strategy invited by the sonnet's doubled and tripled connotations: a rereading and reinterpretation, which is itself an effective illustration of how gender and sexuality are not definable and delimited by the social and political binaries into which we confine them.

A sonnet's structure shifts argument in the final six lines (the 'volta' moment) and Shakespeare explicitly shifts the rhetorical impact of his doubled language ('And for a woman wert thou first created'), where the line's ambiguity hangs on its second word: does this mean 'as a woman' or 'for women to desire', or perhaps both? This segues immediately into the crux of the sonnet, withheld for a line in a grammatical sub-clause, 'And by addition, me of thee defeated / By adding one thing to my purpose nothing'. There can be no doubt that the 'one thing' here is a physical reference to a penis, implying both the physical gender of the beloved as a man (opposed to the 'nothing' that was slang for a woman's vagina) and the difficulty of expressing erotic desire for that physical being in a male poet's voice. The subsequent line ('But since she pricked thee out for women's pleasure') doubly evokes the writing out of gender – 'pricking' meant setting down in list – and the physical attribute of the penis. Shakespeare's pun gives Nature an active function in 'pricking' out a male body. This returns us to the beginning of the poem: the body of the beloved has a woman's face in the first line and a man's 'prick' in the penultimate. If we return to line 3's descriptor, 'not acquainted', the slang connotations (ac'cunt'ed) of the word are orally clear and would have been immediately understood by an early modern audience: 'quaint' as a slang pun for 'cunt' was well known in the period (*OED*), and the pronunciation was as 'ac(q)ernted' (Crystal, 2005: 8). The beloved does not only not behave like a false woman, he/she *is* a false woman, because s/he does not have a 'cunt'. The final line reiterates conventional early modern notions of relationships between men and women as heterosexual: with a male body, women can have him for 'use' (that is, sex) and, with that male body and soul, the poet can share a platonic love that transcends that of the body. However, that very idea of trans(cendence) implies a crossing of both physical and conceptual boundaries – as contemporary trans* theories (Enke, 2012: 5) have illuminated. The doubleness of the beloved's body, the deferred sense of identity, the crossing and interchangeability of characteristics and bodies all problematize notions of a stable physical body that is either female or male, of desire that is either hetero- or homo-oriented, and of all notions of binaries. This sonnet, in its deliberative puns, its reading arc that forces us always to go backwards and ask what is meant and in its foregrounding of sexual difference and desire as non-normative, non-binary, and both spiritual and physical, enacts some of the complex networks of meaning, desire, power and identity that Shakespeare's plays debate and enact.

Sonnet 130 is not concerned with gender in the same way, but rather with how women are written by men. The discursive convention to which it responds is the pervasive tradition of the blazon (see Chapters 1 and 3). The blazon was a convention of love poetry, used prolifically by Petrarch and adopted by many English poets, in which the female subject of the male writer's text is anatomized, part by part, in a series of standard conceits (satirized in Figure I.1). To help understand Sonnet 130, let us first look briefly at a conventional blazon. Edmund Spenser's *Epithalamion* describes the arrival of the maiden on her wedding day:

> Her goodly eyes like Sapphires shining bright,
> Her forehead ivory white,
> Her cheeks like apples which the sun hath rudded,
> Her lips like cherries charming men to bite,
> Her breast like to a bowl of cream uncrudded,
> Her paps like lilies budded,
> Her snowy neck like to a marble tower,
> And all her body like a palace fair,
> Ascending up with many a stately stare,
> To honours seat and chastity's sweet bower.

Spenser dismembers the spectacle of virginal womanhood. About to be married, the subject is 'ripe' but her chastity is clearly asserted. The extract from stanza 10 reproduced here presents a standard set of blazon conceits, comparing the young woman to a series of natural images, starting with precious items – 'sapphires', 'ivory' – and segueing into familiar pastoral signifiers of abundance – 'apples', 'cherries', 'cream', 'lilies'. These all present the woman in a state of anticipation, the virgin before the wedding night when the man will fulfil her natural purpose: the apples have ripened in the sun, the cherries lure men to eat them, the cream is as yet 'uncrudded'. An exercise in poetics and rhetoric, the anaphora of 'Her …' and sheer excess of the description, locate the subject beyond the realms of actual earthly womanhood. In the subsequent stanza he summarizes, 'There dwells sweet love and constant chastity, / Unspotted faith and comely womenhood, / Regard of honour and mild modesty': a woman who is beautiful and chaste, honourable, pious and modest and a spectacle for the 'gaze' of others rather than in possession of agency or voice of her own. By contrast, in Sonnet 130 Shakespeare de- and re-constructs the blazon convention with the meticulousness of his own approach to female beauty. Starting with his

Introduction

Figure I.1 'The Poet's Dream Realised', from Charles Sorel (1654) *The Extravagant Shepherd*, London: Thomas Heath, plate facing p. 22.

'mistress' eyes', Shakespeare refutes each of the blazon's standard conceits. He follows the inventory that anatomizes the woman part by part, yet in each line's negated conceit, Shakespeare resists the dismemberment of his sonneteering predecessors. This is still a male gaze upon a woman; yet she remains present and cohesive, seen but also heard.

Sonnet 130
My mistress' eyes are nothing like the sun;
Coral is far more red than her lips' red;
If snow be white, why then her breasts are dun;
If hairs be wires, black wires grow on her head.
I have seen roses damask'd, red and white,
But no such roses see I in her cheeks;
And in some perfumes is there more delight
Than in the breath that from my mistress reeks.
I love to hear her speak, yet well I know
That music hath a far more pleasing sound;
I grant I never saw a goddess go;
My mistress, when she walks, treads on the ground:
    And yet, by heaven, I think my love as rare
    As any she belied with false compare.

This sonnet is frequently misread as a declaration of how much the voice loves the subject *despite* her flaws: at best, an expression of love beyond physical attraction. Yet this reductive reading 'belie[s]' the sonnet as much as Shakespeare suggests other flatterers 'belie' its subject. This reading exposes rather the bias of its readers, as Zadie Smith reveals in *White Teeth* (2002), in which Irie, a girl of colour, suddenly sees a 'reflection' of herself in this sonnet, an insight quickly quashed by her white teacher:

'I just thought … like when he says, here: *Then will I swear, beauty herself is black*, … And the curly hair thing, black wires –' …
  'No, dear, you're reading it with a modern ear. Never read what is old with a modern ear. In fact, that will serve as today's principle – can you all write that down please.'
  5F wrote that down. And the reflection that Irie had glimpsed slunk back into the familiar darkness. (2002: 235)

Irie recognizes that Shakespeare challenges whiteness as a measure of beauty, presenting a beauty unlike that of the fair Caucasian women that are the standard subject of English love poetry. Where Spenser's subject has a décolletage like 'a bowl of cream uncrudded', breasts 'like lilies budded' and a 'snowy neck like to a marble tower', Shakespeare's mistress possesses no such whiteness. Her 'breasts are dun', a light brown colour, and her hair is 'black'. These features are in direct denial of the convention's blazon's conceits: 'If hairs be wires, black wires grow on her head' recalls the yellow locks of golden wire frequently praised in conventional sonnets. The common practice of reading this sonnet as insulting its subject or as a presentation of love 'despite' physical shortcomings unconsciously assumes the same white standard of beauty displayed in conventional love poetry of four or five centuries ago: Shakespeare identifies such readings as false comparisons and asks us to question whether and why 'dun' should be used pejoratively? Such (mis)readings rely upon a white, Eurocentric bias, conscious or unconscious, that equates whiteness with beauty.

This sonnet's volta is crucial to understanding the sonnet's presentation of female attractiveness. The second part of the eighth line jars, with apparently further insulting language in which he describes the mistress's breath ('reeks'). Yet this concrete detail connotes this woman who 'walks on the ground' and is viscerally present in the sonnet not via the 'gaze' of others but by her specific features: her smell and, crucially, her voice. The following line reveals the purpose of the woman's mouth in very different terms to the conventional blazon in which it is chastely shut, while erotically ripe and ready to be possessed by a man (Spenser's 'lips like cherries charming men to bite'). Shakespeare's volta refocuses on both his subject's and his own voice ('I love to hear her speak'). His resolution in the final couplet draws attention not to the conventional falseness of woman, but on the falseness of those who would flatter her with blazons: men. It is the subject who is 'belied'; she is not the trickster, spirit or 'goddess'. She is humanized: but we need not read this talkative, dark-skinned, black-haired woman as lovely *despite* but rather *for* these very features.

Sonnets 20 and 130 both reveal the complexity and doubleness of Shakespeare's representations of the self and others: language, genre and form emphasize the hybrid nature of bodily identity and its linguistic representations. Shakespeare plays with notions of norms, inverting our comfortable notions of what gender identity and ideals might be – disturbing bodily and cultural norms to suggest, perhaps, those 'other sexes', which Virginia Woolf hypothesized in *A Room of One's Own* in 1929.

How to Read This Book

Shakespeare and Gender offers a series of case explorations in which close textual reading, contextual resources and theoretical approaches open up discussion. We draw attention to the topic's complexity through ideas, readings and examples that demonstrate the richness and validity of Shakespearean scholarship and performance on gender and sexuality. This book offers a resource for students, educators and practitioners seeking to explore approaches to gender and sexuality in Shakespeare's drama as a springboard for further research and contemplation.

Each chapter includes early modern sources to contextualize the plays and emphasize the validity of incorporating literary and social contexts into how we might read Shakespeare today. To balance this broadly cultural materialist understanding of Shakespeare, we explore recent productions of the plays, to debate how gender is performed on the modern stage. Our readers may want to use chapters on specific texts to provide a viewpoint on gender and sexual relations, such as exploring father–daughter relationships in *King Lear* (Chapter 6), or Beatrice's voice in *Much Ado About Nothing* (Chapter 1), or marriage and violence (Chapter 3). Other chapters explore a single issue in a collection of texts, such as gender and space (Chapter 7). Alternatively, a reader may explore how early modern beliefs influence the text, such as how we understand the early modern idea of the body politic (Chapters 2 and 9); how Hamlet and Ophelia's 'madness' relates to medical discourses of the time (Chapter 5); how notions of fragile masculinity speak to both then and now (Chapter 8). All chapters refer to recent productions to illuminate how gender and sexuality perform on stage. Conclusions and specific suggestions for further work alongside short annotated bibliographies complete each chapter.

Chapter 1 explores the woman's voice in Shakespearean drama via a case study of *Much Ado About Nothing*'s Beatrice. The 'battle of the sexes' narrative parallels a modern romantic comedy genre; contemporary viewers can find it challenging to move away from such narrative familiarity and generalized double-standard sexual politics towards a nuanced understanding of the complex issues of the woman's voice in an early modern context. This chapter situates Beatrice in terms of the female 'wit', male silencing and Shakespeare's linguistic constructions of feminine voices in the context of the early modern all-male performance. A range of textual moments in performance situate the play within a rhetoric of gender in the context of *querelles de femmes* pamphlet discourse and Beatrice's engagement with the masculine blazon tradition. It challenges our definition of a 'female' voice on the early modern all-male stage, examining how we might overlay our contemporary concept of 'speaking truth to power' to explore Beatrice and Paulina (*The Winter's Tale*) speaking back to and disrupting patriarchal authority.

Introduction

In Chapter 2, Shakespeare's history plays are considered in the context of the early modern understanding of the sociopolitical and geographical nation in terms of the body politic analogy. Focusing on *Richard II*, this chapter asks how the body of the king actualizes the idea of the nation as body, contextualizing this within a pervasive trope of the female land. Richard is frequently portrayed as an 'effeminate' king, and we explore how this gendering plays out in the deposition scene, examining productions and early modern sources. Comparisons are made across the history plays to the synergy between kingship and the male body in *Henry IV, Henry V* and *Richard III*. Adjoa Andoh's 2019 production (with Lynette Linton, Sam Wanamaker Playhouse) used a cast and production team made up exclusively of women of colour, and explored how compounded oppressions are interrogated through the play including through the body of the king 'himself', played by Andoh. This chapter focuses on this production and is followed by an extensive interview with Adjoa Andoh on her concept, direction and performance.

Chapter 3 shows how Shakespeare's comedies engage with and challenge the classic comic plot of the trials and tribulations of courtship, family disapproval and approval, sexual rivalry, and an inclusive wedding. The chapter shows that by assuming a sophisticated audience sceptical of the romance narrative and the logic of heteronormative plots, these plays (*Taming of the Shrew, Much Ado About Nothing* and *All's Well That Ends Well*) debate the power and erotics of sexual behaviour in a strictly patriarchal society. Although plots and characters challenge dramatic and social conventions, these plays still close on the marriage celebrations of multiple heterosexual couples and between fictional characters who are dressed as man / woman couples. Shakespeare problematizes expected gender norms in sexual courtship practices (in contra-distinction to the binaries of conduct manuals and sermons). This destabilization effectively questions the masculine prerogative and the cultural injunction on female passivity and silence.

Chapter 4 discusses this problematizing of the heteropatriarchal plot in plays where cross-dressing dominates narrative and action, in particular the characters of Viola and Rosalind in *Twelfth Night* and *As You Like It*. These two characters are often central to debates about Shakespeare's supposedly radical representation of women. Cross-dressing is discussed in the context of the material early modern theatrical practice (all female parts were played by adolescent boys), as plot device and as meta-theatrical commentary. We debate whether cross-dressing is a conservative homoeroticism, a misogynist demonstration of femininity or a liberatory space to play with

13

women's voices and identities. The actors' cross-dressing and the fictional cross-dressing of the characters, we suggest, create playful uncertainties about stable gender identities. Such indeterminacy is literally played out by the plot(s) where triadic love stories foreground homoeroticism as parallel to heteroeroticism, validating desire as crossing all genders and all sexualities. The plays' finales continue this indeterminacy: Viola is not returned to her woman's clothes, remaining as Cesario, visually reinforcing the appearance of a marriage of two men. *As You Like It* is Shakespeare's only play closing on a woman's voice with Rosalind's speech moving between character and actor and the two genders each represents, a visual and verbal fluency paradigmatic of the plays' simultaneous playfulness and serious intent. This chapter is followed by an interview with actor Lucy Phelps, who discusses her acclaimed performance of Rosalind, as well as *Measure for Measure*'s Isabella, at the RSC in 2019.

Debating the dynamic state of Hamlet's 'antic disposition' frequently forms the basis of learning and teaching *Hamlet*. Chapter 5 scrutinizes this to explore the gendered nature of madness in *Hamlet* in the context of the burgeoning taxonomy of mental afflictions in early modern England. By contextualizing the play within key early modern classifications of perceived mental ill-health, such as 'the Mother', 'hysteria', lovesickness and melancholy, we argue Shakespeare's construction of the characters of Hamlet and Ophelia engenders *and* subverts proto-medicalization of madness. Ophelia's ghost appears to return in Shakespeare's late collaboration with John Fletcher in *The Two Noble Kinsmen*, in which the Jailor's Daughter's mad songs and near-drowning mirror Ophelia's fate, yet she survives to face a 'cure' of marriage and sex on the orders of a darkly comic doctor. The Elizabethan approach to female madness in *Hamlet* meets the Jacobean medicalization in *Kinsmen* to reveal the doubly vexed status of the 'madwoman' in early modern culture and performance.

Chapter 6 focuses on *King Lear* and the relationship between paternity and patriarchy. With particular interrogation of the father–daughter relationship in a patriarchal model that straddles domestic and public life, the chapter examines how a carnivalesque reversal of parent and child is compounded in *Lear* by the doubled inversion constituted by the male–female inversion of power throughout the play. In both *Lear* and *The Tempest*, a geography of paternity and patriarchy are mapped onto daughters that present the only possibility for the continuance of patriarchal power while their female bodies present a threat to patrilineage. A focus on Richard Eyre's television film (2018) exposes the politics of casting in presenting *Lear* in the twenty-first century.

Introduction

Chapter 7 shifts focus from family politics to the gendered economics of sexual space. Looking at *The Comedy of Errors, Measure for Measure, Twelfth Night, Antony and Cleopatra* and *Pericles*, we examine how men, women and their bodies are located in different spaces, with women's bodies as sites for commercial and representational exchange. The nascent economic and cultural model of capitalism impacted on expressions of gender and sexuality on and through the stage, and contemporary feminist geography helps us understand how Shakespeare points to, uses and challenges dramatic space as constitutive of (gendered and sexualized) identities.

The impact of feminism on how we think about gender and sexuality has been equally fundamental to debates about masculinity. Chapter 8 focuses on how early modern fears about cuckolding fuel anxieties of masculine failure and female betrayal in the context of marriage, sexual desire and sexuality. Fears of women's inconstancy and the inherently 'hidden' nature of female sexuality were rife because heredity remained crucial to social order. In *Othello* Shakespeare presents the trickster who can manipulate fears about female sexuality, because of common notions of what masculinity should be, to manipulate those around him; whilst in *The Winter's Tale* such stereotypes about male anxiety enable the self-destruction of the central male character, who is punished by the tragic loss of his family because of such notions. The language, motifs and plotting of anxious masculinity and the modelling of a fear of 'dangerous' female sexuality in juxtaposition with the plays' tragic or chaste resolutions offer ways into reading masculinity in these plays.

The final chapter focuses explicitly on the performative connotations of the female maternal body, through the dual prism of early modern humoral and physiological theory and contemporary embodiment theories (Bordo, 2003; Grosz, 1995; Young, 1984, 2005). In the *Henry VI* trilogy Margaret of Anjou's role (echoing Joan of Arc's embodiment and narrative arc from saviour to demonized scapegoat) focalizes the life history for an early modern woman – virgin, wife, mother and crone – through gendered bodily attributes and performance. This chapter discusses Shakespeare's exploration and manipulation of the visual embodiment of the female body as one with agency (albeit represented through the body of an adolescent boy). Focusing in particular on the representation of the maternal or pregnant body as a literal visual embodiment of woman-as-other in *Henry VI, Measure for Measure, All's Well That Ends Well* and *The Winter's Tale*, we discuss whether Shakespeare's late plays (literally) reconfigure that body as one central to the literal and metaphorical figuration of the human. The coming-alive of Hermione's statue through the physical midwifery of her servant

Paulina literally plays out the trope of female agency as bodily (re)birth: masculinity is dramatically counterweighted with a fructive femininity in both generations.

The whole book can be read in any order, individually by chapters or as a whole. The structure allows readers independent pathways; you might begin with a familiar text before moving onto untried topics and plays, or you might focus on one genre, such as comedy, and reorder the chapters to accommodate your focus. The book is effectively cyclical: as Kristeva (1975) suggests, non-linear, non-chronological critical writing welcomes and emphasizes repetitions, waves, connections and cycles in reading, viewing and studying performance and literature. Recent reconfigurations about how 'queer time' disrupts linear notions of the self in and through histories show us alternative conceptions of how we might imagine and (re)perform our pasts and our past texts. History is layered and layering – just as performance is. Starting and ending with chapters that feature *The Winter's Tale*, a text predicated on natural cycles as well as on a fantastical version of the passing of time, we invite the reader to take an active role in approaching our book and the topic, to enjoy, interrogate, challenge and explore *Shakespeare and Gender* with freedom and autonomy.

CHAPTER 1
THE WOMAN'S VOICE
Key Text: *Much Ado About Nothing* with *The Winter's Tale*

J.K. Rowling, the most commercially successful female author of our times, identifies the double bind of women speaking in the public sphere: 'every woman I know who has dared express an opinion publically has endured ... abuse at least once, rooted in an apparent determination to humiliate or intimidate her on the basis that she is female'.[1] As public and private speech is increasingly blurred by online communication, female voices have both greater access to the public ear and greater exposure to censure. It is timely, then, to explore what Shakespeare's women tell us about how the female voice functioned in their early modern context and in production today. This chapter holds a lens over one character, *Much Ado About Nothing*'s Beatrice, to explore both contextual and theatrical expectations of women and the power wielded by speech and voice on the early modern stage.

From her first appearance in the opening scene of the play Beatrice demonstrates a female voice resounding outside of archetypal expectations, both disrupting and flouting them. Fatherless, brotherless and unmarried, Beatrice is freer of patriarchal control than her peers and deeply reluctant to be forced into constraint via marriage. It is her verbal proficiency and unchecked loquacity that allows her to transgress hierarchical structures within *Much Ado About Nothing*'s play world. As Gina Bloom writes, 'female characters who embrace, instead of attempting to overcome, their unpredictable vocal flows are able to elude patriarchal regulation' (2007: 11). Beatrice's only patriarch, her uncle, Leonato, gives mere lip service to controlling his niece, yet exhibits an unyielding attitude towards his own daughter, Hero, later in the play, wishing her rather dead than dishonoured (4.1.116–17). Beatrice's apparently unchecked freedom of speech, often in public, provides us with a

---
[1]J.K. Rowling (@jk_rowling), Twitter thread, 9 June 2017.

fascinating model of female verbosity from an age when many texts have it that the unequivocal ideal of womanhood was located in silent acquiescence.

We meet Beatrice very early in *Much Ado*, when she speaks, both publicly and critically, of a man of power and influence, Benedick. The play's opening conversation is between men, Leonato and a messenger, discussing the victorious outcome of a military campaign. This constitutes a conventional inaugural scene, functioning to establish the context and characters for the play. However, Beatrice interrupts – and disrupts – this patriarchal convention. Shakespeare inserts a female voice into his standard opening and, specifically, one that questions the masculine narrative. Beatrice interjects with ridicule, not only of Benedick himself (whom we are yet to meet) but, more broadly, of the male spheres of public discourse and military knowledge. Specifically, she exposes to mockery the masculine language of prowess in battle and male camaraderie, the effect of her humour heightened by the deadpan messenger:

LEONATO
    What is he that you ask for, niece?
HERO
    My cousin means Signior Benedick of Padua.
MESSENGER
    O, he's returned; and as pleasant as ever he was.
BEATRICE
    He set up his bills here in Messina and
    challenged Cupid at the flight; and my uncle's fool,
    reading the challenge, subscribed for Cupid, and challenged
    him at the bird-bolt. I pray you, how many
    hath he killed and eaten in these wars? But how many
    hath he killed? For indeed I promised to eat all of his
    killing.
LEONATO
    Faith, niece, you tax Signor Benedick too
    much; but he'll be meet with you, I doubt it not.
MESSENGER
    He hath done good service, lady, in these wars.
BEATRICE
    You had musty victual, and he hath holp to
    eat it: he is a very valiant trencherman; he hath an
    excellent stomach.

MESSENGER
    And a good soldier too, lady.
BEATRICE
    And a good soldier to a lady: but what is he to
    a lord?
MESSENGER
    A lord to a lord, a man to a man; stuffed with
    all honourable virtues.
BEATRICE
    It is so, indeed; he is no less than a stuffed man:
    but for the stuffing, – well, we are all mortal.

(1.1.30–56)

Beatrice's raillery attacks Benedick's masculinity in line with archetypal standards. First, she challenges his martial ability (39–42), undermining his reputation as a 'good soldier', re-asserting, instead, her own confident challenge to his status. The messenger's apparent confusion and obliviousness to Beatrice's wordplay places her at the advantage at every point in this conversation with a man. She becomes more daring in her assassination of Benedick's masculinity when she hints at a lack of sexual prowess, in the *double entendre* of 'but for the stuffing, – well, we are all mortal' (55–6). On the surface this serves as a basic truism of mortality but the comment also heavily implies the 'stuffing' (a common sexual euphemism) is under par, via the elliptic aphorism 'well, we are all mortal' replacing a more brazen attack.

So how can we read Beatrice's bold voice in the play in the context of the silent female archetype of the early modern period? The ideal of a chaste, silent, obedient woman permeates many writings of the early modern period and is widely explored in scholarship of women's representation in the drama and literature of the time. Poetic expressions of female perfection idealize chastity of body and of speech: in effect, the less speech the better. Sidney's blazon, 'What Tongue Can Her Perfections Tell?' (1590), for instance, effects an exhaustive geographical exploration of the female body as object of male gaze and desire. The 'perfections' do not, however, include movement or sound and the effect is the presentation of a feminine perfection predicated in stillness and silence. Indeed, the subject's silence, or at least a sort of chaste taciturnity, is clearly a great virtue – or rather, a positive attraction:

> But who those ruddy lips can miss,
> Which blessed still themselves do kiss?
> Rubies, cherries, and roses new,
> In worth, in taste, in perfect hue,
> Which never part but that they show
> Of precious pearl the double row,
> The second sweetly-fenced ward
> Her heav'nly-dewed tongue to guard,
> Whence never word in vain did flow.

Sidney eulogizes silence, or at least the bare minimum of speech among the 'perfections'. The visceral eroticism of Sidney's description of the subject's 'ruddy lips' contrasts immediately with the chastity to be found *within* her mouth, both figuratively and literally. Her 'precious pearl' teeth act as pure white jailers to her tongue, which never moves 'in vain'. While we may read here a simple praise of the discernment of the woman's speech, the language of restraint and imprisonment ('ward', 'guard') cannot be ignored. Such literary presentations of the desirability of self-enforced female silence and the more forthright instruction that women must stay quiet and avoid public speech (see Resource 1.a) contextualize Beatrice's verbosity and Shakespeare's response to these ideals.

Shakespeare's mockery of the blazon tradition itself and the standards of female perfection it peddles, can be found scattered across several texts. In *Twelfth Night*, for instance, Olivia expresses her exasperation at the constant pestering praise sent by Count Orsino by providing 'divers schedules of my beauty: it shall be inventoried, and every particle and utensil labelled to my will: as, item, two lips, indifferent red; item, two grey eyes, with lids to them; item, one neck, one chin, and so forth' (1.5.236–40). Olivia's 'inventory' though, will not be set out by a man's pen: it will be 'labelled to my will', reclaiming ownership of her own body and voice. Most famously and openly, however, the blazon convention is mocked in Sonnet 130, 'My mistress' eyes are nothing like the sun …', in which Shakespeare takes a clear swipe not only at the absurdity and literary limitations of the convention, but in the very standards of beauty and attraction it expounds, notably female silence ('I love to hear her speak …'; see Introduction). In *Much Ado About Nothing*, it is Beatrice who, in a festive moment of reversal, is identified as the female creator, not the female subject of a blazon, when she employs comic conceit and witty punning to describe sulky young Claudio as 'civil as an orange, and something of that jealous complexion'. 'I'faith Lady,' replies the prince,

'I think your blazon to be true' (2.1.270–2). In Beatrice, the witty, speaking woman, not the 'guard[ed]' tongue of chaste silence, is presented as desirable.

When Beatrice first encounters her adversary, Benedick, it is to pick up what has already been framed as an ongoing battle of words and wits that has begun long before the action of the play:

BEATRICE
    I wonder that you will still be talking, Signior
    Benedick: nobody marks you.
BENEDICK
    What, my dear Lady Disdain! are you yet
    living?
BEATRICE
    Is it possible disdain should die, while she
    hath such meet food to feed it as Signior Benedick?
    Courtesy itself must convert to disdain, if you come in
    her presence.
BENEDICK
    Then is courtesy a turncoat. But it is certain
    I am loved of all ladies, only you excepted: and I would
    I could find in my heart that I had not a hard heart; for,
    truly, I love none.
BEATRICE
    A dear happiness to women: they would else
    have been troubled with a pernicious suitor. I thank
    God and my cold blood, I am of your humour for that:
    I had rather hear my dog bark at a crow than a man
    swear he loves me.
BENEDICK
    God keep your ladyship still in that mind!
    so some gentleman or other shall 'scape a predestinate
    scratched face.
BEATRICE
    Scratching could not make it worse, an 'twere
    such a face as yours were.
BENEDICK
    Well, you are a rare parrot-teacher.
BEATRICE
    A bird of my tongue is better than a beast of
    yours.

> BENEDICK
> I would my horse had the speed of your
> tongue, and so good a continuer. But keep your way,
> o' God's name; I have done.
> BEATRICE
> You always end with a jade's trick: I know you
> of old.
>
> (1.1.110–39)

Beatrice's first remark to Benedick is to suggest he talks without audience, that his speech is inconsequential to his male companions: 'nobody marks you'. Her first attack, therefore, is both on his speech and his status among men. Rhetorical skills, as well as physical vocal control, were important tools in establishing men's authority and position, as Gina Bloom writes:

> Whereas early modern women and children were discouraged and even barred from certain forms of vocal expression, men were often coached from an early age in the skill of oratory in an effort to prepare them to speak effectively.
>
> (Bloom, 2007: 9)

The evenness of the verbal and vocal battle between Beatrice and Benedick, then, and her suggestion that his fellow men do not attend to his speech, undermines his accomplishment and power as a man among men. The exchange then soon descends into further insult, in which the only point of agreement is shared rejection of marriage. Beatrice identifies herself with Benedick's 'humour', referencing her 'cold blood', associated with the feminine balance of humours but through which she feels safe from lovesickness. It is in this exchange that Benedick attacks Beatrice for 'the speed of [her] tongue', reminding the audience of the archetypal criticism of women's tendency to loquacity that ought to be curbed. Yet Beatrice has the advantage of the audience, who have already shared her jokes at Benedick's expense. Benedick's attacks here are therefore not to be taken as expressions of the play's ideological standpoint. While, later, her uncle will warn Beatrice she will never secure a husband 'if thou be so shrewd of thy tongue' (2.1.17), by contrast the most politically powerful patriarch, Don Pedro, will profess that, on the contrary, her 'silence most offends' him (2.1.305).

The Woman's Voice

Later, after an exchange at the masked revels, Benedick presents himself as a victim of Beatrice's speech. Her words are weaponized; her voice is a danger to his person:

> She told me, not thinking I had been
> myself, that I was the prince's jester, that I was duller
> than a great thaw; huddling jest upon jest with such
> impossible conveyance upon me that I stood like a man
> at a mark, with a whole army shooting at me. She
> speaks poniards, and every word stabs: if her breath
> were as terrible as her terminations, there were no living
> near her; she would infect to the north star. I would
> not marry her, though she were endowed with all that
> Adam had left him before he transgressed.
>
> (2.1.222–31)

Benedick's affront at Beatrice's verbal attack, albeit under the guise of mistaken identity at a masked revel, displays his fear of her disapproval and her power. His speech admits military defeat, recalling to the audience the 'good soldier' described by the Messenger (1.1.50) but now retreating from his enemy, 'a whole army shooting at me', all alone in the face of an overwhelming foe. While apparently insulting her, Benedict's metaphor simultaneously concedes defeat in the conventionally masculine sphere of battle. Likening her words to 'poniards', presents her speech as dangerous to his masculine identity. She is given a male weapon both literally and figuratively: a small, slender dagger connoting the phallic conceit of her penetrative words that 'stab'. Benedick's next reference is Biblical, referring back to the Fall and thus calling to mind the woman's first fault, that she tempted Adam to transgress. As poet Aemilia Lanyer would challenge in her seminal work, *Salve Deus Rex Judaeorum* (1611), the premise of Eve's fault in the Fall of man had served as a fundamental basis on which the inferiority of women could be based. Lanyer shows this was founded on the unsound logic that man is master of woman, yet could not resist the temptation she placed before him. The alluring Eve and all the pleasures of the first garden are invoked here as the ultimate temptation for the first man – but Benedick would resist all this, rather than marry Beatrice. Rounding off his protestations with 'I cannot endure my Lady Tongue' (2.1.251-2), Benedick finally identifies Beatrice metonymically *as* her voice. He thus re-genders it female after a rage-fuelled foray in which he has segued into presenting her not only as an equal but a superior adversary in war. He will, of course, soon alter his intention; once the love trick is underway, Benedick ceases to express any reservations about Beatrice's loquacity.

Act 2, Scene 1 is a pivotal moment at which Shakespeare provides – in the festive, carnivalesque reversal of masked revels – an opportunity for a woman to assess the perfections of a man, as Beatrice talks of the dangerous Don John:

> BEATRICE
> How tartly that gentleman looks! I never can
> see him but I am heart-burned an hour after.
> HERO
> He is of a very melancholy disposition.
> BEATRICE
> He were an excellent man that were made just
> in the midway between him and Benedick: the one is
> too like an image and says nothing, and the other too
> like my lady's eldest son, evermore tattling.
> LEONATO
> Then half Signior Benedick's tongue in Count
> John's mouth, and half Count John's melancholy
> in Signior Benedick's face, –
> BEATRICE
> With a good leg and a good foot, uncle, and
> money enough in his purse, such a man would win any
> woman in the world, if a' could get her good-will.
>
> (2.1.3–15)

Here it is both the silent 'melancholy' man and the 'tattling', verbose one who are considered lacking. Hero identifies Don John as melancholy, probably a somewhat flattering piece of excuse-making, as Shakespeare does not represent him as representing this disposition (see Chapter 5); he seems, rather, to be the malcontent revenger or villain of a tragedy who has found himself misplaced in this comedy. Indeed, silence is not a particular indicator of melancholy. In any case, Don John is not silent when it comes to male company. Despite what is said here, speech is Don John's weapon of choice throughout the play, the means whereby he manipulates the men around him as 'a plain-dealing villain' (1.3.29–30). It is the men's gullibility, the trust they place in the authoritative male voice – even the openly villainous Don John's – that nearly leads the plot into tragedy. Significantly,

Benedick will choose, later, to believe Beatrice's words over Don John's, the woman's over the man's, leading him to become Hero's defender ('think you in your soul the Count Claudio hath wronged Hero?' (4.1.325–6)). Beatrice's criticism of Benedick as 'tattling' resembles concerns more usually directed at women (see Resource 1.a): that he talks too much and to little purpose. She suggests the ideal man ought to be a combination of the two men, since 'the one is too like an image and says nothing, and the other too like my lady's eldest son, evermore tattling' (2.1.9). Rather than being the subject of poetic admiration or judgement, in the carnivalesque inversion permitted by the festive scene, the woman can appraise the men, subjecting them to her gaze and critique – and she finds them wanting. Furthermore, Beatrice's presentation of the perfect man crucially argues that he would still require a woman's consent to 'win' her, presenting female agency as central to the process of courtship.

Resource 1.a: From John Dod and Robert Cleaver, *A Godlie Forme of Householde Gouernment* (1598)

Let her auoide such occasions as may draw her from her calling. She must shake off slouth, and loue of ease: she must auoide gosseping, further then the lawe of good neighbourhoode doth require. *S. Paul* would haue a woman a good *home-keeper*. The vertuous woman is neuer so well, as when shee is in the middest of her affaires. She that much frequenteth meetings of gosseps, seldome commeth better home: some count it a disgrace to come much abroad, least they should be counted gosseps: which name is become odious: but they must haue tatlers come home to them, to bring them newes, and to hold them in a tale, least they should be thought to be idle without a cause. They perceiue not how time runneth, nor how vnto wardly their busines goeth forward, while they sit idle. They know not, that great tale-bringers, be as great carriers, and that such make their gaine of carrying, & recarrying. The wise woman will be warie, whom shee admitteth into her house, to sit long there, knowing that their occupation is but to marke & carrie. Towards her neighbours she is not sowre, but courteous, not disdainefull to the basest, but affable, with modestie: no scorner, nor giber, but bearing with infirmities, and making the best of things: not readie to stomacke them for euery light matter, and so to looke big: but passing by offences, for vnities sake, not angrie, but milde: not bold, but bashfull: not full of words, powring out al in her

> mind, & babling of her household matters, that were more fitter to be concealed, but speaking vpon good occasion, and that with discretion. Let her heare and see, and say the best, and yet let her soone breake off talke, with such in whom shee perceiueth no wisedome, nor fauour of grace. Let her not be light to beleeue reports, nor readie to tell them againe, [note: Silence is a grauitie, when she abstaineth and holdeth her peace from speaking when it doth not become her to speake.] to fill the time with talke: for silence is farre better, then such vnsauorie talke. Let her not be churlish, but helpefull in all thinges, to preuent breaches, or else to make them vp againe, if by the waiwardnesse of others there be any made.
>
> (pp. 93–5)

Following Hero's abuse at the hands of her future husband, Claudio (4.1), only Beatrice and Benedick are left onstage. After they declare their love, Benedick offers 'bid me do anything for thee' yet refuses Beatrice's command to 'kill Claudio' (4.1.287–8), sparking renewed conflict. Beatrice expresses her frustration and fury not only at the appalling behaviour of the other men, but at the restrictions of her own gender that render her unable to take revenge. In questioning both Benedick himself and patriarchal power more broadly, Beatrice speaks entirely without fear or apology in her language:

BENEDICK
  Is Claudio thine enemy?
BEATRICE
  Is 'a not approved in the height a villain, that
  hath slandered, scorned, dishonoured my kinswoman?
  O, that I were a man! What, bear her in hand until they
  come to take hands, and then, with public accusation,
  uncovered slander, unmitigated rancour? O God, that I
  were a man! I would eat his heart in the marketplace.
BENEDICK
  Hear me, Beatrice –
BEATRICE
  Talk with a man out at a window! A proper
  saying!
BENEDICK
  Nay, but Beatrice, –

BEATRICE
    Sweet Hero! She is wronged, she is slandered,
    she is undone.
BENEDICK
    Beat –
BEATRICE
    Princes and counties! Surely, a princely
    testimony, a goodly count! Count Comfit, a sweet
    gallant, surely! O that I were a man for his sake! Or
    that I had any friend would be a man for my sake!
    But manhood is melted into curtsies, valour into
    compliment, and men are only turned into tongue,
    and trim ones, too. He is now as valiant as Hercules
    that only tells a lie and swears it. I cannot be a man
    with wishing, therefore I will die a woman with grieving.
BENEDICK
    Tarry, good Beatrice. By this hand, I love thee.
BEATRICE
    Use it for my love some other way than
    swearing by it.

                                              (4.1.299–327)

Here, Beatrice's language, while furious and emotionally charged, concerns an offence to her family honour and expresses not an archetypal feminine 'grie[f]' but a more conventionally masculine prioritization of duty. Beatrice bemoans a sense of lost masculine strength, in which 'manhood is melted into curtsies, valour into compliment' (317), and physical valour is supplanted by verbal aggression, as we have seen played out in Claudio's cruelty at the abortive wedding. In Kenneth Branagh's film (1993), this verbal violence is augmented with physical abuse, in which Claudio (Robert Sean Leonard) hurls Hero (Kate Beckinsale) brutally to the ground. While the play text may suggest a physical 'handing back' of Hero to her father in the indicative syntax of Claudio's line, 'There, Leonato, take her back again' (4.1.29), there is little further textual justification for this extreme physical violence, which further problematizes the plot's final resolution. Claudio's attack on Hero, in the text, is verbal: he 'only tells a lie and swears it' (320), epitomizing the verbal cruelty and cowardice Beatrice describes. Indeed, echoing Benedick's metonymy in 2.1, when he labels Beatrice 'my Lady Tongue' (252), Beatrice reverses the insult to represent masculine failings,

Figure 1.1 Emma Thompson as Beatrice and Kenneth Branagh as Benedick (4.1), *Much Ado About Nothing* (Kenneth Branagh, 1993).

in which 'men are only turned into tongue' (318). Beatrice's response is to mourn her feminine constraints, both societal and physical, that force her to need the help of a man 'friend' (264) to take physical revenge for the violation both of Hero herself and their shared family honour, when Claudio has 'slandered, scorned, dishonoured my kinswoman' (301). Her emphasis on the compromise of family and female honour, though, is paired with an understanding of the specific, gendered social death to which Hero is condemned, in which, her chaste reputation stolen: 'she is undone' (311).

However, Beatrice does not simply wish to find a male supporter to carry out revenge on her and Hero's behalf. Instead, her speeches are littered with the desire to be re-gendered male, for the sake of carrying out revenge. Beatrice makes three almost identical ejaculations to this purpose: 'O that I were a man!' (301), 'O God, that I were a man!' (304–5) and 'O that I were a man for his sake!' (315). Apostrophizing, she calls upon God in her hopeless desire to re-sex herself in order to effect apposite, physical vengeance. While Beatrice's righteous indignation in her desire to cast off the restrictions of her sex appears far from Lady Macbeth's demand to 'unsex me' (1.5.41) for nefarious purposes, both seek to cast off their womanhood so they can fulfil their desire to commit violence. Here, the demand – even prayer – is juxtaposed with images of bloody violence: 'O God, that I were a man! I would eat his heart in the market-place' (304–5). In between her cries of 'that I were a man', Beatrice's vehemence displays a linguistic power that compromises archetypes of feminine and masculine language, occupying a liminal space between what she states is a failure of men to live up to the expectations of 'manhood' (317) and the inability of a woman to take over those manly occupations of physical strength and violence when, as she sees it, the situation demands it. This verbal power and physical frustration is often accentuated with mock violent gesture in modern performance, as in Emma Thompson's portrayal of Beatrice in Branagh's 1993 film adaptation (Figure 1.1).

Beatrice's language reverses archetypal standards of masculine and feminine behaviour – or rather perceived faults – when it comes to loquacity and taciturnity. Dod and Cleaver represent a popular and representative view that women's talk is both insubstantial and excessive (see Resource 1.a) but should in fact be sparse and careful: 'Silence is a gravity, when she abstaineth and holdeth her peace from speaking when it doth not become her to speak' (Resource 1.a). So, even where women appear to seek to keep their place at home and avoid the shameful and unchaste label of 'gossip', they *seek* gossips to bring their tales into the home. Women talking to women is undesirable and dangerous to the patriarchy. Women must strive, therefore, to limit their talk altogether and to avoid believing secondhand gossip, 'for silence is far better, then such unsavoury talk' (Resource 1.a). Yet it is Shakespeare's male characters in *Much Ado About Nothing* who engage not only in gossip but slander, believing scandalous 'reports' told abroad on two occasions. First, Claudius is drawn into Don John's disruptive plot (2.1), at which he becomes silent and 'civil as an orange' (270) until ordered by a woman to talk, when Beatrice directs him 'speak count, 'tis your cue' (280) in a self-reflexive, metatheatrical moment. His silence represents, to the audience, his defeat by Don John, and undermines his position in a male hierarchy, since 'loss of vocal control is often indexical of male characters' social and political disempowerment' (Bloom, 2007: 9). Here, and in the post-wedding scene with Benedick, Beatrice highlights the reversal of gender roles: men become silent at points when they should know what to say. Benedick's 'so attir'd in wonder [he] knows not what to say' (4.1.144–5) connotes speechless-ness as powerless-ness. When men also display the archetypal female characteristic fault ('evermore tattling' (2.1.9)) and become speakers of 'lie[s]' and 'slanders' by 4.1, male speech is scrutinized as fiercely as female speech has been. Both 2.1 and 4.1 are scenes of festivity: a masked ball and a wedding, where carnivalesque conventions allow roles to be reversed and order disrupted. Within these moments, Beatrice uses this space of and for verbal freedom to identify weakness and hypocrisy in men conventionally in a position to control women. Yet, Beatrice's disgust at masculine failings (4.1.318–22) itself relies on an accepted archetype of male physical power and sense of duty. She is appalled that 'manhood is melted into curtsies, valour into compliment, and men are only turned into tongue', assuming that men's reliance on speech over action has undermined their masculinity and stripped them of their right to power. Women are not silenced in her new social model. Beatrice is not critical of verbosity but of slander, gossip, vacuous 'tattl[e]' – the modes of speech, in other words, more usually (but not in *Much Ado About Nothing*) attributed to women. Even the comic relief provided by Dogberry and his comrades is centred on *male* circumlocution and garrulity, while the allegation made against Hero, as we have seen, is in fact male-generated, groundless 'gossip'. The accusation itself, too, centres on an invented 'talk[ing] with [a] man' (4.1.86), where speech and sex elide: to Hero's accusers, it does not matter whether voice or body is unchaste, whether 'talking' at her window is euphemistic or not, since speech in such a context, as much as sex, is forbidden. The irony of a woman being accused of inappropriate speech (*qua* sex) by a group of men who themselves are reliant on the word of another man (who is a proven villain) is clear to the audience but lost to the men on stage.

In raising their voices above, beyond or through patriarchal discourses and conventions, early modern women were leaping into a liminal space between the expected dwelling place of woman, the private sphere, and the male dominion of the public sphere. In *Much Ado About Nothing*, Shakespeare has constructed a female character whose wit and verbal confidence present not an archetypal 'shrew' (see Resource 3.a and Chapter 3) but a desirable, as well as likable, character. Her resistance to male domination through marriage may be made a nonsense by the ease with which she is tricked out of her resolution but this is mirrored by Benedick's simultaneous gullibility, so the switch is not gendered. When Beatrice interrupts the men opening the play with their conventional discourse, refuses any prospect of marriage and demands revenge for the dishonouring of her 'kinswoman' (301), she disrupts the patriarchal narrative and the sociopolitical order around her onstage and off. Yet Beatrice is only a construction, played too by a man; no female Beatrice would be heard until her lines were spoken by later actresses of whom Shakespeare could not have conceived. There were, however, women speaking truth to power in the early modern era. Shakespeare's contemporary, the poet Aemilia Lanyer, offers a logical deconstruction of the use of Genesis to support patriarchal misogyny, while, just a year after Shakespeare's death, nineteen-year-old Rachel Speght responded to a particularly vicious pamphlet by Joseph Swetnam. In her pamphlet *A Muzzle for Melastomus*, she takes down not only his logic but his poor expression and grammar (Resource 1.b). Her defence of women provides us with an example of fearless, competent female rhetoric, in which women write back against the discourse of misogny that forms the foundation of a restrictive patriarchal society. In *Much Ado About Nothing*, we find a female voice interrupting and disrupting; let us compare this to Paulina in *The Winter's Tale*.

Resource 1.b: From *A Movzell [Muzzle] for Melastomus*, Rachel Speght (1617)*

From standing water, which soon putrifies, can no good fish be expected; for it produceth no other creatures but those that are venemous or noisome, as snakes, adders, and such like. Semblably, no better streame can we looke, should issue from your idle corrupt braine, then that whereto the ruffe of your fury (to vse your owne words) hath moued you to open the sluce. In which excrement of your roaring cogitations you haue vsed such irregularities touching concordance, and obserued so disordered a methode, as I doubt not to tel you, that a very Accidence Schollar would haue quite put you downe in both. You appear heerein not vnlike that Painter, who seriously indeuouring to pourtray *Cupids Bowe*, forgot the String: for you beeing greedie to botch vp your mingle mangle inuectiue against Women, haue not therein obserued, in many places, so much as as Grammer sense. But the empriest Barrell makes the lowdest sound; and so we wil account of you.

Many propositions haue you framed, which (as you thinke) make much against Women, but if one would make a Logicall assumption, the conclusion would be flat against your owne Sex. Your dealing wants so much discretion, that I doubt whether to bestow so good a name as the Dunce vpon you: but Minority bids me keepe within my bounds; and therefore I onlie say vnto you, that your corrupt Heart and railing Tongue, hath made you a fit scribe for the Diuell.

(fo.B1^v-B2^r)

*Her response to misogynist pamphlet writer Joseph Swetnam

Leontes' unjustified, abusive, jealous rage has cast out his wife and queen, the heavily pregnant Hermione (see also Chapter 9). Paulina risks all rather than stand for the brutal injustice suffered by her queen – and friend. While, ultimately, Beatrice engages a man to challenge Claudio on her behalf,

Shakespeare and Gender

Paulina faces the king herself, carrying in her arms Hermione's newborn daughter. As she enters, Leontes chides Paulina's husband, Antigonus, for failing to control his wife, 'What, canst not rule her?' (2.3.45) to which Paulina concludes, 'He shall not rule me', (2.3.49) asserting her autonomy and moral agency. Like Beatrice, Paulina disrupts the assumed male hierarchy, inserting a female voice into public life:

> PAULINA
> Good queen, my lord, good queen; I say good queen;
> And would by combat make her good, so were I
> A man, the worst about you.
> LEONTES   Force her hence.
> PAULINA
> Let him that makes but trifles of his eyes
> First hand me: on mine own accord I'll off;
> But first I'll do my errand. The good queen,
> For she is good, hath brought you forth a daughter;
> Here 'tis; commends it to your blessing.
>   *Laying down the child*
> LEONTES   Out!
> A mankind witch! Hence with her, out o' door:
> A most intelligencing bawd!
> PAULINA   Not so:
> I am as ignorant in that as you
> In so entitling me, and no less honest
> Than you are mad; which is enough, I'll warrant,
> As this world goes, to pass for honest.
> LEONTES   Traitors!
> Will you not push her out?
>
>   (2.3.58–72)

Leontes attacks Paulina with a tirade of gendered insults centring on the archetypal 'witch': 'a gross hag', 'bawd' and 'callat' (scold). He rails against the men present as 'traitors' for failing to remove her physically from him and prevent her speech. He presents her as the nagging wife who is 'Of boundless tongue, who late hath beat her husband / And now baits me!' (89–91), a danger to patriarchal order and an abomination. Leontes' fury is directed, too, towards Antigonus for failing to assert his authority over her, 'thou art worthy to be hang'd, / That wilt not stay her tongue' (107–8).

Ultimately, Paulina's voice cannot be silenced, even as Leontes hurls misogyny with increasing verbal violence and ultimately threatens 'I'll ha' thee burnt' (112). At this point, Paulina's efforts to be heard become a form of martyrdom. Paulina responds to murderous misogyny with commitment to a sense of truth and complete defiance:

> PAULINA   I care not:
> It is an heretic that makes the fire,
> Not she which burns in't. I'll not call you tyrant;
> But this most cruel usage of your queen,
> Not able to produce more accusation
> Than your own weak-hinged fancy, something savours
> Of tyranny and will ignoble make you,
> Yea, scandalous to the world.
> LEONTES   On your allegiance,
> Out of the chamber with her! Were I a tyrant,
> Where were her life? She durst not call me so,
> If she did know me one. Away with her!
> PAULINA
> I pray you, do not push me; I'll be gone.
>
> (2.3.112–23)

Shakespeare presents Paulina as morally right in confronting the jealous and deluded king. Her visual presence is maternal: carrying an innocent baby, she simultaneously presents female resistance while holding the visual evidence of female reproductive power, the power that has so terrified Leontes (see Chapter 9). She turns the vitriolic king's threat to 'ha' thee burnt' to the pervasive iconographic image of the burning martyr that would have been familiar to contemporary audiences, not least from the bestseller, John Foxe's *Actes and Monuments* (known as the *Book of Martyrs*): 'It is an heretic that makes the fire, / Not she which burns in't'. While here Paulina responds to a threat to her own person, throughout the dialogue she displays her purpose as a defence of the wronged queen and her new child. These women, like Hero and *Othello*'s Desdemona, are the victims of patriarchal anxiety (see Chapters 8 and 9) and, in Paulina, Shakespeare presents the oppressed but righteous woman speaking truth to power.

At the end of *The Winter's Tale*, too, the woman's voice resonates through Hermione rather than Paulina. Wrongly accused of sexual treachery by her husband, Hermione, retreats into hiding, believed to be dead, for some sixteen years. Just as *Much Ado About Nothing*'s Hero is hidden and given out to be dead until her name is cleared, Hermione is hidden by her female friend who has asserted Hermione's innocence from the first. Paulina vows to use her voice as a positive force: 'I'll use that tongue I have: if wit flow from't / As boldness from my bosom, let 't not be doubted / I shall do good' (2.2.51–3). The plots of both plays show the power of sexual accusation to force women further into the private sphere – in these cases in the complete silence of a sort of death. However, whereas in *Much Ado About Nothing* Hero's return is conditional on the proof of her innocence and Claudio's repentance, Hermione's revival at the end has no specific 'reveal' of innocence (which effectively occurred at the end of Act 3 with the oracle's announcement). On the return of her long-lost daughter, the aptly-named Perdita, Hermione returns to 'life'. Presented by Paulina as a statue to her husband, Hermione descends from her plinth and, in many productions, is shown to reconcile with Leontes, as the text suggests in Polixenes' 'she embraces him' (5.3.111). However, Hermione's speech is not addressed to her husband but to her daughter:

> You gods, look down
> And from your sacred vials pour your graces
> Upon my daughter's head! Tell me, mine own.
> Where hast thou been preserved? where lived? how found
> Thy father's court? for thou shalt hear that I,
> Knowing by Paulina that the oracle
> Gave hope thou wast in being, have preserved
> Myself to see the issue.
>
> (5.3.121–8)

Although her words establish the importance of female lineage, Leontes still has the literal last word, and he effectively silences the woman who has spoken out earlier in the play – 'O, peace, Paulina! / Thou shouldst a husband take by my consent, / As I by thine a wife' (135–7) – after which, Paulina is silent. In *Much Ado About Nothing*, Beatrice's voice sounds clearly in the very first scene, while her verbosity is also endorsed by the most powerful male in the play's society. The prince, Don Pedro, corrects

Beatrice's self-chastisement 'I was born to speak all mirth and no matter', avowing on the contrary that 'your silence most offends me' (2.1.305). Despite Don Pedro's admiration of Beatrice's discourse, Shakespeare provides Beatrice with a verbal combatant as a love interest, dramatizing the *querrelles de femmes* for comic entertainment. Both Paulina and Beatrice are ultimately silenced and out-talked by men. Moreover, with no *actual* female bodies on stage, Shakespeare and his contemporaries could only ever ventriloquize women's voices through male actors (and indeed, in terms of public drama at this time, created by male writers); women are still, in effect, dumb in the public theatre until the Restoration. This effects an 'institutionalised practice of female impersonation' (Callaghan, 2002: 7), via which recognized archetypes of female behaviour (and any performative attempts to subvert them) are still only acts of 'impersonation', at risk of tipping into a parody, rather than a representation, of early modern womanhood. However verbose Beatrice may be, her speech was not heard from a contemporary woman's mouth.

More broadly, it is also important to think about how Beatrice and Shakespeare's other verbose women meet their endings. Women are often ultimately silenced in Shakespeare and his contemporaries' drama either by death or marriage. In tragedy, women who begin to disrupt the patriarchal system of power are silenced by death via accident, suicide or grief, such as *Hamlet*'s Ophelia (whose speech is briefly disruptive before being permanently ended; see Chapter 5) or Lady Macbeth, both of whom are first presented as losing their mental balance. Women who speak truth to power directly, however, are rarely 'punished' by Shakespeare; for example, a silencing by violence, as suffered by Emilia in *Othello*, is treated as an abomination and Cordelia's death is presented as the enactment of Lear's grief and regret (see Chapters 6 and 8). *The Merchant of Venice*'s Portia uses logic and eloquence to triumph over male lawmaking to restore, rather than disrupt, order, though she has to dress as a man to do it, as does Viola, when reasoning with Orsino on the women's capacity for constancy in *Twelfth Night* and Rosalind when testing Orlando's attitudes to marriage in *As You Like it*. In *Much Ado About Nothing* Beatrice's silencing in Benedick's symbolic kiss and declaration 'Peace! I will stop your mouth' (5.4.97) marks the end of Beatrice's voice. Earlier in the play, Beatrice's instruction to Hero, 'Speak, cousin, or, if you cannot, stop his mouth with a kiss and let not him speak neither' (2.1.285-6), foreshadows, in festive reversal, her own silencing by marriage in the end.

Conclusions

1. What can we do with the inconsistencies of Shakespeare's final words – and silences – of his talkative women? The question is vexed. In the face of mainstream, popular misogyny, such as Dod and Cleaver's, Shakespeare's presentation of talkative women as representing moral right (such as Emilia at the end of *Othello*, Paulina's defence of Hermione, Beatrice's moral outrage at Hero's slander) might be read as radical, allying with early modern proto-feminist writings, such as Rachel Speght's *Muzzle*.
2. However, we cannot ignore that, ultimately, these women are silenced by men. Beatrice is silenced by Benedick's kiss (symbolizing marriage) and the King, as in *The Winter's Tale*, still leaves his voice resounding in the theatre as the play ends (see Chapter 9). Understanding the open misogynies of Shakespeare's contemporary patriarchal society and the value placed on female chastity, silence and obedience offers a key context for the plays.
3. There is a consistent sense across many of Shakespeare's plays, as well as emergent in the poetry, that women's silence is not clearly a desirable quality to be strived towards, even if, ultimately, we feel keen disappointment as a modern audience when, in the end, women are not allowed the last word.

Further Work

As You Like It

Rosalind's transformation into Ganymede affords her freedoms she has not been able to access as a women in either her father's or her usurping uncle's court. How does Rosalind speak to men as herself and as Ganymede? Do you find any difference in her expression or approach? How does the central friendship between Rosalind and Celia present women's language among themselves?

Twelfth Night

Like Rosalind, Viola cross-dresses as a man for most of the play. Look at her conversation with Orsino in Act 2 Scene 4 ('She sat like patience on a monument / Smiling at grief ...', 2.4.113–14) and consider how Viola presents female silence. Compare this moment with the all-female scenes between Viola and Olivia. Does Viola / Cesario maintain a consistent voice?

Further Reading

Gina Bloom, *Voice in Motion: Staging Gender, Shaping Sound in Early Modern England* (University of Pennsylvania Press, 2007). **Explores the physical voice on stage, particularly on how manipulations, changes or failures of voice engender and gender meaning in early modern drama.**

Penny Gay, *As She Likes It: Shakespeare's Unruly Women* (Routledge, 1994). **Classic on the 'unruly' women of Shakespeare's comedies, both textually and in terms of the pragmatics of performing, encapsulating a moment when feminist critical approaches to Shakespeare were gaining ground in the theatre, of interest in light of twenty-first-century projects such as 50:50 casting commitments.**

Marianne Novy, *Shakespeare and Feminist Theory* (The Arden Shakespeare, 2019). **Introduction to current feminist approaches to Shakespeare, exploring the variety of feminist readings of Shakespeare now and over the past few decades.**

CHAPTER 2
THE MALE BODY, KINGSHIP AND THE BODY POLITIC
Key Text: *Richard II*, with *Henry IV Part 1*, *Henry V*, *Richard III*

Medieval and early modern political theory analogized the state as body, and from this bodily metaphor it is a simple step to rationalize the monarch as 'head', rightfully controlling the nation. In Shakespeare's England, this body politic model was pervasive, anthropomorphizing society to make sense of its complexities and to establish its hierarchies (Gosbee, 2001: 109). This corporeal analogy was also gendered male. Under a female monarch, as England was from 1558 to 1603, the sanctity and chastity of a virgin queen, connoting an untouched state, was crucial. Shakespeare wrote his cycle of History Plays during this time, all of which feature male monarchs. His *Henry V*, for example, 'may have been popular in 1599 in part because it depicts the role of a male monarch, a king who is a martial hero and who serves as a point of identification for those audience members weary of the rule of a woman' (Howard and Rackin, 1997: 4). The monarch's body in all of Shakespeare's History plays is gendered male, reflecting a patriarchal male body politic by embodying past kings onstage. Threats to – and fragmentation of – this male body, in both its figurative and literal sense, are explored in numerous ways. This chapter focuses particularly on *Richard II*, in which the male body of the king and state is a site of both order and disorder, particularly in the context of a gendered body politic where a 'feminized' king or fluid monarchic gender disrupts both the masculinity of kingship and the king's relationship with his feminized land.

Resource 2.a: From Edmund Plowden, *Reports* (1588, trans. 1761)

For the King has in him two Bodies, *viz.* a Body natural, and a Body politic. His Body natural (if it be considered in itself) is a Body mortal, subject to all Infirmities that come by Nature or Accident, to the Imbecillity of Infancy or old Age, and to the like Defects that happen to the natural Bodies of other People. But his Body politic is a Body that cannot be seen or handled, consisting of Policy and Government, and constituted for the Direction of the People, and the Management of the public-weal, and this Body is utterly void of Infancy, and old Age, and other natural Defects and Imbecillities which the Body natural is subject to, and for this Cause what the King does in his Body politic cannot be invalidated or frustrated by any Disability in his natural Body.

(p. 213)

The body politic model of political theory is a means by which to reconcile the potential discord inherent in the diverse range of elements, with differing needs, necessary for society to function. John Norden's lengthy poetic work *Vicissitudo Rerum* (1600, Resource 2.b) expresses the concept as a balance between these elements (stanza 95), just as the body is a balance of humours (Arikha, 2007: Chapter 5) (stanza 93) and the home is a patriarchal structure of husband, wife and offspring (94). The body politic, analogous to these systems, allows for a functional society in which, in line with Aristotle's concept of synergy, the whole is greater than the sum of its parts (95). This justifies any incumbent hierarchy: its 'expression of organic theory and of anthropomorphic analogy in Renaissance England ... was above all a defence of the hierarchical status quo' (Gosbee, 2001: 109). Dissent, corruption and disagreements over succession could easily be rationalized as sickness, disease or injury to the body politic. Re-/de-gendering the king, too, destabilizes the monarchy; and indeed, many critical readings and productions present Richard II as an 'effeminate' king. Across Shakespeare's Histories, the male body of the King is a site of conflict and anxiety, sometimes fragile, sometimes terrifyingly mortal (Resource 2.a) but always embodying, on stage, the body politic. When the future King Richard III bemoans his 'deform'd, unfinish'd' (*Richard III*, 1.1.20) body, or Richard II deconstructs his kingship body part by body part at his deposition at the hands of his rival

The Male Body, Kingship and the Body Politic

(*Richard II*, 4.1), Shakespeare is deconstructing, challenging, subverting – and sometimes validating – the male body of the king as a fundamental symbol of political power.

Resource 2.b: Extract from John Norden, *Vicissitudo Rerum* (1600)

93.
In humane *bodies* is a *discord* set,
Choler and *blood*, *phlegm* and *melancholy*,
These four the four *complexions* beget:
Among them *Nature* hath sent enmity.
Yet stands the *body* of this contrary,
Which could not live, if one alone did reign:
One too too strong, the other three complain.
94.
All other *bodies* are compos'd as this,
Not of a like, but of unlike in kind.
As praised body *Economic* is,
Of *husband*, *wife*, and *children* them assign'd,
Lord and *slave*, *master* and *servant* wee find
To live unlike, yet in good harmony,
If true concording *discord* beautify.
95.
A body *politic*, or public *state*,
Hath like dissents, which yet assenting stands:
The *King*, the *subject*, and the magistrate,
Noble and *base*, *rich*, *poor*, *peace*, and warlike *bands*,
Law, *religion*, *idle*, working *hands*,
Old, *young*, *weak*, *strong*, good men and evil bee
Dislike in parts, yet in *consort* agree.

(D3^v-D4^r)

The *actual* body of the king is crucial to the idea of heredity and ultimately to the argument for the divine right to rule. However, plays that explore the deposition or change of lineage of kings, such as *Richard II* and *Richard III*, suggest ideas – but also often dangers – of meritocracy, a burgeoning early modern concept in which certain traits enable men to become, rather than be born, kings. Shakespeare's plays were written at a time of crisis for the English succession. Elizabeth's lack of offspring, combined with her apparent indecision over her successor kept the nation in apprehension and uncertainty for some years. As Charles R. Forker writes (in the Introduction to the Arden edition):

> As Elizabeth I aged, it became increasingly common to identify her with Richard II. Her remark to William Lambarde [her royal archivist] in 1601, 'I am Richard II. Know ye not that?', is only the best known of several such comparisons.
>
> (Forker, 2002: 5)

The most infamous link between Elizabeth, precarious monarchy and Shakespeare's play is a performance directly before (and linked to) the Essex Rising of 1601, which may or may not have aimed to depose Elizabeth. With a woman on the throne – a childless woman – the very definition of the monarch was in flux (Axton, 1977). If there was no clear successor, even among those who claimed the right, there loomed the notion that there may need to be some judgement on fitness, or even personal skill and merit, to decide the question.

Resource 2.c: From Simon Patericke's 1602 translation of Innocent Gentillet's *A discourse upon the meanes of wel governing*

The distinction of the proprietie of the goods of this world, wherby every man ought to be master and assured possessor of his owne, hath been introduced by the law and right of nature, which wils, That to every man be yeelded that which belongeth unto him, or els by the right of nations, which comes all to one end. This distinction of proprietie maintaineth the commerce and trafficke amongst men, it entertaineth buyings and sellings, permutations, loanes, and such like, which are the bonds of all humane societie: and if the distinction of proprietie of goods, be not maintained in the world, all commerce is destroyed, & all consocietie decayed and resolved. For although some poets and philosophers praise the communitie of goods, remembring us of that old golden world of *Saturne*, yet it is plainely evident to all people of judgement, that communitie induceth and brings a carelesnesse, idlenesse, discord, and

> confusion into the commonweale, as learnedly *Aristotle* demonstrateth in his Pollitiques. Therefore very necessary it is, that the naturall right therein be observed, and every man maintained in the enjoyance of his owne good, and that to every man be rendered that which is his owne: yea, this right ought to bee so observed, that it is not lawfull for the prince to breake or violate it: because by reason of naturall right it is inviolable, and none can derogate from it. And hereunto agreeth the divine right, whereby it is shewed unto us, that *Achab,* a king, ought not to take away the vineyard from *Naboth* his subject: and hereunto also accord the rules of civile right, whereby it is said, That the right naturall, and the right of nations are inviolable, in such sort, as that right civile and positive, neither can nor ought to derogate any thing from them.
>
> (p. 168)

In *Richard II*, we find a narrative of deposition in which the horror of destroying the anointed king is at odds with a different kind of right to rule: the military success and popularity of the pretender, Bolingbroke. Yet this situation is brought about only when the King oversteps his power and fails to see that, in the divine right model, Bolingbroke must be allowed to follow his own natural course of succession. The ideals of kingship in the play are not entirely clear, given the torn sense of horror at deposing a rightful king and sympathy with Bolingbroke's grievance. The play exists in a moral and political paradox. While the deposition of a king is unnatural, Richard's theft of Bolingbroke's rightful inheritance, in the same system, is equally so. As Gentillet (trans. Patericke) (Resource 2.c) demonstrates:

> To every man be rendered that which is his owne: yea, this right ought to bee so observed, that it is not lawfull for the prince to breake or violate it: because by reason of naturall right it is inviolable, and none can derogate from it.

An early modern audience faces a quandary. Which is more heinous, Richard's brazen seizure of Bolingbroke's rightful property or Bolingbroke's rebellion against and deposition of the king in response? The result is a play that encapsulates the problem of how far the divine right carries beyond the body of one man (see Resource 2.c). Richard sees his own body as 'anointed' but he strips himself of any divine protection long before he hands the crown to Bolingbroke in defeat. We may read this in York's outrage after the death of Gaunt:

> RICHARD
> Think what you will, we seize into our hands
> His plate, his goods, his money and his lands.
> YORK
> I'll not be by the while. My liege, farewell.
> What will ensue hereof there's none can tell;
> But by bad courses may be understood
> That their events can never fall out good.
>
> (2.1.209–14)

York identifies Richard's unnatural act and prophesies disorder. The rhyming couplets suggest a sense that each character is attempting to have the final word, given the conventional use of couplets as endings. However, York's final proverbial style implies he is returning to an accepted 'truth', simplifying the dispute into a binary of 'bad' and 'good', regardless of the king's status.

Under threat of impending deposition, throughout his eponymous play Richard II asserts his divine right to rule and presents his kingship as provided, maintained and embodied by male powers, rejecting any threat as futile in terms of deposing a true king:

> Not all the water in the rough rude sea
> Can wash the balm off from an anointed king;
> The breath of worldly men cannot depose
> The deputy elected by the Lord.
> For every man that Bolingbroke hath pressed
> To lift shrewd steel against our golden crown,
> God for his Richard hath in heavenly pay
> A glorious angel. Then, if angels fight,
> Weak men must fall, for heaven still guards the right.
>
> (3.2.54–62)

The struggle is specifically against 'men' denoting a broader idea of mankind while retaining clear connotations of its masculine sense. Naming Bolingbroke specifically, Richard identifies the threat but is convinced (or convinces himself) that God will defend him against 'weak men'. Referring

The Male Body, Kingship and the Body Politic

here to what is known as the 'great chain of being' (in which the monarch is mortal but holds divine rights over others and is closer, therefore, to God; see Dolan, 2001; Tillyard, 1943), Richard establishes his ordained right and appears to take this literally as actual protection on earth. Here, his defiance is based entirely on ideological belief. Real, 'worldly' threats to his person are sidestepped: kingship itself is enough to preserve him from peril.

However, as defeat grows more and more likely, Richard increasingly verbalizes the problem of the monarch's body: its mortality and fragility on earth. While Hamlet concludes that even 'Imperious Caesar, dead and turn'd to clay, / Might stop a hole to keep the wind away' (5.1.206-7), Richard despairs over the mortality of kings:

> Let's talk of graves, of worms and epitaphs,
> Make dust our paper and with rainy eyes
> Write sorrow on the bosom of the earth.
> Let's choose executors and talk of wills.
> And yet not so, for what can we bequeath
> Save our deposed bodies to the ground?
> Our lands, our lives and all are Bolingbroke's,
> And nothing can we call our own but death
> And that small model of the barren earth
> Which serves as paste and cover to our bones.
> For God's sake, let us sit upon the ground
> And tell sad stories of the death of kings –
> How some have been deposed, some slain in war,
> Some haunted by the ghosts they have deposed,
> Some poison'd by their wives, some sleeping kill'd –
> All murder'd. For within the hollow crown
> That rounds the mortal temples of a king
> Keeps Death his court; and there the antic sits,
> Scoffing his state and grinning at his pomp.
>
> (3.2.144-63)

Richard places his life, body and kingship in a context of a continuum of 'sad stories', chronicling himself and the lineage he sees as part of a discourse of kingly bodies abused and opposed, 'all murder'd' for the 'hollow crown' (56, 60). Ultimately, the actual mortality, bodily fragility, problematizes the supremacy of a divine right to power.

Responding to Richard's despondency, Aumerle suggests regrouping via his father's army, specifically to re-establish the body politic that has fragmented, 'and learn to make a body from a limb' (3.2.187). However, he speaks here of a body politic clearly distinct from the body mortal of the king; the former is miraculous, free from the laws of nature. This implicit dismemberment is echoed when Richard finally, reluctantly, gives up his crown to Bolingbroke. He deconstructs his body piece by piece, 'undo[ing] [him]self' (4.1.203), symbolically dismantling this iteration of the body politic model with a divine monarch at its head. Richard nihilistically fragments his kingly person:

> Ay, no. No, ay; for I must nothing be.
> Therefore no 'no', for I resign to thee.
> Now mark me, how I will undo myself:
> I give this heavy weight from off my head,
> 	[*Gives crown to* BOLINGBROKE]
> And this unwieldy sceptre from my hand,
> 	[*Takes up sceptre and gives it to* BOLINGBROKE]
> The pride of kingly sway from out my heart;
> With mine own tears I wash away my balm,
> With mine own hands I give away my crown,
> With mine own tongue deny my sacred state,
> With mine own breath release all duteous oaths.
> ...
> Make me, that nothing have, with nothing grieved,
> And thou with all pleased, that hast all achieved.
> Long mayst thou live in Richard's seat to sit,
> And soon lie Richard in an earthly pit!
> 'God save King Henry', unking'd Richard says,
> 'And send him many years of sunshine days!'
> What more remains?
>
> (4.1.201–22)

Deconstructing the physical body, here, merges with the destruction of the divine monarch, the 'King's two bodies' (Kantorowicz, 1957), in which Richard's mortal submission erases his immortal divine power, as 'with [his] own tears' he 'wash[es] away' that 'balm' that has anointed his body as king and that he had claimed 'Not all the water in the rough rude sea ...

[could] wash ... off' in 3.2 (54–5). Ironically, only the king has the power to *de*-anoint, or 'unking', the king. Richard takes his 'self' apart, fragment by fragment, from thinking 'head' to active 'hand', feeling 'heart', to voice and very 'breath'. As all parts of his body have relinquished their kingship, the symbolic body politic is dismembered and we are left with 'nothing'. 'Nothing' was certainly common slang for the vagina, a female genital space. Femaleness is a state of absence, of nothingness, existing only in relation to a lack of male 'something' (see Sonnet 20, Introduction). Here, Richard applies this common trope to his monarchic emasculation. He is not just no longer a King but no longer a man and, finally, must ask, 'what more remains?' A literal reading would see this remark simply as questioning what further ceremony he should undergo but, rhetorically and corporeally speaking this is a statement of his resulting (feminized) 'nothing[ness]' (222).

Throughout *Richard II* despair itself is coded as female. Distinguishable clearly from the conventionally masculine, noble struggles of melancholy (see Chapter 5), despair and despondency is empirical, responding to specific events. This emotional reaction is frequently gendered female, associated with aspects of femininity or linked to the female body itself. The Queen, for instance, has a lengthy conversation with Bushy in 2.2, in which she describes her state of 'grief' upon having parted with her husband. Bushy reminds her that she has promised to be 'cheerful', but she finds she cannot keep her promise:

> To please the King I did; to please myself
> I cannot do it. Yet I know no cause
> Why I should welcome such a guest as Grief,
> Save bidding farewell to so sweet a guest
> As my sweet Richard. Yet again, methinks,
> Some unborn sorrow, ripe in Fortune's womb,
> Is coming towards me, and my inward soul
> With nothing trembles.
>
> (2.2.5–12)

The Queen's extended metaphor of pregnancy paradoxically highlights her childlessness. Instead of an heir, her body grows an 'unborn sorrow, ripe in fortune's womb', in which her foreboding is undefined despite being as tangible as a pregnancy. Her 'inward soul / With nothing trembles', her female self embodying the growing sense of threat in its barren articulations, unable to bear forth a reason for her fear and despair. Femininity is associated with nothingness, proleptically foreshadowing Richard's later words.

The Queen continues in the same discourse of pregnancy, her female rhetorical devices providing more than a match for Bushy's platitudes:

> QUEEN
>   I cannot but be sad – so heavy sad
>   As thought on thinking on no thought, I think,
>   Makes me with heavy nothing faint and shrink.
> BUSHY
>   'Tis nothing but conceit, my gracious lady.
> QUEEN
>   'Tis nothing less. Conceit is still derived
>   From some forefather grief. Mine is not so,
>   For nothing had begot my something grief,
>   Or something hath the nothing that I grieve.
>   'Tis in reversion that I do possess –
>   But what it is, that is not yet known what,
>   I cannot name. 'Tis nameless woe, I wot.
>
>   (2.2.30–40)

'Sad[ness]' and 'heav[iness]' are linked together here, where 'heav[iness]' might be taken to mean both trouble of mind and a pregnant metaphor. Forker notes that this speech resembles one of the play's apparent sources, the anonymous play *Woodstock*, in that the Duchess of Gloucester declares she is 'full of fear and heaviness', while arguing that the source lacks 'Shakespeare's distinctive image of pregnancy' (Forker, 2002: 275). Editors do not tend to recognize a potential pregnant image in the idea of 'heav[iness]' of mind relating to the state of being 'heavy' with child, and thus the gendering of sadness. The contrast between the Queen's feminization of grief, the masculine body politic and body of the king earlier in the play is stark. The metaphors of female nothingness and prophecy as pregnancy are clear in the Queen's sustained 'conceit'. Shortly later, the Queen's pregnant woes come to fruition when she receives from Green the news of Richard's overwhelming enemies:

> So, Green, thou art midwife to my woe,
> And Bolingbroke my sorrow's dismal heir.
> Now hath my soul brought forth her prodigy,

And I, a gasping new-delivered mother,
Have woe to woe, sorrow to sorrow joined.

(2.2.62–6)

The Queen brings her earlier metaphor to graphic conclusion, in which the physicality of birth is evoked. The labour is one of despair, as the 'gasping new-delivered mother' is delivered only of misery. Green, too, is feminized in this analogy, becoming a 'midwife', delivering, via his news, the sorrow-child she has been carrying, creating a female space in which her prophesy is realized.

Further, just as Richard will see his deposition as a descent into 'nothing[ness]', the Queen plays verbal games with the dichotomy of 'something' and 'nothing' in her presentation of the nebulous and intangible sense of dread that she cannot shake off ('For nothing had begot my something grief / Or something hath the nothing that I grieve' (36–7)). The inevitability of a developing pregnancy lends the framework for the fear and sadness growing within her mind and body. Editors have not seen her something–nothing word games as gendered: Arden's Forker, for instance, sees 'nothing' as a 'prominent motif' in the play that is simply picked up here in the Queen's language (Forker, 2002: 277). However, the common usage of 'something' / male and 'nothing' / female cannot be ignored. Elsewhere in Shakespeare's work the common euphemism abounds. In *Hamlet* the Prince goads Ophelia with this when he puns on Ophelia's 'I think nothing my Lord' to imply 'nothing' as vagina: 'That's a fair thought to lie between a maid's legs' (3.2.116–17). Similarly, the same trope is adopted in Sonnet 20's 'And by addition me of thee defeated / By adding one thing to my purpose nothing' (see Introduction). In these contexts, the play's 'prominent motif' of nothingness in the deposition of a monarch, in the loss of identity of a man, carries a clear sense of his defeat as feminized.

Feminine sadness is portrayed as something to be feared among men of war and stately power, in which their masculine identity in a male body politic is threatened by womanishness, like Hamlet's 'unmanly grief' (1.2.94). The idea of women as being constituted more of the element water than men, and therefore unsound and leaky, is common in early modern discourses of gender, so watery tears become metonymic of both grief and femininity. In *Henry V*, for example, when Exeter is overcome with the sorrow of relating the elaborate deaths in battle of both Suffolk and York, he excuses himself for his feminine behaviour:

EXETER
> The pretty and sweet manner of it forced
> Those waters from me which I would have stopped,
> But I had not so much of man in me,
> And all my mother came into mine eyes
> And gave me up to tears.
>
> HENRY   I blame you not,
> For hearing this I must perforce compound
> With my full eyes, or they will issue too.
>
> (4.6.28–34)

Here, when Exeter refers to 'the mother [coming] into his eyes', he means the womb, commonly known as 'the mother' in early modern medical discourse (see Chapter 5). Exeter thus equates his tearfulness with a fundamental transformation of sex, in which a wandering womb moves up into his masculine eyes and renders them female, when he had 'not so much of man in me' to overpower his female emotion. Henry, though, appears a confident king and is unconcerned by Exeter's emotional response: 'I blame you not'. Further, he is willing to admit his own eyes to be in danger of 'issu[ing]' with Exeter's, where 'issue' has clear connotations of birth that reiterate not only a feminine identity for sorrow but also a specific sense of birthing grief that is reminiscent of Queen Isobel's extended metaphor of pregnancy. Yet, in *Richard II*, in contrast to Henry's confident response to Exeter's sadness, Richard observes 'Aumerle, thou weep'st, my tender-hearted cousin!' (3.3.160) and suggests they may dig 'their graves with weeping eyes' (3.3.169). Richard's anguish at his loss of kingly power, as we have seen, leads him to contemplate the mortality of his person, as opposed to the kingship he represents. This results in a despair in which he writes his grief in the ground where his body will lie, he will 'Make dust our paper and with rainy eyes / Write sorrow on the bosom of the earth' (3.2.146). These 'rainy eyes' feminize Richard, both according to early modern associations of the watery female and time-honoured assumptions that crying is a fundamentally female trait. The earth's 'bosom' may not necessarily be read as female, given that the term need not be gendered. Yet the Histories often present the land as a dangerous and/or an endangered female body that contrasts starkly with the masculinized body politic embodied in the onstage the king (see also Chapter 7).

The Male Body, Kingship and the Body Politic

Threats to both literal and figurative bodies of the king – from deposition, civil war, revolution or invasion – constitute the action of Shakespeare's Histories and in these cases the land is assigned a female gender, in contrast to the masculinity of the monarch. In *Richard II*, the king presents the nation as mother and her feminine chastity as threatened by the monstrosity of civil war:

> Tell Bolingbroke – for yon methinks he stands –
> That every stride he makes upon my land
> Is dangerous treason. He is come to open
> The purple testament of bleeding war;
> But ere the crown he looks for live in peace,
> Ten thousand bloody crowns of mothers' sons
> Shall ill become the flower of England's face,
> Change the complexion of her maid-pale peace
> To scarlet indignation and bedew
> Her pastors' grass with faithful English blood.
>
> (3.3.91–100)

The double meaning of the 'bloody crowns' of dead English soldiers and the moment of birth, as the baby's 'bloody crown' emerges from its mother is continued into a horror of the violation of the female virginal body of England, 'chang[ing] the complexion of her maid pale-peace / To scarlet indignation', presenting Bolingbroke's civil insurrection as a rape of the feminine kingdom, in which she will be desecrated by the spilling of her own blood. A trope of a female England defiled by civil war appears elsewhere in the Histories, such as in *Richard III* when, in his closing speech, Richmond mourns that 'England hath long been mad, and scarr'd herself' (5.5.23). Unruly feminine madness is the conceit for a disorderd kingdom. The men of these plays relentlessly feminize disorder despite the chaos being orchestrated by men while women persistently attempt, unheeded, to warn of the dangers ahead (see also Chapter 9).

The trope appears, too, in *Henry IV, Part 1*, where the idea of a mother earth elides with a specifically feminized land, mapping the dangerous, unruly female body onto the nation space. The King's description of the uprisings of a violent 'mother' kingdom opens the play, posing a threat to the king's literal and figurative bodies:

> So shaken as we are, so wan with care,
> Find we a time for frighted peace to pant

And breathe short-winded accents of new broils
To be commenc'd in strands afar remote.
No more the thirsty entrance of this soil
Shall daub her lips with her own children's blood;

(1.1.1-6)

The land itself, here, is dangerous – and clearly gendered. A land sullied by civil war is fashioned as a monstrous and unnatural mother. François Laroque argues that Henry 'turns [the earth] into an infanticidal and cannibalistic mother, a ghoul that drinks fresh blood' (Laroque, 1991: 91), but does not interrogate the gendering of such horrors. The explicit and visible irony in personifying a female land simply to blame her for the bloody acts of men is a critique of this kind of ideology. The dangerous, unruly female body, so often presented as a passive site and metaphor for disorder, is here actively expressing her most terrifying and unnatural upheavals.

Henry's shocking feminization echoes and contrasts John of Gaunt's description of the nation as 'This blessed plot, this earth, this realm, this England, / This nurse, this teeming womb of royal kings' in *Richard II* (2.1.51-2). Rather than anthropomorphizing the land into a woman to construct her as brutal and self-destructive, Gaunt's female England is nurturing ('nurse') and fertile. It is the unnatural act of a monarch that causes the land to be sullied. In Gaunt's despair at the civil unrest and division he foresees, we might focus on his extended metaphor of the king as landlord and the land as mere 'tenement or pelting farm' (2.1.60). However, having clearly gendered England 'this blessed plot, this earth' (as opposed to the social structure that stands upon her land), Gaunt neither demonizes the land for the unrest nor deploys the misogynistic tropes of Henry IV's speech. Instead, Gaunt uses language of tenancy and of female reputation (read chastity). England is a maternal, fertile space, well loved but, being sold, her reputation will be destroyed: 'this dear dear land, / Dear for her reputation through the world, / Is now leased out' (2.1.57-9). Beyond the obvious language of land commerce, here, is the language of the female body as a site of trade, in which the prostitution of England destroys her chaste reputation and thus her value in the patriarchal model.

Richard II might be read as presenting a gendered and politicized dichotomy, in which Richard represents the feminine and Bolingbroke the masculine. The idea of Elizabeth as 'King', in which, while her body was biologically female, it somehow housed a masculine ruler, may have been

The Male Body, Kingship and the Body Politic

expressed even by the Queen herself (see Resource 4.a). However, any kind of fluidity or duality in the monarch's patriarchal body might be seen as dangerous to the body politic it represents: 'the binary opposition personalized in the conflict between Bullingbrook [sic] and Richard is implicated in an early modern ideology of "masculine" and "feminine"' (Howard and Rackin, 1997: 142). For instance, Richard's response to the crisis of his monarchy is emotional, rather than pragmatic: he retreats to Flint Castle to 'pine away' in his 'kingly woe' (3.2.210), expressing an archetypal feminine response of emotional overwhelm. By contrast, Bolingbroke's approach to Richard shortly afterwards emphasizes the contrast of his military power and ruthless determination, when he threatens the consequences if Richard fails to meet his demands: 'I'll use the advantage of my power / And lay the summer's dust with showers of blood' (3.3.42–3). Howard and Rackin see this as a gendered division:

> In *Richard II*, the king's patrilineal authority is vitiated by his womanish tears and his effeminate behaviour: he has no taste for foreign wars, he talks when he should act, and he wastes his kingdom's treasure by indulging in excessive luxuries. Bullingbrook [sic], who has no hereditary right to the crown, acquires it by the successful performance of masculine virtues.
>
> (Howard and Rackin, 1997: 142)

Yet Richard's characterization must be read, too, in the context of how monarchic succession can be decided. The relinquishment of rule from the verbose, reflective Richard to the man of action and military leader, Bolingbroke, arguably proposes the power of conventional masculinity as ideal rule. In today's performances, too, this binary distinction between an effeminate Richard and a macho Bolingbroke can crystallize into a binary of weakness and strength. This risks perpetuating archetypes we most recently term 'toxic masculinity', in which, among other things, manhood is fundamentally defined by strength as opposite to feminine weakness. Further, when Richard's lack of a perceived 'masculine' mental and political strength is portrayed via distancing him from heteronormative male behaviours, 'all-too-modern links between effeminacy and sexuality … harden into stereotype' (Higginbotham, 2014: 60). Links between both weakness and femininity, and effeminacy and non-hetero male sexuality are implied by this kind of critical reading, casting and direction.

Gregory Doran's 2013 production of *Richard II* for the RSC, for instance, starred David Tennant, clothed in an androgynous white garment that reviewer Peter Kirwan identifies as 'Christ-like' robes (2014: 198), contrasting starkly with the warlike clothing of the other men and particularly with his deposer, Bolingbroke (Figure 2.1). His hair worn long and flowing, Tennant's styling resembles the gender-fluid beauty of the well-known anonymous portrait of Shakespeare's patron, Henry Wriothesley, 3rd Earl of Southampton,[1] and presents Richard in a liminal space between the palpably binary male and female costumes in the production. Yet the image of Wriothesley depicts an individual of power and influence. His beauty does not undermine his command, any more than the ornateness of the armour he wears makes it less impenetrable. Tennant's Richard, though, was read by some critics as feminine:

Figure 2.1 Nigel Lindsay as Bolingbroke and David Tennant as Richard, *Richard II* (Gregory Doran, Royal Shakespeare Company, 2013). Photo by Kwame Lestrade © RSC 2013.

---

[1]This painting is online in the collection of the National Portrait Gallery (UK): https://www.npg.org.uk/collections/search/portrait/mw05918/Henry-Wriothesley-3rd-Earl-of-Southampton?LinkID=mp04202&role=sit&rNo=0 (accessed 30 March 2019).

Where Bolingbroke, Northumberland and their men wore stark armour, Richard restricted himself to fine cloths or a golden breastplate. Where heavy-set, efficient and clipped modes of speech defined the relationships between Richard's uncles and their sons, Tennant adopted a high register, tripping lightly over Richard's dialogue.

(Kirwan, 2014: 197–8)

Kirwan does not directly mention the androgyny of, or claim effeminacy in, Tennant's Richard, but he does note that the actor uses a 'high[er] register' than his usual speaking voice. The high pitch at which Tennant speaks, his long, loose hair, his dress-like garb all compromise his traditional masculinity in contrast to the warlike appearance of his adversary – and ultimate – Bolingbroke. Yet, on the all-male stage of Shakespeare's time, how can we imagine Richard was played? It is scarcely believable that a boy actor, used to women's parts, would be cast as Richard to make him 'effeminate' and, on a stage in which all Queens are boys or men, the audience must accept some transgressions of the firmness of binary genders, as Chapter 4 will scrutinize. Tennant's physical feminization of his voice hints at an effeminate king, in which the high pitched voice is a clear marker for the audience to know they must register the male actor as female in the play world especially in the context of Shakespeare's all-male theatre (and revived in original practices today). This vocal register would have been important to convincing doubling but, more crucially, necessary to cross-dressed parts such as Viola and Rosalind (Gamboa, 2018). In modern casting, too, a man whose voice is familiar to his audience raising his vocal register is likely to be read as a specific act of feminization.

Focus: All-Female History Productions

The Histories feature predominately male characters. Many, such as *Richard II*, only include a couple of female parts, and those have comparably few words to say. In practical terms, this offers challenges to modern theatres trying to explore ways in which to create a 50:50 representation on stage, as well as restricting roles available to leading women actors. Using gender-blind casting, in which characters are cast regardless of the gender of the actor, is growing in popularity, while female actors playing main lead roles such as Henry V or Richard II is far from a new phenomenon. This approach identifies the kingly person as physically differing from 'his' fellow powerful male presences and draws attention to themes of gender and power. The performative potential of enacting an all-female History play reaches far beyond the practicalities of providing equal opportunities. It is an act of theatrical occupation of the traditionally patriarchal ownership of Shakespeare and his works. As far back as the early twentieth century we see all-female Histories, such as Marie Slade's 1921 production of *Henry V* at Stratford. For example, in Phyllida Lloyd's 2016 all-female cast production of *Henry IV* (an amalgamation of both parts into a short, single play), Harriet Walter's portrayal of a hyper-masculine king involved exaggerated archetypal male postures, such as sitting with her legs spread apart and head high. She used a lower register to create Henry's voice, too, and her short hair and androgynous prison uniform all served to blur the gender of the king embodied onstage. The power structure created by embedding the play, too, into a women's prison setting, allowed the audience to reread the concept of the monarchic body in a specifically female space.

In *Henry V*, we find a very different monarch to both Henry IV (his father), and Richard II, the king his father deposed. He is vital, confident and assured in his right of invasion and his own monarchy is undisputed. Yet the concept of Henry's right to absolute power is challenged the night before his biggest battle, when, not knowing he addresses the King himself, a soldier expresses his fear for the souls of men blindly following their king into battle. Early in their interaction, Henry has established the mortality of the king's body explicitly, sharing knowing humour with the audience when he declares:

> I think the king is but a man as I am: the violet smells to him as it doth to me; the element shows to him as it doth to me; all his senses have but human conditions; his ceremonies laid by, in his nakedness he appears but a man;
>
> (4.1.102–6)

Henry establishes a monarchic body that is appropriately mortal; he is human, one of the men, without Richard's angst over kingly mortality. Indeed, this is a motif scattered through the play, in which powerful kingship is represented in a confident self-awareness of mortality and pragmatism. For example, this is clear even in the wooing of Katherine at the very end, in which Henry's logical arguments take shape, when he speaks 'plain soldier' (5.2.150) to argue, 'take me, take a soldier. Take a soldier, take a king' (165), deconstructing again the division between man and monarch. Unlike Richard II's medieval adhesion to divine right throughout the play, Henry V seems an anachronistically modern monarch, a great rhetorician and soldier, rather than an 'anointed' body that must represent the body politic as a living metaphor. Henry's declaration of the king's mortal person, however, appears to embolden the soldier, Williams, in his critique of the king's responsibilities:

> But if the cause be not good, the King himself hath a heavy reckoning to make, when all those legs and arms and heads, chopped off in battle shall join together at the latter day and cry all 'We died at such a place', some swearing, some crying for a surgeon, some upon their wives left poor behind them, some upon the debts they owe, some upon their children rawly left.
>
> (4.1.134–41)

Dismembered fragments are monstrously assembled and reanimated as a body of everyday people that may challenge the accepted constitution of the body politic.

The body politic in peril is represented here and elsewhere by male physical dismemberment, in which body parts are itemized with anatomical precision. We have seen this trope in *Richard II* when the king deconstructs his kingship. Across Shakespeare's History plays, the fragmentation of a male body presents a ghastly masculinization of the dissected body of the blazon convention (see Introduction and Chapter 1). The anatomization of a dismembered kingly body demonstrates a fundamental fear of demasculation via the loss of bodily cohesion both in the male body and the body politic. Indeed, after his confrontation with Williams, Henry shows clear awareness of a precarious right to rule in his anxious reflection on how he came to be king, following his father's (Bolingbroke/Henry IV) deposition of Richard:

> O not today, think not upon the fault
> My father made in compassing the crown.
> I Richard's body have interrèd anew,
> And on it have bestowed more contrite tears
> Than from it issued forcèd drops of blood.
>
> (4.1.290–6)

Here, Richard's royal person is re-honoured, despite compromising Henry's own claim to the throne and hence his perceived legitimacy; he is one of those kings Richard II imagines to be 'haunted by the ghosts they have deposed' (*Richard II*, 3.2.158). Henry's rule is presented as, in some ways, meritocratic: he is a successful leader who foils plots against him and is victorious in war. Yet 'Richard's body' haunts Henry's thoughts at the very moment that he must claim absolute right to lead, on the eve of battle. This is especially troublesome in the context of a divine right model, since Henry is not fighting to retain his own crown, but attempting to effect a deposition in France. By re-interring the deposed antecedent and weeping over his body, Henry acknowledges Richard's rights as king, yet his 'contrit[ion]' is limited, as he still views himself as rightful monarch. Richard's 'two bodies' – mortal and divine – are laid to rest and with them their medieval model of kingship, while Henry offers a more modern, cohesive sense of the king 'in his nakedness ... but a man' (4.1.102–6).

The significance of soundness and cohesion in the king's physical body is brought most sharply into focus in *Richard III*, which centres on an improper rise to power and deconstructed kingship. Richard opens the play in soliloquy, starting with a monosyllabic, adverbial reminder of the potential for the play's immediacy as well as its representation of the past: 'Now is the winter of our discontent.' Richard's self-identification as 'deformed' pre-establishes his rise to power as a deliberate act of 'villain[ny]', in which he challenges himself to cause maximum disruption to the status quo: a body politic in chaos and disorder. Just as *Much Ado About Nothing*'s Benedick is disgusted at men's feminized behaviour in peacetime (2.1.8–21), Richard presents men's actions outside of wartime as unmanly, 'instead of mounting barbed steeds ... caper[ing] nimbly in a lady's chamber' (1.1.10–12). He presents his own dissatisfaction with his disabled body as a rationale for his desire for both power the chaos of 'villain[y]':

> I, that am curtail'd of this fair proportion,
> Cheated of feature by dissembling Nature,
> Deformed, unfinish'd, sent before my time
> Into this breathing world, scarce half made up,
> And that so lamely and unfashionable
> That dogs bark at me as I halt by them –
> Why, I, in this weak piping time of peace,
> Have no delight to pass away the time,
> Unless to spy my shadow in the sun
> And descant on mine own deformity.
>
> (1.1.18–27)

The Male Body, Kingship and the Body Politic

Richard's bitterness at being 'cheated ... by dissembling Nature' presents a basis for the havoc he wreaks for the duration of the play, predicated on the prevailing early modern belief in disability as monstrosity. Richard is characteristically solipsistic here, yet there are hints at the female root of his problems, both in 'dissembling Nature', where nature is exclusively gendered female in early modern discourse (see Chapter 6) and also in terms of his problematic gestation and birth. Throughout the play, while Richard's dangerous masculinity threatens the stability of the nation, his own perceived physical shortcomings are frequently traced back to his birth and his mother's truncated pregnancy, when he was 'sent before [his] time / Into this breathing world, scarce half made up'. His 'deformed, unfinish'd' male body manifests his unnatural ascension to the throne, upsetting the cohesion of the body politic and causing unrest in the nation. Yet the fact of his disability existing since birth allows Richard to assign blame on the female, biological author of his body, rather than on himself for those actions represented as inevitable due to his portentous disassociation from physical normalcy, regardless of his consistently solipsistic attitude elsewhere in the play ('Richard loves Richard, that is I am I' (5.3.183)). The corruption of the body politic in Richard's rise to power is mirrored throughout by a 'deform'd, unfinished' body of the king and its origin as female fault. Richard is not king when he makes his opening speech but the audience sees him as inevitable king and, by drawing attention to Richard's physical 'deform[ity]' in the character's own words, Shakespeare presents a prolepsis of the disorder of the body politic to come, via the disorder of the future king's body on stage.

Richard utilizes, too, the systemic gynophobia and ableism of his world to blame women convincingly for his crimes and turn the powerful men around him against them. This rhetorical tactic means women's warnings are more thoroughly silenced as Richard creeps towards power (such as Queen Margaret's fury in 1.3). Initially, Richard summons a specific fear of female rule in order to encourage fear of disorder and divert attention from his own guilt:

Why, this it is, when men are ruled by women:
'Tis not the king that sends you to the Tower:
My Lady Grey his wife, Clarence, 'tis she
That tempers him to this extremity.

(1.1.61–4)

Here Richard creates a plausible lie based not only the archetypal assumptions of the false woman but the fear of an inversion of patriarchal power where 'men are ruled by women', to ensure the success of his deception. Later, Gloucester will deploy another core archetype of womanhood as demonic to lend credence to his own counter-storytelling, when he presents his own arm as evidence of female witchcraft:

> Then be your eyes the witness of this ill:
> See how I am bewitch'd; behold mine arm
> Is, like a blasted sapling, wither'd up:
> And this is Edward's wife, that monstrous witch,
> Consorted with that harlot strumpet Shore,
> That by their witchcraft thus have marked me.
>
> (3.4.67–71)

Here, again, Richard lays the blame for his non-conforming kingly body squarely on women – this time not his own mother but the witchcraft of two women he accuses of having transformed his arm. Richard gains power partly by assigning the shortcomings of his physical form to women, establishing a gendered threat to the state, the monarch's body and the monarchy itself. The audience are aware throughout of Richard's true actions and this undermines the idea that the threat to the nation genuinely comes from women. It suggests instead, in Richard's unruly masculine body, an embodiment of a body politic in disorder. Nevertheless, we might well imagine that Richard's dangerous pronouncement that this is what happens when 'men are ruled by women' might have brought knowing laughter to an audience of Elizabethans.

Production in Focus: *Richard II*, Dir. Adjoa Andoh, with Co-direction by Lynette Linton, 2019, Sam Wanamaker Playhouse

As the first ever all women of colour production of a Shakespeare play in a mainstream theatre (in both casting and production team), director and leading actor Adjoa Andoh made history, in both senses, with her 2019 production of *Richard II*. Amid the divisions brought to light by Brexit debates, and in the midst of the Windrush scandal, the production openly stated its relevance to the political landscape and was scheduled deliberately to run across the date when Britain's exit from the EU was originally to take place.

Embodying Richard as a woman, at a symbolic level alone, disrupts patriarchal critical judgements of the effeminacy of the king. The female

The Male Body, Kingship and the Body Politic

body onstage inverts the power structure on which that reading relies and past productions have also used cross-casting (such as Fiona Shaw playing Richard in Deborah Warner's 1995 production at the National Theatre). Andoh's production does not simply cast a female actor as king: an all women of colour production defies the limitations of previous all-female productions. While some all-female Shakespeare productions have adopted so-called 'race-blind' casting practices (such as the Donmar Trilogy, Phyllida Lloyd, 2016), arguably this risks supressing the significance of the oppressions to which women of colour are and have been exposed that cannot be encompassed in simply re-embodying the king. Unlike theoretical debates over intersectional feminism, the production's approach exposes and explores more complex issues of patriarchy and of empire, of nationhood and ethnicity, of how we might understand ancestral identities, while layering these over issues of gender to reveal compounded issues of white imperial patriarchal oppression, both historical and current.

The sheer power Andoh exudes as Richard is expressed in a confident, nimble physicality that defies the Richard-as-weak-king trope. Richard's royal person, which must be in some ways the literal incarnation of the body politic, is, in Andoh's performance, agile and self-assured. This production's engagement with the myths of nationhood and empire intersect with the challenges to gendered norms of power that the female cast present. The auditorium, for instance, is adorned with images of the female ancestors of the play's production team and cast. This immerses the audience, beyond the stage world, in a space in which women of colour form the basis both of the nation portrayed in the fiction in front of them and the nation outside the theatre walls. This meta-theatrical design elides the boundaries between player and spectator and bridges the gap between the England onstage and off, creating a body politic that is represented not by the white male body of an English king, but by a collaborative, diverse conglomerate of evident female bodies of colour. It establishes a visibility that resonates clearly through the space, reconfiguring these women of colour as nation-builders who, in defiance of a whitewashed imperial version of history, are instead remembered, revealed, revered.

Within this environment, there were moments of lucidly specific cultural equivalence, where no art was necessary to achieve the specific association between *Richard II* and today's divided nation. At the performance we attended (12 March 2019), murmurings were clearly audible in the audience when Indra

Ové gave Mowbray's speech on being banished (deported) and stripped of his voice, made overtly poignant in the context of the Windrush scandal:

> The language I have learnt these forty years,
> My native English, now I must forgo,
> And now my tongue's use is to me no more
> Than an unstringed viol or a harp.
>
> (1.3.159–62)

Shortly after the production run, Andoh herself gave this speech at a UNHCR event for Refugee Week (2019), presenting it in a Ghanian accent and situating it in the narrative of contemporary displacement and diaspora. Banishment, for Mowbray, becomes a silencing in which, by being exiled, he must lose both language and voice. Yet beyond the uncanny relevance of this moment to a specific, long-term scandal at the time of the performances, this has even wider significance. The concept of silencing via statelessness is not only relevant to a literal deportation, but a summary denial of national belonging effected by the cultural silencing and historical erasure of those ancestors by whom modern England was built. Not only are these words physically spoken by a woman of colour, the audience is drawn to contemplate silencing, both literal and figurative, via the circle of women of colour who look on from the past through the portraits hanging ceremonially from the gallery.

Richard II, often fragmented and known widely by quotation, has produced the most well-used 'evidence' of Shakespeare's English patriotism in John of Gaunt's 'this England' speech. Frequently anthologized in an incomplete state, the speech is usually cut off in its many appropriations before it takes a turn into, as we have seen, a female conceit for England as a 'teeming womb of royal kings'. In Andoh's production, as Dona Croll gave the speech in the intimate Wanamaker theatre while Brexit and Windrush might be debated in parliament only minutes away, we heard audible murmurs once again across the theatre's intimate space as the speech continued into its despair at a divided nation, the body politic at risk. When Ové's Mowbray mourns lost nationhood, Croll's John of Gaunt despairs at the division of 'this England' and Andoh's Richard faces deposition, the body politic is re-examined, challenged and newly exposed, both literally in the bodies onstage and figuratively, in exposing the tenets of white patriarchy that have historically formed its anatomy.

Conclusions

1. The body politic was the pervasive model by which sense could be made of a complex sociopolitical system and hierarchy in early modern England. However, early modern political theory and practice was evolving in terms of how both those in power and the nation as a whole would see monarchy and succession, with ideas of meritocracy and widespread, growing doubt over the validity of the medieval divine right of kings. Shakespeare's Histories explore the precariousness of kingship via the embodiment onstage of diverse 'kings' during a time of female monarchic rule that problematized the patriarchal political system.
2. The ill-judging and unstable king of *Richard II* has been viewed by critics, directors and audiences as representing archetypal effeminacy in contrast to the ultra-masculine Bolingbroke, a view examined via our textual analysis here.
3. When modern productions of *Richard II*, particularly Andoh's ground-breaking all women of colour production (2019), have embodied Richard II in a female actor, they have challenged what we mean by kingship and the body we see on stage in the context of a white patriarchal history. All-female productions of other histories, in particular *Henry V*, present a political challenge to the inherent masculinity of the kingly body politic through presenting a monarch that transgresses gender binary definition.
4. By interrogating and challenging the equation of strong monarchy and the idea of the body politic as fundamentally masculine, while 'his' land is gendered feminine, we can explore how Shakespeare's Histories present the flaws and faultlines in the body politic analogy both in his own time and, as Andoh and Linton did in 2019, at other times of national crisis.

Further Work

Richard III

Consider how Shakespeare utilizes early modern anxieties over disability, which arose out of older superstition, religious fears and contemporary concerns regarding witchcraft, all clashing with burgeoning medical understandings of anatomy. How does Richard's 'different' body disrupt the cohesion of the body politic?

Henry V

This play has frequently been understood as presenting a paragon of English kingship, successful leadership and ideal masculinity. However, Henry is a young and inexperienced king and leads his troops into peril on a precarious claim. How does Henry compare to royal antecedents, particularly his father and the deposed Richard II, in his interpretation of kingship?

Further Reading

Jean E. Howard and Phyllis Rackin, *Engendering a Nation: A Feminist Account of Shakespeare's English Histories* (Routledge, 1997). **Seminal feminist approaches to the Histories, exploring ideas of nationhood and gender in the texts and productions.**

Regina Schulte (ed.) *The Body of the Queen: Gender and Rule in the Courtly World, 1500–2000* (Berghahn Books, 2006). **Thorough, diverse assessment of female monarchic bodies, including the early modern period. Useful for comparison to this chapter's focus on the masculine body of the king: see particularly Louis Montrose and Rachel Weil's chapters.**

Emma Smith, *Shakespeare's Histories* (Blackwell, 2004). **Includes an excellent chapter on 'Gender and Sexuality', offering a pathway into understanding a range of feminist and other approaches to Shakespeare's Histories.**

PRACTITIONER PERSPECTIVE: ADJOA ANDOH

Director and actor Adjoa Andoh reflects on her concept for, direction of and performance in *Richard II* at the Sam Wanamaker Playhouse in 2019 (see cover image). The interview was held at BAFTA, London, 24 June 2019.

What drew you to directing and starring in *Richard II*?

I went to see Globe artistic director Michelle Terry in 2018 about a different project and she offered me the first play in the history cycle they would be mounting the following year. That following year included March 29th, the date we were supposed to be Brexiting the EU and we would be performing throughout that time. *Richard II* is a play about the nature of power within the great conversation around nationhood, a play that holds at its heart the great 'This sceptr'ed Isle' paean to a lost and longed-for England; to stage that play as we Brexited became instantly, fabulously appealing. We would be in the Zeitgeist, addressing the questions on everyone's mind; who is English? What does it mean to be English? Who has the right to call themselves a citizen of this country? Within Brexit, the 'plucky little England standing on her own like she did in the war' narrative is heard a lot. I want to reply, 'no, England didn't get through the wars, Great Britain had an empire. England got through the wars *with the sacrifice* of empire. Beware empire cannot be called upon to shore up the nation this time.'

There is a huge conversation to be had about the contribution of the empire to the wealth and prosperity of this country. So, I wanted to have the conversation within the context of *Richard II*, from the perspective of empire, through the voices and bodies of the people who are always at the bottom of the heap – the women and people of colour.

I wanted the thought experiment of hearing and experiencing the story anew in a production that was entirely created and realized by women of colour, from text edit, to direction to voice direction, fight direction, design, composition, actors, stage management, lighting design. Why? To show that through colonization and trade, the ownership of that story and the creators of this nation, have been expanded; and equally as creative artists, to demonstrate that we women of colour are capable of mounting such a production in all aspects. We can iterate this story afresh, and make the invitation appealing to a broader cross-section of our communities than a usual Shakespeare production might attract. Astonishingly in 2019 there has *never* been an all women of colour production on a major British stage, before us.

All of that is what drew me and co-director Lynette Linton in!

How did you read Richard as a character?

I wanted to look at a little boy whose father died when he was three, whose grandfather died when he was ten, who was stuck on a boat and sent from France to an unfamiliar country, England, and told, 'be a king. Get on with it'. Without role model, guidance nor unconditional love, Richard operates on instinct and mimicry alone – in psychoanalytical terms he might be classed as *insecurely attached* – and so he becomes this *performative* king, with no space to investigate who he really might be. I think many of us live our lives in that way, doing and being what's expected, rather than living the lives we are gifted for.

In the arc of this play, one could say, when Richard is possessed of all worldly wealth, he is an attractive, yet frightened, needy bully, acting out divine majesty rather than inhabiting a true sense of self. As he cedes all the trappings and power of kingship to his ambitious, and probably more innately magisterial, cousin Bolingbroke, in his brokenness, Richard gains a deeper understanding of his true self and what it means to be human. In jail, deposed by his cousin, crownless, friendless and abandoned, shortly before his assassination, Richard reveals to us his new found understanding, he says: '… but whate'er I be, / Nor I nor any man that but man is / With nothing shall be pleased, till he be eased / With being nothing' (5.5.38–41). Nothing will make us happy until we understand that we are nothing, no greater or lesser than any other human being and that they are no greater or lesser than us.

For me, this understanding speaks back into the conversation about being women of colour; one of the most moving things in our rehearsal period was to have all these women from African, West Indian, South East Asian, East Asian, Middle Eastern heritage, suddenly all being in a room together *not* having to represent all women, or all people of colour. For once we could all simply come into the room and be an artist, because *everyone* is a woman of colour. For once, just breathe out; nobody's watching you, waiting for you to mess up or be brilliant, just come and play, be an artist, be your unique and brilliant self in the space. And people broke down. Actors, some who had been doing this for forty years, broke down with the relief of not having to be that performative, representative person – because we do it all the time. It's exhausting. Never being able to tell if you are being judged purely on what you have given as an actor, or if you are being judged through the prism of your judge's own baggage around women or people of colour. Race and gender specifically because these are undisguisable visual signifiers. Of course, we could be having another intersectional conversation about disability and sexuality, which of course is also part of woman of colour's potential life.

It was really important to me after thirty-five years as an actor, with my director's hat on to have people come and just be judged on their work, to be encouraged and emboldened, to try things, fail and fail better, knowing they're not letting down the race or womankind, just having another go at something – and that's ok.

We took the performative king and looked at the way *we* are all obliged to be performative in our lives – because it's not just about women of colour, everybody is in that position. You can be an upper-class, wealthy white boy who actually loves car mechanics or would be a great nurse, but because of the family you're born into you're obliged to join the family firm or go into politics. It's not just a race thing, it's not a gender thing; it's a human thing.

How did you approach broadening your audience?

For me, Shakespeare is the great humanitarian and as with the very best artists, in *Richard II* he creates work that not only talks about history, but fundamentally talks about human beings and their freedom or lack of it, to be who they are. Too often, Shakespeare has become the preserve of elitism, a badge of education and of wealth. Has Shakespeare only got something to say to the moneyed, so-called cultured classes? I do not see that in any of his work. In fact, in his love and generosity towards our human frailties, I see quite the opposite.

So, in presenting *Richard II* in an all women of colour production, I wanted to explore the nature of the unique human spirit, the performative nature of a human being, to give the artists involved a creatively unencumbered space and to make a strong invitation to those potential non-traditional Globe audiences; to say 'Look, here we are! We're all brown women. Not your general fare. Maybe you're not the general fare for a Shakespeare audience? Come and see what we can do. We are doing it with a special invitation to you'.

I wanted to do that in the poster: my big brown face in front of the flag of St. George. We wanted to shift the target audience, in marketing and in pricing. To this end the Globe, with added BAME support, expanded the locations and media for marketing, and ring-fenced some lower ticket prices; because if you're paying £62 for a ticket, that's someone's weekly shopping bill – at that price, why would you take a punt on a Shakespeare play, when it's not something you normally do?

I am interested in telling the story well and in a way that is clear for people who aren't experts on Shakespeare. I wanted to mount an all women of colour production that talks about the uniqueness of each individual human being. By being all women of colour on stage, there is no significance around the interplay of race and gender. In our cast those differences have been neutralized, so the audience and cast are free to simply read straight into the unique nature of each character. I know that we have done our job when somebody who has perhaps never set foot in a theatre to watch a piece of Shakespeare before, comes to our production and does not feel intimidated, out of place, or lost as to what's going on. When that person can engage with *Richard II* and feel like they are carried along by the story, discover something new, be moved, appalled, laugh out loud in the company of others, then we on stage know we have succeeded.

How did your production respond to the space of the Sam Wanamaker Playhouse?

Dominic Dromgoole had the Sam Wanamaker painted black for a Jacobean production a while ago. That does not work for people of colour in space lit purely by candlelight. Black sucks the light out of the space and unless you light extremely fiercely, when *we of colour* are onstage it's a radio play. Subliminally it says people of colour are not meant to be on this stage and by extension nor in this audience.

So, with our lighting designer Prema Mehta, we had to mitigate against the space. I had everything clad in bamboo; first, because bamboo is a material you would find in East Asia, South East Asia, Africa, the Middle East and the West Indies – mirroring the geographical histories of the bodies onstage; secondly because Bamboo is light in colour, and light

Practitioner Perspective: Adjoa Andoh

bounces off bamboo, which would help us enormously. We had a floor that was striated by a bright, gold-coloured reflective metal, and earth. Colonialism was all about exploiting raw materials be they bodies, plants or minerals. Earth, as something to fight for and be supported by, is a theme that is returned to throughout the play; everybody is fighting for this earth, 'this sceptr'd isle'.

In terms of setting the play, we're in the halls of royal power throughout; given that I determined we would be an empire-wide all women of colour production, the thought was 'tell me in what setting women of colour hold the reins of power and I will set it there'. Given that no such place exists, I decided that we would set it in a collective ancestral place that was based on the bodies of the actors in the space.

I remembered my great-grandmother's house, long, wooden, on stilts, set in a huge courtyard, in Cape Coast, Ghana, in the 1970s. The main room was probably about a hundred feet long. On the smooth, polished, wooden walls hung these huge sepia photographs of family members going back as many generations as the art of photography. It reminded me of the stately homes and palaces of Western Europe with all their ancestral paintings of Lord and Lady 'Blahblahblah'. I decided I wanted to take those images from my great-grandmother's house, those sepia photos lining the walls and recreate them. Instead of Lord and Lady 'Blahblahblah', or my sepia-toned family members, we had the photographs of the mothers, grandmothers, aunts and carers of every member of our team: all the women who have got us to where we are today. For every woman of colour involved in the production, there was a photograph, reprinted on linen, hung around the walls of our court, in Rajha Shakiry's design for our halls of power. So that, in the production, when we talk about Richard II's father, there is a photograph of my grandmother, Mamaa. When we talk about the Duke of Gloucester, there's a picture of Sarah Lam's (Duchess of Gloucester) mother. I wanted us to be surrounded by our ancestors, because the way one progresses in this world is still largely based on networks; on who you know and how they push you forward. Yet the people who have pushed us forward, quite often, have been those unsung women. I wanted to acknowledge them as our ancestors, our royalty and the reason that we go forward. It was a huge encouragement every night, to see those women, in their beauty, in their power, in their *survival* looking down on us. Mamaa, my grandmother, that's my lineage, upon whose shoulders I stand. Because of them, we are. That's what we were doing with the pictures. We call them Ancestors because that is the language that has cultural currency for all of us.

Shakespeare and Gender

What were your approaches to costume and cultural custom in the production?

As I said the cultural references flowed out of the bodies of the actors on the stage. In terms of costume design, Richard, for example, is wearing the headdress of an Ashanti chief and carrying the Chief's fly-whisk denoting office, so that's like the crown and sceptre, which are the symbols when given up in 4.1, which denote Richard's deposition from Kingship; but Richard is also wearing the costume of an Indian prince in his pomp. All the costumes have that blend. In terms of cultural custom, there's a scene where the Queen is in the garden and she's talking to her lady-in-waiting. What is she doing in the garden? Leila playing the Queen offered that maybe she's getting her armpits waxed? So that's what we did and given Leila (Farzad's) Iranian heritage, we did it as an Iranian woman would with sugar (which you'll find also in North Africa) and strips of fabric. And because it's recognizable, it was funny, it was arresting. It made the queen relatable to everyday women from all cultures, going through that pestilential process. It humanized the story.

In that garden scene, the tree is a baobab tree, shaped from bamboo, because the baobab is a venerated ancient tree to be found in all our geographical heritage locations. When greeting a respected person, one touches the ground, a gesture of obeisance – a West African tradition; when greeting a beloved person one touches their foot, a gesture of love – an Indian tradition. The trumpets, alarums and songs composed by Dominique LeGendre are based on West Indian road-marching songs. The instruments and vocals used hail from Europe, Africa, China, Pakistan, and India. We were trying to fold in all those different elements, so that whatever you are reading on that stage is part of a coherent narrative that really concretizes the story.

What are your thoughts on women playing men in this production?

I think we are all on a gender spectrum. One of my kids is trans, so it becomes a lived thought experiment for me to ask, what makes a human being a human being? Is it their genitalia? Is it their melanin? Or is it who they are in and of themselves?

I'm much less interested in the idea 'you're a woman playing a man'. What does that even mean? I know as many different kinds of women as there are grains of sand, similarly with men. So, no playing gender. We just needed to think about who this human being is: who are they scared of, who do they love, what power do they need, what power do they fight against, where do they decide to put their allegiances, what will make them betray or remain loyal. I didn't want us to think about male or female, because who goes around thinking about that? You just move through your day thinking 'I've got to get the bus ... oh my god, I didn't get that job .... I really miss that person .... I've got to renew the insurance'. I don't go around thinking 'hey, I'm a black woman!'. I only think about that when someone throws it at me or when it is made an obstruction.

I wanted us simply to play the person, to think about what our character stakes are and play those stakes. So, there's John of Gaunt. His nephew's banished his son, how does he feel about that? How does he feel about the state of his country? There's the Duke of Northumberland; he thinks Richard's a lightweight and will he betray his office and throw his weight behind Bolingbroke to keep his land. Similarly with class, the gardener and his assistant, like working people with little or no power the world over, always want to know what's going on politically. They have to keep their ear to the ground, because as marginalized people they have the least resources to weather any political storm, so they needed to be thoughtful and watchful like economically vulnerable people are, not the working class comedy punchline.

Equally, I didn't want the characters who were women in it to be whiners. I *loathe* seeing Shakespeare productions where the women are whiners; why are they? Because of the director's baggage? Forget that. I wanted the Duchess of Gloucester and the Queen to be mighty in this production, completely present in all their scenes. The Duchess witheringly calls out John of Gaunt's cowardice in 1.2. The Queen is not necessarily in 1.4, our money scene, but I really wanted her central to that. I wanted her with a fag on the go, glasses on, doing the accounts. I wanted her central to Richard's vision – two abandoned kids making common cause to survive along with Richard's beloved cousin Aumerle. Later in 5.1, when the Queen is saying goodbye to Richard on the street, I wanted the audience to see that woman saying 'my God, the power is slipping away. My protection, my love is slipping away. How do I survive? How do I manage?'. Single mothers, women fleeing with their children, with just what they could carry, the ancestors looking down on us, these are not whiny women. I wanted to see the necessary strength of survivor women. Whining is not in the text! It's dreary. And who are the majority of theatre-ticket buyers? Women. Why pay for the privilege of sitting through mighty men and whiny women? Not interesting. Those were the gendered things in the production I wanted to swerve.

Shakespeare and Gender

Overall, how do you feel the production responded to ideas of citizenship in the contexts of heritage and empire?

We, in this production, are all daughters of empire in an *in*voluntary relationship. We are all here because somebody from here went to where our ancestors lived and did something to us that was not of our choice, changed the course of our lives forever and as a result we ended up here. What binds us is our group survival. I'm not the only one in the company, who was the child of someone who had to flee their country as a result of the damage of colonialism. There are many of us who understand the bag by the front door that is always packed, because you never know when you will have to run. So, you grow up with that mentality. There were other people in the cast whose parents, to this day, still have the bag packed and ready to go. Look at Windrush. I would say proudly, we are daughters of empire, survivors of empire, makers of empire; because the empire exists through the contributions, voluntary and involuntary, made all across this nation and the empire, including our antecedents from here and from there, it is all our history.

Nonetheless we are also daughters of this particular history, who may have had a completely *different* history, had it not been for the colonial adventurism and capitalist aspirations of this country. So, the production is both a celebration and a rebuke, a rehistorying, an enriching expansion we hope, of a narrow story told of this nation's past, in the spirit of its great humanitarian creator, William Shakespeare.

CHAPTER 3
TESTING THE MARRIAGE PLOT: FORM, VIOLENCE AND GENDER
Key Texts: *The Taming of the Shrew, Much Ado About Nothing, All's Well That Ends Well*

The Taming of the Shrew opens with an induction scene, before the play proper commences. It offers a generic frame through which Sly (and the audience) might view what follows. Like Hamlet's instructions to the players (3.2.1–36), such framing moments must be taken in their performative contexts. Sly has now been (almost) convinced that he is a lord, and that the woman by his side is really his 'wife'. The audience already know this premise is an elaborate con by the Lord and his men – that Sly is really an itinerant drunkard, who owes money to the tavern and prefers ale to wine. The tricking of Sly extends over several days, and culminates here in the arrival of the players to perform a comedy:

> SERVANT
> Your honour's players, hearing your amendment,
> Are come to play a pleasant comedy;
> For so your doctors hold it very meet,
> Seeing too much sadness hath congealed your blood –
> And melancholy is the nurse of frenzy –
> Therefore they thought it good you hear a play
> And frame your mind to mirth and merriment,
> Which bars a thousand harms and lengthens life.
> SLY
> Marry, I will. Let them play it. Is not a comonty a
> Christmas gambol or a tumbling trick?
> BARTHOLOMEW
> No, my good lord, it is more pleasing stuff.
> SLY
> What, household stuff?
> BARTHOLOMEW   It is a kind of history.

SLY
> Well, we'll see't. Come, madam wife, sit by my side
> And let the world slip: we shall ne'er be younger.
>
> (Induction 2.125–38)

The 'pleasant comedy' (126) offers more 'pleasing stuff' (135) than gambolling or tumbling, or the connotations of Sly's malapropistic 'comonty' (a fusion of 'common', 'comedy' and 'commodity'): a 'kind of history', 'mirth and merriment', which can 'frame your mind' and 'lengthens life'. Sly's own comment as the 'real' play begins similarly frames playing both as rejuvenation, and as something he watches conjugally: 'Let the world slip; we shall ne'er be younger' (138). Comedy is thus simultaneously about 'household stuff', 'history' (136) and the populist forms invoked by Sly, and transformative in its effects. The induction highlights two key issues through the prism of the performance of gender and class: the nature of comedy and its impact. It acknowledges that theatrical practice produces affect and emotion; audience response to what is represented and fictionalized is wrapped into the play's meanings. The 'frame' of our induction into the fictional world of Padua is Sly's viewpoint and experience, on comedy, gender and marriage.

Shakespeare's first comedy was probably *The Comedy of Errors* (*c.* 1592), self-consciously beholden to Roman comedies by Plautus, which were taught, translated and rehearsed in the grammar school system in which Shakespeare and his contemporaries were educated (Baldwin, 1944). It was innovative in fusing the emerging tradition of English theatre's fascination with domestic conflict and minutiae (for example, the anonymous tragedy *Arden of Faversham* (?1592)) with the elegance of the ancient Roman classic comic plot. This plot consisted of two interrelated strands: a conflict – generational between parent and son, or between a rival lover or brother – and a romance – between the son and a supposedly unsuitable or unobtainable young woman (Barber, 2011). The plot was usually resolved through trickery involving a faithful slave and concluded simultaneously in a shift in power from the older to the younger generation and a heterosexual marriage. Genre reinforced an ideological imperative to celebrate marriage as the means through which young men not only come to sexual adulthood and autonomy but simultaneously to political and social power in their community. Comedy itself thus both echoes and reinforces social codes of key rites of passage into adulthood for young males. Plautus's comedies were amongst those studied and debated by young men in grammar schools, universities and Inns of Court. Such narratives were common currency and central to the construction of masculinity. Framed through conflict with an older generation, masculine identity was expressed through playful trickery alongside camaraderie with other young men and consummated in a heterosexual and socialized marriage.

Shakespeare – more than any of his contemporaries – excelled in this plot arena. Alan Boone (1989) argues that the marriage plot is a dominating trope in Western fiction in which the romance of courtship, seduction and marriage retains an erotic charge that fuels the popularity and reception of the novel, helping model bourgeois notions of identity as heterosexist and standardized. Equally significant, however, is the 'counter tradition' which redefines the marriage plot through formal challenges to happy endings, in particular through open-ended novels and multiple voices. Feminist scholars – including Nancy Armstrong (*Desire and Domestic Fiction*, 1987) and Eve Kosofsky Sedgwick (*Between Men*, 1985) – have shown how this dominant plot trope is particularly challenged by looking at female agency (characters and writers) and seeing masculinity as constructed through the exchange of women between men.

The classic comic plot centres round the trials and tribulations of courtship, family disapproval and approval, sexual rivalry, ending on an inclusive wedding party. *The Taming of the Shrew* self-consciously challenges and parodies all these conventions, assuming a sophisticated audience sceptical of both the romance narrative and the logic of heteronormative plots. The plays discussed in this chapter debate the power and erotics of sexual behaviour in a strictly patriarchal society and continue to resonate today both in Western heteronormative societies and cultures which advocate arranged (hetero-) marriages. Although plots and characters challenge dramatic and social conventions, these plays close on the marriage celebrations of multiple heterosexual couples.

Baptista's first words delineate the story as an explicit marriage plot and himself as patriarch who must arrange the ordered marriages of his daughters:

> BAPTISTA
> Gentlemen, importune me no farther,
> For how I firmly am resolved you know:
> That is, not to bestow my youngest daughter
> Before I have a husband for the elder.
>
> (1.1.48–51)

Shakespeare and Gender

Katherina's first words ('I pray you is it your will / To make a stale of me amongst these mates?' (57–8)) explicitly and wittily draws attention to that patriarchal model: that a father's 'will' dominates both the agency and identity of a daughter, and that marriage is figured as an arrangement between men about women. With her semantic play on 'stale' and 'mates' (prostitute and impasse in chess, sexual partner and husband) she tropes her status as both sexual object and subject to a political game. Structurally this initial scene is emblematic; of 250 lines, Katherina speaks eleven and a half, and Bianca four (80–4): a gender (im)balance of approximately 1:15 words spoken by women. Aurally, men's words dominate. Katherina is accused of shrewishness, but the audience hear men clamouring. Amidst these words, the men talk about both love and how to wrangle access to women: delivery and plot show men debate between men about possession of women.

We are introduced to Petruccio in the subsequent scene, in which his knock-about physical dialogue with Grumio establishes his mastery of his servants as physical and verbal. When his commands are met with incomprehension and/or resistance, his response is physical violence ('*he wrings him by the ears*' (1.2.17)). It is in this context that he considers marriage ('haply to wive and thrive as best I may' (55)), and welcomes Hortensio's offer of the possibility of 'a shrewd, ill-favoured wife? … yet … rich' (59–61):

PETRUCCIO
    Signor Hortensio, 'twixt such friends as we
    Few words suffice; and therefore, if thou know
    One rich enough to be Petruccio's wife –
    As wealth is burden of my wooing dance –
    Be she as foul as was Florentius' love,
    As old as Sibyl, and as curst and shrewd
    As Socrates' Xanthippe or a worse,
    She moves me not – or not removes at least
    Affection's edge in me – were she as rough
    As are the swelling Adriatic seas.
    I come to wive it wealthily in Padua;
    If wealthily, then happily in Padua.

(1.2.64–75)

Resource 3.a: Anon., *The Cruell Shrow; or the patient man's woe* (c. 1640)

To the tune of cuckolds all a-row
Come Batchelers and Maried men,
  and listen to my Song;
And I will shew you plainely then,
  the injury and wrong
That constantly I doe sustaine,
  by the unhappy life,
The which does put me to great pains,
  by my unquiet wife.
She never linnes her bauling,
  her tongue it is so loud,
But alwaies shee'le be railing,
  and will not be contrould:
For shee the Briches still will weare,
  although it breedes my strife,
If I were now a Batcheler,
  I'de neuer have a Wife.

  *

When I for quietnesse sake desire,
  my wife for to be still;
She will not grant what I require,
  but sweares shee'le haue her will:
Then if I chance to heaue my hand;
  straight way she'le murder cry:
Then iudge all men that here doe stand,
  in what a case am I.

  *

Thus to conclude and make an ende,
  of these my Verses rude,
I pray all wives for to amende,
  and with peace to be endude:
Take warning all men by the life,
  that I sustained long,
Be carefull how you'le chuse a Wife,
  and so Ile ende my Song.

(pp. 1–2)

Boasting and celebrating 'Twixt such friends as we' (64), Petruccio invents an active verb for courting and marrying ('wive' (55, 74)). The alliterative and assonant connections between marriage and fortune (wive/thrive and wive/wealthily, 55, 74–5) semantically pattern out the play's articulation of masculinity as hunting and gathering and femininity as a passive source of wealth. Physical violence against his servant, initially appearing to be a harmless *commedia dell'arte* type of physical theatre, tips into the discourse of mastery as courting and husbandry. Scenic structuring here plays out male courtship within a context of violent physicality, between men, and about the competitive gaining of wealth. The 'proof' of this behavioural model lies in the fable at the heart of the play's plot: the female shrew who is mythically the worst type of woman, a nag who will wear away at a man's self and income, and disturb the household order. Petruccio's list of women are anti-types of the ideal woman (67–70): all women are commodified, as exemplified in the early modern popular ballad *The Cruell Shrow* (Resource 3.a).

Grumio's admiring comments on Petruccio's courting style ('he will throw a figure in her face and so disfigure her with it that she shall have no more eyes to see withal' (1.2.112–13)) draws attention to the active/passive dynamics of Petruccio's wooing and the violent metamorphosis the wife-to-be must undergo. Simultaneously, however, the connotative semantics echo: words are 'thrown' and 'disfigure' – Katherina is physically assaulted, alerting the audience to the material and affective realities of the marriage plot.

When Petruccio meets Katherina (2.1.180–277) his wooing strategy has already been flagged: his extravagant language (and later excesses) are framed as deliberative performances, aimed at 'wiving'. Their encounter is lively and witty on both sides, with a relatively equal balance of speeches between them (although Petruccio's are longer). However, the encounter closes with:

PETRUCCIO
   Marry, so I mean, sweet Katherine, in thy bed.
   And therefore, setting all this chat aside,
   Thus in plain terms: your father hath consented
   That you shall be my wife, your dowry 'greed on,
   And will you, nill you, I will marry you.
   Now, Kate, I am a husband for your turn,
   For, by this light whereby I see thy beauty –
   Thy beauty that doth make me like thee well –
   Thou must be married to no man but me,

Testing the Marriage Plot: Form, Violence and Gender

> For I am he am born to tame you, Kate,
> And bring you from a wild Kate to a Kate
> Conformable as other household Kates.
> Here comes your father. Never make denial:
> I must and will have Katherine to my wife.
>
> (2.1.269–82)

Petruccio's 'plain terms' underline the marriage as a negotiation between men, connoting a legal agreement and the antithesis of conventional lovers' discourse and the protestant ideal of a mutual equality within marriage. His dismissal of the process of courtship as 'All this chat' (270) emphatically reminds us that this is a transactional negotiation ('will you, nill you' (273)) where Katherina has no voice. The transaction ('your father has consented') literally obliterates Katherina ('nill you'). His insistence on re-naming her as 'Kate' and 'Katherine' in this speech (contra to her designation in the Folio text as 'Katherina') is a linguistically imposed, and aurally sensory experience erasing her name. By troping on her denomination as 'Kate'/'household cates' (279–80) (the provisions a good housewife provided) Petruccio underlines her construction as an ideal wife. Semantics, scenic construction, and aural denomination all coincide to alert an audience to gender conformity in married relations as socially constructed.

The Elizabethan Church settlement of 1558 made sermon-making subject to licence: publishing official homilies which local priests (if they lacked a preaching licence) were expected to preach. *The Homilies* share a common message about obedience to God and monarch, and the evocation of a hierarchical social order. This language of patriarchal obedience and submission is echoed throughout Petruchio's assumptions.

Resource 3.b: *An Homily of the State of Matrimony* (1583)

Now as concerning the wife's duty. What shall become her? Shall she abuse the gentlenesse and humanitie of her husband, and at her pleasure turne all things upside down? No, surely. For that is far repugnant against God's commandement. For thus doeth St. Peter preach to them: *ye wives be ye in subjection to obey your owne husbandes*. To obey is another thing than to controle or command, which yet they may doe to their children and to their familie. But as for their husbands, them must they obey, and cease from commanding and perfourme subjection. For this surely doth nourish concord very much, when the wife is ready at hand at her

> husbandes commandement, when she will applye herself to his will, when she endeavoureth her selfe to seeke his contentation and to doe him pleasure, when she will eschewe all things that might offend him. For thus will most truly be verified the saying of the poet: a good wife by obeying her husband shall beare the rule, so that he shall have a delight and a gladness, the sooner at all times to returne home to her. But on the contrarie part, when the wives be stubberne, froward and malapert, their husbandes are compelled thereby to abhor and flee from their owne houses, even as they should have battaile with their enimies.
>
> (p. 158)

The events at Petruccio's home see explicit, visible violence visited upon servants and Katherina. Petruccio, increasingly manic and distempered, reminds an audience of the populist puppet character Punch, from the Italian *commedia dell'arte*. Grumio complains about being beaten, describes Petruccio's beating his horse, offers himself to beat Curtis, and argues Petruccio is 'more shrew than she' (4.1.75). The master's physical and verbal violence extends to the refusal of food to Katherina because it has not been properly prepared, and the tearing up of new clothes. Sustenance and provision, in the forms of food, drink, rest and clothes are successively denied: all the 'cates' which Katherina needs are brought onto stage, waved around, and sent off again. Is this simply knock-about comedy or theatrical diegesis of the extremity that patriarchal ideologies can produce? There is no definitive answer but the intersection between frame, genre and male characterisation suggests a critique of this part of the fiction.

Two theatrical productions that have performed these scenes in divergent ways help illuminate this issue. Bill Alexander's *The Taming of the Shrew* (RSC, 1992) brought Sly back into the frame here, casting the Lord's servants as Petruccio's servants and Grumio as a metatheatrical master of ceremonies. By contrast, Toby Frow's Globe production (Shakespeare's Globe, 2012) plays the scenes for slapstick laughs, with slight tinges of discomfort about the violence realized through audience-facing grimaces by Katherina (Smantha Spiro) and Grumio (Pearce Quigley).

Petruccio's soliloquy – spoken directly to the audience at the end of the scene – amidst this chaotic violence is chillingly instrumentalist:

Thus have I politicly begun my reign,
And 'tis my hope to end successfully.

Testing the Marriage Plot: Form, Violence and Gender

> My falcon now is sharp and passing empty,
> And till she stoop she must not be full-gorged,
> For then she never looks upon her lure.
> Another way I have to man my haggard,
> To make her come and know her keeper's call:
> That is, to watch her, as we watch these kites
> That bate, and beat, and will not be obedient.
> She ate no meat today, nor none shall eat;
> Last night she slept not, nor tonight she shall not.
> As with the meat, some undeserved fault
> I'll find about the making of the bed,
> And here I'll fling the pillow, there the bolster,
> This way the coverlet, another way the sheets.
> Ay, and amid this hurly I intend
> That all is done in reverend care of her;
> And in conclusion she shall watch all night,
> And if she chance to nod I'll rail and brawl
> And with the clamour keep her still awake.
> This is a way to kill a wife with kindness,
> And thus I'll curb her mad and headstrong humour.
> He that knows better how to tame a shrew,
> Now let him speak; 'tis charity to show.
> (4.1.177–200)

This speech can be quite jarring; Jonathan Pryce as Petruccio (Bogdanov, RSC, 1978) undercut the actor's usual typecasting as a sexy pin-up. As a soliloquy, it is delivered in the liminal space and persona of a character breaking the 'fourth wall' through a direct address to the audience ('Now let him speak', (200)). Metaphors ('my falcon now is sharp'; 'kites that bate and beat', 'man my haggard' (179, 184–5, 182)) are explicitly gendered and aggressive, where marriage is framed as a violent hunt. Femininity is figured as passive prey ('kill a wife with kindness' (197)) and masculinity as though it is naturally aggressive ('man my haggard'). Violence ('fling ... hurly' (190)) is defended as a politic 'reverend care' (193). By stepping *aside* from the action, Petruccio asks the audience to take a view *on* that action ('now let him speak' (200)). The taming story, the exaggerated physical comedy, the physical and linguistic exuberance of Katherina and the mania of Petruccio are all juxtaposed as open to judgement.

What is the impact of this dramaturgical moment? Petruccio self-characterizes as a patriarchal householder expecting obedience and deference from a wife. Second, by addressing the audience directly, he disturbs mimetic representation, and in so doing asks the audience to judge language and actions. Third, Petruccio draws attention to the 'politic' nature of his actions, a self-consciousness reminding us that identity can be constructed and performed. Dramaturgical strategy and the breaking of a genre's mimetic continuity disturb notions of what is 'natural' on stage: the play helps us question who and what we are, might or can be.

This insight has implications for the scenes that follow. For example, as Petruccio and Katherina return to Padua, we witness an apparent conversion on the road as Katherina compromises her account of the world literally to match what Petruccio says, in response to Hortensio's pragmatic urging ('Say as he says, or we shall never go' (4.4.10)). Her acquiescence ('Forward, I pray, since we have come so far, / And be it moon or sun or what you please, ... Henceforth I vow it shall be so for me' (12–15)) is then demonstrated by her behaviour in their encounter with a convenient old man they meet. Petruccio welcomes him as a beautiful young woman, and Katherina plays out this fiction with performative gusto (4.4.38), including reversing her welcome to an apology when Petruccio points out she has the man's gender wrong. Katherina elaborates on Petruccio's fantastic notions within his narrative frame, self-consciously drawing attention to how we perform identities through speech and action. *The Taming of the Shrew* shows how women conform to men's views of the world and how fluidity of identity and crossing of identity boundaries (of gender or class) can create social success. This play's 'marriage-plot' suggests companionate, humorous acknowledgement of societal norms: playfulness and fluidity existing alongside the discourse of domination and subordination, of both the play's title and its staged physical violence.

The Taming of the Shrew's thematized assumption of identities allows gender and class identity to be, and be seen to be, about clothes and prosthetics, from the disguises adopted by Lucentio and Tranio's swapping of costumes (1.1.203) and Petruccio's mad-cap anti-wedding gear (3.2.96–182), to the Sly frame story where the dressing up of a boy actor as a tantalizing woman is played out. It is not the body-underneath that makes the plot or identity, the husband or the wife, but the body displayed on top; success lies in performative identities. The scene at Petruccio's country house with the dress maker (4.3), for example, radically dis-plays physical identity as a construct: Katherina's physical appearance is constructed in layers that can be put on and taken off, a visual scenic moment emblematizing the play's kaleidoscopic gender construction.

Testing the Marriage Plot: Form, Violence and Gender

In the play's finale, Petruccio wagers his wife's obedience as absolute, his confidence in her 'taming' confirmed when Katherina alone comes at her husband's call and makes her final speech:

> Fie, fie, unknit that threatening unkind brow,
> And dart not scornful glances from those eyes
> To wound thy lord, thy king, thy governor.
> It blots thy beauty as frosts do bite the meads,
> Confounds thy fame as whirlwinds shake fair buds
> And in no sense is meet or amiable.
> A woman moved is like a fountain troubled,
> Muddy, ill-seeming, thick, bereft of beauty
> And while it is so, none so dry or thirsty
> Will deign to sip or touch one drop of it.
> Thy husband is thy lord, thy life, thy keeper,
> Thy head, thy sovereign: one that cares for thee
> And for thy maintenance; commits his body
> To painful labour both by sea and land,
> To watch the night in storms, the day in cold,
> Whilst thou liest warm at home, secure and safe,
> And craves no other tribute at thy hands
> But love, fair looks and true obedience –
> Too little payment for so great a debt.
> Such duty as the subject owes the prince,
> Even such a woman oweth to her husband;
> And when she is froward, peevish, sullen, sour,
> And not obedient to his honest will,
> What is she but a foul contending rebel
> And graceless traitor to her loving lord?
> I am ashamed that women are so simple
> To offer war where they should kneel for peace,
> Or seek for rule, supremacy and sway
> When they are bound to serve, love and obey.
> Why are our bodies soft, and weak, and smooth,
> Unapt to toil and trouble in the world,
> But that our soft conditions and our hearts
> Should well agree with our external parts?
> Come, come, you froward and unable worms,
> My mind hath been as big as one of yours,

>   My heart as great, my reason haply more,
>   To bandy word for word and frown for frown.
>   But now I see our lances are but straws,
>   Our strength as weak, our weakness past compare,
>   That seeming to be most which we indeed least are.
>   Then vail your stomachs, for it is no boot,
>   And place your hands below your husband's foot:
>   In token of which duty, if he please,
>   My hand is ready, may it do him ease.
>
>   (5.1.142–85)

Katherina demonstrates her physical obedience to husband, according to the strictures of the Elizabethan church and state (using terms from the official wedding service, 'serve, love and obey'), and her belief in it through giving voice to that ideology in her character ('our weakness past compare'). This kind of articulation of identity within the language of a particular ideology has been described as 'interpellation' by the neo-Marxist theorist Althusser (2014). The plot shows Katherina succumb to, and then speak from, the position of her subjection as a woman in a patriarchal culture. The marriage plot, so starkly delineated in the opening act as a masculine hunt for fortune is finally demonstrated as successful only when a wife can both articulate and *perform* subordination (Katherina offers to place her hand under his foot (185)). Knowledge and performance of a self-proclaimed essential, subordinate (and subordinated) gender identity is seen as necessary to marriage. Shakespeare's play seems to lie firmly within Elizabethan homiletic gender norms, but the male priest's discourse is delivered by a woman.

However, the play arguably points in other directions, producing a choral undercurrent of dis-ease with this dominant gender ideology. The structural framing of the Sly story and scenes foregrounds performativity as the dominant mode of social identity, femininity as constructed by clothing, desire for the 'other', and interpretative contexts. Second, the scenic structure and plot ordering display marriage arrangements as the simultaneous masculine pursuit of wealth and as arrangements between older and younger men, a cultural arrangement in which women are visibly objectified and commodified (see also Chapter 6). Finally, the fast-paced actions and physical comedy arguably displace the narrative from mimetic representation of marriage. By introducing farce to the plot, Shakespeare distances the play from 'reality', saving performances from a mimetic misogyny.

Testing the Marriage Plot: Form, Violence and Gender

Many productions acknowledge that it is only by enabling these choral undercurrents to be performed explicitly that the play can succeed on the modern stage. This is often achieved through casting. If Petruccio is a well-known heart-throb (Douglas Fairbanks in the 1929 film (dir. Sam Taylor), or Jonathan Pryce in the 1978 RSC version), his implicitly violent misogyny is counterbalanced by what the audience already feel or think they know about the actor. Equally, the casting of Katherina can tilt interpretation towards an explicitly feminist reading. The casting of Paola Dionsetti as Katherina (Bogdanov, RSC, 1978) acted as a heavyweight counterpart to Pryce; her ironic removal of her hand from his foot, and the explicit reiteration of the frame at the end of the performance, enabled the feminist viewing position to be explicitly part of the play's meaning. Casting and direction can torque the tale into a feminist resistance to the male (and heteronormative) marriage plot. The film *10 Things I Hate About You* (Junger, 1999, USA) makes popular teenage viewing as a teen romcom story of female empowerment but ignores the endemic misogyny of the original and rewrites the submissive ending. Phyllida Lloyd's all-female casting of the play for Shakespeare's Globe (2003) emphasized the constructed and theatrical nature of gender using cross-casting to estrange gender.

Suspension of disbelief is fundamental to the play's theatricality: 'frame your mind to mirth and merriment' (Induction, 231). The 'comonty' (Induction, 133) raises serious issues about gender identity, the gendered and innate misogyny of the marriage plot and the constrained nature of women's speech, but to achieve this it holds Katherina in a double-bind. 'Freedom' to speak as a married woman comes at the price of subordination. However witty and exuberant her and Petruccio's exchanges, however much we perceive that identity is performative and marriage an economic bargain, in the end the play asks her (and other wives) to submit.

Much Ado About Nothing's plot consists of courtship and marriage, complicated with the device of parallel courting couples to establish divergent outcomes so the audience is encouraged to 'read' these plots against each other. The courting of Hero by Claudio follows a conventional Petrarchan model (1.1.181–90) which is juxtaposed by the parallel anti-courting between Beatrice and Benedick. Equally, the plot juxtaposes two perceptions about love, gender and behaviour. For example, here Benedick recounts how love has changed Claudio:

> I have known when there was no music with him but the
> drum and the fife, and now had he rather hear the tabor
> and the pipe. I have known when he would have walked

ten mile afoot to see a good armour, and now will he lie ten nights awake carving the fashion of a new doublet. He was wont to speak plain and to the purpose, like an honest man and a soldier, and now is he turned ortography; his words are a very fantastical banquet, just so many strange dishes. May I be so converted and see with these eyes? I cannot tell; I think not. I will not be sworn but love may transform me to an oyster, but I'll take my oath on it, till he have made an oyster of me he shall never make me such a fool. One woman is fair, yet I am well. Another is wise, yet I am well. Another virtuous, yet I am well. But till all graces be in one woman, one woman shall not come in my grace.

(2.3.13–29)

Benedick's uncompromising position against erotic love is based on an argument grounded in expected male gender roles: reinforced by his rhetorical repetitions and questions ('I have known …'; 'I am well'; 'graces … my grace' (13, 27, 28-9)). Martial commitment ('drum and fife' (13)) is explicitly contrasted to the music of love ('tabor and pipe' (14–15)). Armour, physical exercise, plain speaking and soldierliness are successively opposed to fashion design, excess speech and courtly banqueting: 'true' masculinity implicitly opposed to Claudio's current changed character under the influence of a woman. Benedick's ideal woman intensifies his characterizations of masculinity as dominant and idealized: his wife will be rich, wise, virtuous, fair, noble, educated and artistic.

By contrast, Balthasar's song in the same scene suggests a different view of gender and love. By prefacing his song with the caveat, 'There's not a note of mine that's worth the noting' (2.3.55), he echoes the play's titular proverb that words and performance are trivial. However, the line's oral effect ('not a note … worth(e) not(h)ing', with the elision of 'th/the') signals the central significance of words and song.

> Sigh no more, ladies, sigh no more,
>   Men were deceivers ever;
> One foot in sea, and one on shore,
>   To one thing constant never.
> Then sigh not so, but let them go,
>   And be you blithe and bonny,

Testing the Marriage Plot: Form, Violence and Gender

>   Converting all your sounds of woe
>   Into 'Hey, nonny, nonny'.
>
> Sing no more ditties, sing no more,
>   Of dumps so dull and heavy;
> The fraud of men was ever so,
>   Since summer first was leavy.
> Then sigh not so, but let them go,
>   And be you blithe and bonny,
> Converting all your sounds of woe
>   Into 'Hey, nonny, nonny'.
>
> (2.3.60–75)

Addressed to the 'ladies' of the audience and in a woman's voice (albeit sung by a man) masculinity is associated negatively with military adventure. Radically, the song urges women to follow their own desires ('let them go / And be you blithe and bonny'), not constrained by male discourses ('the fraud of men was ever so') and reject masculinist conventions of male behaviour.

The play's closure echoes this song's choral function, suggesting a marriage plot in which masculinity is re-drawn. When Beatrice despairingly cries 'O that I were a man … O God that I were a man!' and 'Or that I had any friend would be a man for my sake!' (4.1.302–15, see Chapter 1), Benedick commits himself to believing her version of events and agreeing to act. By being such 'a man' Benedick offers a model of masculinity that fuses lover and soldier. In the scene in which he challenges Claudio to trial by combat (5.1), Don Pedro suggests that Beatrice has 'trans-shape[d] thy particular virtues … what a pretty thing a man is when he goes in his doublet and hose and leaves off his wit!' (5.1.166), attacking Benedick's essential ('particular') and physical ('trans-shape') manliness ('virtue' – from the Latin 'vir', man). The plot shows that the aggressive masculinity of Don John, Pedro and Claudio positions women as physical casualties: Hero's shaming and apparent death have been caused by their arrogance. While Benedick's challenge to Claudio foregrounds chivalric masculinity as a defender of female honour, this is supplemented by additional versions of Benedick's masculinity that are moderated by Beatrice (he is 'trans-shaped'), and wedded to her non-conventional femininity. Henry Smith's *A Preparative to Marriage* (Resource 3.c) establishes conventional notions of gender roles and relationships: Beatrice's characterization is neither silent nor obedient although chaste, acting as an active foil to Benedick's 'trans-shaped' masculinity (see Chapter 1).

Resource 3.b: Henry Smith, *A Preparative to Marriage* (1591)

Every Wife is called Goodwife; therfore if they be not goodwiues their names doo belie them, and they are not worth their titles, but answer to a wrong name as Players doo upon a stage. This name pleaseth them wel: but beside this a Wife is called a *Yoke fellowe*, to shewe that she should helpe her Husband to beare his yoke, that is, his griefe must bee her griefe; and whether it bee the yoke of povertie, or the yoke of enuie, or the yoke of sicknesse, or the yoke of imprisonment, she must submit her neck to beare it patiently with him ... she is called *a Helper*, to helpe him in his businesse, to helpe him in his labours, to helpe him in his troubles, to helpe him in his sicknesse, like a woman Phisition, sometime with her strength, and sometime with her counsel ... It becomes not the Mistris to be Master, no more than it beseemeth the Master to be Mistris, but both to saile with their owne winde.

Lastly, wee call the Wife ... house wife, not a street wife like *Thamar*, nor a field wife like *Dinah*, but a house wife, to shew that a good wife keepes her house: & therefore *Paule* biddeth *Titus* to exhort women that they be chast, & keeping at home: presently after *Chast*, he saith, *keeping at home*, as though *Home* were Chastities keeper. And therefore *Salomon* depainting the Whore, setteth her at the doore, now sitting vpon her stalls, now walking in the streetes, now looking out of the windowes, like curled *Iezabel*, as if she held forth the glasse of temptation, for vanitie to gaze uppon.

As it becommeth her to keepe home, so it becommeth her to keep silence.

(pp. 71–8)

The plot device of Hero's near (or apparent) death (like Hermione's in *The Winter's Tale* and Helena's in *All's Well that Ends Well*) is a visual and dramaturgical demonstration and enquiry into the harm created by misogynist notions of femininity. By staging this in a public and sacred forum (church), Shakespeare's plot functions as a critical engagement in cultural gender practices and prejudices: although the audience know the accusations against Hero are manufactured by John, Claudio holds off his accusation until the marriage day in church, so we see this shaming as both premeditated and unfounded. Beatrice and Benedick's witty dialogues and our privileged viewing behind the scenes use plot and dramaturgy actively to encourage us to align with Hero and Beatrice.

Testing the Marriage Plot: Form, Violence and Gender

The play's finale stages a visual pageant that simultaneously problematizes and resolves the marriage plot. Hero's father has arranged a 'new' marriage for Claudio with a supposed niece. Claudio's acquiescence in this arrangement after his defeat in the duel displays heteronormative marriage as 'forced': a veiled Hero is handed over to Claudio ('this same is she and I do give her to you' (5.4.54)), the marriage formalized ('give me your hand before this holy Friar' (58)), and only then does Hero unveil. Her account of the transaction ('One Hero died defiled, but I do live / And surely as I live I am a maid' (63–4)) reinforce female chastity prior to marriage as essential to both life and status, simultaneously splitting her identity and her history. This short sequence literally stages the passing of woman as object between father and husband (veiled, she is everywoman). Marriage is visually staged as a transaction manoeuvred between men, with a woman's voice complicit in acquiescing in an ideology suggesting death is better than un-chastity. Claudio's words ('Another Hero!' (62)) imply she is an endlessly replaceable model.

Beatrice's and Benedick's union is equally problematic: Benedick's 'Come I will have thee. But by this light, I take thee for pity' and Beatrice's 'I yield upon great persuasion' (5.4.91–5) model marriage as a sparring, reluctant union. Benedick's final comments to the Prince ('Get thee a wife, get thee a wife! There is no staff more reverend than one tipped with horn' (5.4.120–1)) suggests a man's duty to 'get' a wife will always place him in the paradoxical position of authority (over her as a woman) and vulnerability (to cuckoldom via sexual betrayal – 'tipped with horn'), echoing the underlying fear of the Claudio/Hero plot. Plot structure and finale display the marriage plot as a necessary social fantasy: a dark interpretation going against many productions celebrating the 'witty' and sexy relationship between Beatrice and Benedick (see Chapter 1).

The complexity of these views of eros, marriage and politics are condensed visually and via casting in Joss Whedon's *Much Ado About Nothing* (2012, USA). The LA-redolent wealthy house-party setting emphasizes the sexual chemistry and the dangerousness of erotic desire as passions that disrupt social cohesion. The casting of Fran Kranz (a popular Hollywood and Broadway actor) as a young Claudio allowed a nuanced representation of the entitlements and uncertainties of contemporary masculinity. Often the casting in recent years has privileged the pairing of Beatrice/Benedick (Tamsin Greig and Joseph Milson – dir. Marianne Elliott, RSC, 2006; Vanessa Redgrave and James Earl Jones – dir. Mark Rylance, 2013), which arguably detracts from the play's serious examination of the problematics of the marriage plot.

Perhaps Shakespeare's most radical engagement with the marriage plot is *All's Well that Ends Well* (1604/5). Whereas in *The Taming of the Shrew* and *Much Ado About Nothing* theatrical framing, characterization and plot partially displace conventional patriarchal and heteronormative assumptions about gender roles in marriage, *All's Well that Ends Well* questions male agency in sexual choices through inverting conventional plots, the notion of the male gaze and masculine identity as a paramount model for adult behaviour.

Plotting is foregrounded by the play's action. In the opening scene, Helena explicitly tells the audience of her love for Bertram in terms which echo and invert the language of masculine desire for the unobtainable woman:

> ... my imagination
> Carries no favour in't but Bertram's.
> I am undone: there is no living, none,
> If Bertram be away. 'Twere all one
> That I should love a bright particular star
> And think to wed it, he is so above me:
> In his bright radiance and collateral light
> Must I be comforted, not in his sphere.
> The ambition in my love thus plagues itself:
> The hind that would be mated by the lion
> Must die for love. 'Twas pretty, though plague,
> To see him every hour; to sit and draw
> His arched brows, his hawking eye, his curls,
> In our heart's table; heart too capable
> Of every line and trick of his sweet favour:
> But now he's gone, and my idolatrous fancy
> Must sanctify his reliques.
>
> (1.1.84–100)

Her delineation of his physical attributes ('his arched brows ... his curls' (96)) and the sacral imagery ('sanctify his reliques' (100)) echo Petrarchan blazons by men objectifying women (see Introduction and Chapter 1). Metaphor and point of view reinforce staging and dramaturgy: Helena's articulation of desire is performed on stage alone, positioning female voice and body as an active agent in direct conversation with the audience. This early dramaturgical signal of the centrality of female sexual desire and its relationship to female pursuit of marriage directly counters in voice, character and staging the dominant heteronormative plot 'between men'.

Testing the Marriage Plot: Form, Violence and Gender

The overall plot equally gives agency to women, which cumulatively questions the conventions of the patriarchal marriage plot. Bertram's mother, the Countess, observes Helena's love and validates her choice over and above her son's views (1.3). Helena's professional medicinal knowledge and skill cures the King's apparently terminal fistula and, in return, he allows her to choose Bertram as a husband (2.3). When Bertram denies Helena as a wife, she uses the apparently impossible language of his rejection letter to plot out a resolution:

> Look on his letter madam; here's my passport.
> 'When thou canst get the ring upon my finger, which
> shall never come off, and show me a child begotten
> of thy body that I am father to, then call me husband.
> But in such a 'then', I write a 'never'.
> This is a dreadful sentence.
>
> (3.2.56–61)

Two words here, 'passport' and 'sentence', act as puns connoting both a legalized exile from her conjugal rights, and the language of narrative, a story over which Helena might take control. The riddle implicit in the hypothetical 'when … then' provides a hypothesis of (impossible) action that Helena accepts and enacts. When Helena travels to Florence as a pilgrim to find Bertram, she meets with the Widow and Diana and they collectively deceive Bertram into believing he will sleep with Diana before substituting Helena in a bed-trick engineered by women for women. Helena makes this agency explicit when she meets with Diana and the widow:

> Why then to-night
> Let us assay our plot; which, if it speed,
> Is wicked meaning in a lawful deed
> And lawful meaning in a lawful act,
> Where both not sin, and yet a sinful fact:
> But let's about it.
>
> (3.7.43–8)

The action she creates is a 'plot' in both senses: a series of subterfuges to a political end, and a story in which she is active agent. The Countess conspires with Helena to report her death, which drives Bertram to believe he can sleep with Diana and return to Paris without penalty. By passing on her ring to Bertram in the darkened bedroom, Helena ensures she can publicly shame him into the finale's admissions. When Bertram offers the ring in pursuit of another marriage, the King recognizes it as the one he gave Helena. Bertram's denials of both ring and Helena effectively expose, publicly, his character as opposite to his supposedly beloved 'honour' (a word appearing eight times in the final scene, 5.3.98, 180). This exposure has been engineered and plotted by Helena.

There are a number of folktale archetypes lying behind *All's Well that Ends Well*'s plot but they are all reversed to question and challenge traditional sexual and gender relationships and hierarchies of folktale. The story of the low-born clever man who performs an impossible task, and is given a beautiful bride in return, is inverted and defamiliarized. Helena's own story articulates agency through her gaze, through the expression and enactment of sexual desire and through action. The medieval folk story of the loathly lady (known from Chaucer's *The Wife of Bath's Tale*) who is transformed after a night with a prince is complicated in *All's Well that Ends Well* by characterization and plot. Bertram's rejection of Helena evokes those stories where a man is forced into marriage ('a poor physician's daughter my wife!' 2.3.116), including his refusal to kiss her when she demands it (2.5.87). However, the audience never see Helena as a loathly lady: we see the story from her perspective because of a number of structural and dramaturgical guiding devices. First, her soliloquies, via direct address to the audience, invoke our sympathies; second, the older characters (King and Countess) continually tell us and other characters that she is virtuous and clever; third, Bertram's characterization remains throughout at the register of a sulky teenager. Inversion of fairytale and folktale motifs transgress gendered conventions, forcing audiences to reconsider such stereotypes.

The bed-trick plot recurs in a number of folktales and prose stories circulating in renaissance Europe. The plot usually involves a man acting on behalf of a wronged woman so she can obtain a fully legal claim to the man with whom (unknown to him) she sleeps (see the Duke's actions in *Measure for Measure* (4.1)). The duped man usually desires a different woman illicitly and the bed trick acts as a plot device displacing his sexual desire for the 'wrong' woman onto either his wife or his betrothed. The bed-trick thus facilitates the marriage plot to ensure a legitimate marriage, which coincides with the formal closures and resolutions of the story or play. But this plot provides some recompense for women wronged by men (as in *Measure for Measure*) and, in taking control of such a plot device, Helena is empowered as a legitimate agent of her own sexual desires within the frame

Testing the Marriage Plot: Form, Violence and Gender

of the heterosexual marriage plot. The implicit violence of the bed-trick (a woman takes a man both sexually and in law) is performed off stage in *All's Well that Ends Well* (between 4.2 and 4.4), although the 2017 Sam Wanamaker production (dir. Byrne) performed the violent and sexualized actions through the doors, with naked legs and arms emerging suggestively. By juxtaposing this violence with the violence of the men at war, and Bertram's continued lack of contrition for his violent language against Helena, the production trod a fine line between condemnation of both main protagonists.

The parallels between Bertram and Paroles help maintain our critical distance from Bertram, and ally us with Helena. Paroles' actions and attitudes are twinned with Bertram's: they confer and plot to escape Paris and the shackles of Bertram's marriage and discourse on the 'manly' nature of going off to war (2.3.282). Coupled with Paroles' affectionate language to Bertram ('sweet heart' (2.3.270)), there are hints of a homoerotic friendship where masculinity is evoked through male friendship and militarism. However, the play's action critiques this notion of masculinity by parallel plotting: against Bertram by Helena and against Paroles by the soldiers (who trick him into confessing his military treachery and cowardice). These two plots are played out in interlinking scenes in Florence where Helena and Diana plot against and successfully trick Bertram into Helena's bed (Act 4). When Paroles bewails 'who cannot be crushed with a plot?' (4.3.328), his comeuppance echoes into the main story where Bertram is also undone by a plot. Plot and character parallels thereby question the notion that patriarchal authority and gender hierarchies are natural, necessary or desirable.

Dramaturgical plotting positions women as active theatrical agents; excepting the witches in *Macbeth*, this is the only play Shakespeare writes in which women open the speaking. The Countess's views are pivotal, turning the audience away from assumptions about patriarchal agency in an early modern social world. In conversation with Helena, she claims her as more her daughter than Bertram is her son (3.2.68). Through dialogue and characterization, a matriarchal model for marriage plotting counterweighs the conventional marriage plot: two or more women are pitted against one man, a triangular disturbance of the 'between men' model in which woman is always a third party. Two scenes set in Florence (3.5 and 3.7) feature only women speakers. The first involves the widow, Mariana and Diana meeting Helena in the street as they watch and wait for, and then comment upon, men marching from war. They remark on both Bertram's honour ('if he were honester he were much goodlier' (3.5.79–80)) and Paroles' appearance and function (a 'jackanapes with scarves', 84) and, by appearing amidst the crowd, act as commentator figures on military action as defining masculinity, evoking audience complicity into their plots and stories. The play's finale, in which Helena's plotting forces Bertram to acknowledge he has slept with her and that she is pregnant, means the marriage plot is wholly owned by women. However, Bertram's acquiescence appears begrudging; there is no evidence that he has really changed his attitude either to Helena or to women. The closure leaves the audience with feelings of discomfort, suggesting we are culturally uncomfortable with powerful and assertive women who 'plot' their own narratives and marriages.

Helena's reiterated proverbial commonplace 'All's well that ends well' (4.4.35; 5.1.25) denotes a world where she has optimistically spun the best story out of adverse circumstances. By expressing agency, desire and active plotting, a woman's voice and body can credibly legitimize the marriage plot. The first lord's description of 'the web of our life [as] of mingled yarn' (4.3.71), tropes life crises as tapestries of stories: the mingled yarns of both men's women's views are intertwined in this play but the makers of tapestries were women.

Conclusions

1. Traditional festive comedies narrate and perform the courtship between one or two young couples, the generational and paternal obstacles they face, and the final redemptive closure in marriage and festive celebration. The plays discussed here use generic and performative strategies to force an audience to question the genre and its cultural connotations of marriage as festive ending and of the gender roles in a heteronormative marriage plot. In *The Taming of the Shrew*, the induction frame breaks the 'fourth wall' so the subsequent play is viewed as performance and gender as constructed by clothes and situation. In *Much Ado about Nothing*, the marriage plot is dissected as one socially rather than erotically organized, and challenged through the near-tragic repudiation of Hero in the church. In *All's Well that Ends Well*, fairytale plot expectations are inverted and challenged by giving significant professional agency to a female character in the marriage plot.

Testing the Marriage Plot: Form, Violence and Gender

2. These plays do not involve cross-dressing heroines who can use a masculine appearance and speaking position to explore alternate gender identities. Instead, protagonists clash with social and gendered conventions. This places an emphasis on both plot and character. The plays show us that the narratives and stories we use to shape our lives and communal practices (such as love and marriage) are determined by stereotypes: shrews behave in a particular way, the pure woman must have a back-history, boys will be boys and so on. These plays use generic disruption, generic reversal, characterization, framing devices, and choral voices to show how these conventions are limiting and damaging.

3. Masculinity and femininity are exposed as social constructions, through an emphasis on clothing as performative, and by associating masculinity with excessive aggression, militarism, violence and solipsism.

4. Patriarchal control of the marriage market through paternal intervention and decision-making is central to the decision-making of the young men engaged in trying to marry. Such patriarchal control is handed over to husbands: symbolically enabling the marriage plot to be seen as an arrangement 'between men'. The Protestant emphasis on companionate marriage (implicit in Petruccio and Kate's and Benedick and Beatrice's accommodations) sits alongside this theatrical insight in uneasy juxtaposition.

5. Sexual identity and desire is contained by the marriage plot's resolution, but talk about cuckolding and female sexuality show that a desire to control female sexuality lies at the heart of masculine sexual violence. Heteronormative closures to the marriage plots are dependent upon models of gender relying on knowledge about, and control of, female chastity.

6. Audience positioning (through breaking of the fourth wall, or privileged access to scenes showing alternative plots or additional information) is significantly critical of male posturing, plotting and characterization. The cumulative doubling of disguise and courtship in *The Taming of the Shrew* draws attention to courtship as masculine rivalry through parodic repetition. Audience recognition of genre reversal positions us as critical of dominant narratives: songs in *Much Ado About Nothing* and inverted fairytales in *All's Well that Ends Well* chorally comment on main narratives.

Shakespeare and Gender

Further Work

The Taming of the Shrew

How do crossings of class and gender in the Induction inform the play? How does farce (the cumulative repetition of physically ridiculous situations) in Shakespeare's early plays comfort and discomfort audiences? How and why is identity problematized in other characters (see Tranio's 'study what you most affect' (1.1.40))?

Much Ado About Nothing

Marriage and courtship are discussed by different characters in 2.1. Who owns the scene? How do men and women mutually comment on gendered behaviour? How is the audience positioned? How does the formality of staging in 4.1 affect our judgement of events? The language and genres of love are self-consciously debated by Benedick, Margaret and Beatrice in 5.2: how does this influence our reading? How is architectural space gendered and does this help to think about 'plots'?

Further Reading

Kate Aughterson, ed. *Renaissance Woman: An Anthology of Sources and Documents* (Routledge, 1995). **Contains early modern texts on conduct to compare with Shakespeare's plays.**

C.L. Barber, *Shakespeare's Festive Comedy: A Study of Dramatic Form and Its Relation to Social Custom* (Princeton University Press, 2011). **Classic study of 'festive' comedy.**

Catherine Belsey, *Why Shakespeare?* (Palgrave, 2007). **Excellent consideration of Shakespeare's use and transformation of traditional stories.**

Laurence Danson, *Shakespeare's Dramatic Genres* (Oxford University Press, 2000). **Discussion of Shakespeare's thinking about genre.**

Frances Dolan, *Marriage and Violence: The Early Modern Legacy* (University of Pennsylvania Press, 2008). **Excellent debate about patriarchal ideology in theories of marriage in the early modern period and contemporary discourses.**

Leonard Tennenhouse, *Power on Display: The Politics of Shakespeare's Genres* (Routledge, 1986). **The first study to talk about how Shakespeare uses genre and plot for political interpretative ends.**

CHAPTER 4
CROSS-DRESSING AND GENDER TRANSGRESSION(S)
Key Texts: *As You Like It* and *Twelfth Night*, with *The Merchant of Venice*

All drama involves playing and pretending to be someone or something new or different; identity is central to theatrical exploration. Cross-dressing, therefore, is integrally theatrical, a necessary part of the dramatic repertoire for actors, playwrights, performers and audience. The early modern theatre in England was, simultaneously, both joyously self-conscious and deeply anxious about how theatre enabled, displayed, liberated and constrained models of identity. Adolescent boys played women on the public English stage until 1662, a largely unquestioned convention, although women did perform in masques at the royal Court, in private performances and in some touring European companies, and worked in theatre costuming, management and property ownership (Korda, 2011: 1–13). Just like seventeenth-century kabuki theatre (which is still practised in this way), performances were all-male, suggesting a non-mimetic, representational and symbolic theatre. Plays asked audiences to suspend their disbelief when a youth played a woman. If we are overly self-conscious that the actor playing Lady Macbeth is an adolescent boy, we are distracted from the story's political and personal fiction. Cross-dressing was an accepted convention. A significant number of plays include female-to-male cross-dressing as a plot device, sometimes as a means to escape a complicated situation, as protective disguise, or to enable the actor beneath to more naturally 'act' his character. Fewer plays explore male-to-female cross-dressing (exceptions include *Merry Wives of Windsor*, Jonson's *Epicoene*, Middleton's *A Mad World My Masters*). Some of these explicitly draw attention to the convention of cross-dressing and its disruptive possibilities to stereotypical notions of gender and sexuality, often through a framing prologue, induction or epilogue (as in *The Taming of the Shrew* or *As You Like It*). This chapter debates plot-driven cross-dressings within the context of an all-male theatrical tradition.

In the late 1590s, a number of Shakespeare's contemporaries worked at the two boys' company theatres (St. Paul's and Children of the Chapel), an acting tradition that emphasized non-mimetic representation. John Marston's *Antonio and Mellida* (c. 1599), contemporaneous to both *As You Like It* (1599) and *Twelfth Night* (1601), debates cross-dressing:

> FELICE
> Why, what must you play?
>
> ANTONIO
> Faith, I know not what: an Hermaphrodite; two parts in one: my true person being *Antonio*, son to the Duke of *Genoa*; though for the love of *Mellida*, *Pieros* daughter, I take this feigned presence of an *Amazon*, calling my self *Florizell*, and I know not what. I a voice to play a lady! I shall ne're do it.
>
> ALBERTO
> O, an *Amazon* should have such a voice, *virago*-like, not play two parts in one? away, away: 'tis common fashion. Nay if you cannot bear two subtle fronts under one hood, idiot, go by, go by; off this worlds stage. O time's impurity!
>
> ANTONIO
> Ay, but when use hath taught me action, to hit the right point of a Ladies part, I shall grow ignorant when I must turn young Prince again, how but to truss my hose.
>
> FELICE
> Tush never put them off: for women wear the breaches still.
>
> (Induction, 64–77)

By drawing attention to young actors playing men playing cross-dressed women and by explicitly foregrounding the material, physical accoutrements and actions required of the actor ('I a voice to play a lady!' 'to truss my hose' (69, 76)), the Induction frames staged gender performance as playful and effortful but essential to an actor's labour. Alberto's 'if you cannot bear two subtle fronts under one hood, idiot .... off this worlds stage' (71–3) implies that diversity is a social and theatrical requirement and that social and gender performance is central to any 'front[ing]' of identity. Three additional points here recur in debates about early modern cross-dressing. First is the fear that by dressing as a woman the male actor will become a woman and disturb the supposedly 'natural' order of identity, body and gender (see Resource 4.c). The second is the commonplace proverb (implicitly misogynist) that women 'wear the breaches still' (Tilley, 1950: B645). Finally, the third is that such performance creates a new kind of

Cross-Dressing and Gender Transgression(s)

being ('an Hermaphrodite, two parts in one' (65)); crossing gender becomes simultaneously monstrous, theatrical and covertly hermaphroditic – or as we might say now, intersex ('parts' connoting genitalia). This debate is a complex mix of misogyny, playful cross-dressing, self-conscious theatrical discourse and a covert queering of all supposedly stable or binary identities. This interplay of motivations, discourses of cross-dressing as material performance (many boy actors had to do it) and playful signifier, typifies early modern representations of, and playing with, cross-dressing.

How, why and when does Shakespeare foreground cross-dressing? Why might this be important? How is this informed by Elizabethan and Jacobean thinking about gender and erotics? The doubled, and tripled, nature of an audience's response to instances of cross-dressing can make it difficult to answer these questions. We have already seen (Chapter 3) that the Induction to *The Taming of the Shrew* plays with the model of male-to-female cross-dressing as simultaneously erotic (both homoerotic and heteroerotic) and ridiculous.

Recent theorizations of cross-dressing have ranged across a number of interpretative positions, informed by our own changing perceptions of cross-dressing and its relationship to sexual and gender identity, including queer identities. Second-wave feminism (1960s–early 1980s) interpreted cross-dressed heroines as transgressively defiant of patriarchal prescriptive gender norms, seeing Viola, Portia and Rosalind as representing (albeit ventriloquiously) a kind of proto-feminist Elizabethan woman (Jardine, 1983; Woodbridge, 1984). Some third-wave feminists (late 1980s–1990s) argued that the erotic dynamics generated by cross-dressed heroines deconstructed the dynamics of heteronormative desire, including the view that both the early and contemporary postmodern homoerotic gaze was both validated and titillated by the fact of boy actors acting as women dressing as men (Garber, 1992; Jardine, 1992; Orgel, 1996; Zimmerman, 1992). By contrast, New Historicists have argued that apparently liberatory representations of women characters (albeit as men) are finally closed down by the plays' return(s) to normative identities (Dollimore and Sinfield, 1994; McCluskie, 1989; Newman, 1991). More recently, queer theory and fourth-wave feminist articulations of material bodily identities, axes of desire and the power of the subject enable readings of cross-dressing characters and plots in their performative context. They integrate affective theories about audiences to readings of dramatic cross-dressing as part of wider contemporary liberatory debates about power, desire and gender identity (Chess, 2016; Stanivukovic, 2017; Traub, 2016b).

Shakespeare and Gender

Shakespeare's first female character to cross-dress as a man is Julia in *Two Gentlemen of Verona* (c. 1594) when escaping from her father's wrathful imprisonment to seek her banished lover. Finding him in love with another woman, she becomes his page, and a partial resolution to the love triangle eventually follows. Portia's account of her plan in *The Merchant of Venice* (c. 1596–7) to save her husband's friend from his debt necessitates a change of clothes and identity:

> They shall [see us], Nerissa, but in such a habit
> That they shall think we are accomplished
> With that we lack. I'll hold thee any wager,
> When we are both accoutred like young men,
> I'll prove the prettier fellow of the two,
> And wear my dagger with the braver grace,
> And speak between the change of man and boy
> With a reed voice, and turn two mincing steps
> Into a manly stride, and speak of frays
> Like a fine bragging youth, and tell quaint lies
> How honourable ladies sought my love,
> Which I denying, they fell sick and died.
> I could not do withal; then I'll repent,
> And wish, for all that, that I had not killed them.
> And twenty of these puny lies I'll tell,
> That men shall swear I have discontinued school
> Above a twelvemonth. I have within my mind
> A thousand raw tricks of these bragging jacks
> Which I will practise.
> NERISSA   Why, shall we turn to men?
>
> (3.4.60–78)

Portia wants to perform difference convincingly ('think we are accomplished / With what we lack' (61–2)); the audience's conviction – not physical biology – is key. Her anatomization of masculinity through costume ('dagger' (65)), voice ('speak the change between man and boy' (166)), gait ('manly stride' (68)), and discourse ('quaint lies' 'bragging jacks' (69, 77)) delineates a perception of gender as performative and of youthful masculinity as fragile and comical. This perception simultaneously empowers her female-positioned speaking voice as critical of callow young men, destabilizing conventional Elizabethan gender hierarchies in which women are inferior to men, and suggests gender can be performed. Elizabeth I's apocryphal, doubly-gendered speech on the eve of the Spanish Armada in 1588 provided a public model of gender performance as exterior and of two-sexes-in-one (Resource 4.a, contemporaneously recorded as verbatim, although unlikely to have been delivered in person).

Resource 4.a: Elizabeth I, speech to her troops at Tilbury (1588)

My loving people,
We have been persuaded by some that are careful of our safety, to take heed how we commit our selves to armed multitudes, for fear of treachery; but I assure you I do not desire to live to distrust my faithful and loving people.

Let tyrants fear. I have always so behaved myself that, under God, I have placed my chiefest strength and safeguard in the loyal hearts and goodwill of my subjects; and therefore I am come amongst you, as you see, at this time, not for my recreation and disport, but being resolved, in the midst and heat of the battle, to live and die amongst you all; to lay down for my God, and for my kingdom, and my people, my honour and my blood, even in the dust.

I know I have the body of a weak, feeble woman; but I have the heart and stomach of a king, and of a king of England too, and think foul scorn that Parma or Spain, or any prince of Europe, should dare to invade the borders of my realm; to which rather than any dishonour shall grow by me, I myself will take up arms, I myself will be your general, judge, and rewarder of every one of your virtues in the field.

I know already, for your forwardness you have deserved rewards and crowns; and We do assure you on a word of a prince, they shall be duly paid. In the mean time, my lieutenant general shall be in my stead, than whom never prince commanded a more noble or worthy subject; not doubting but by your obedience to my general, by your concord in the camp, and your valour in the field, we shall shortly have a famous victory over these enemies of my God, of my kingdom, and of my people.
(BL Harley 6798, f.87, as transcribed by the British Library, http://www.bl.uk/learning/timeline/item102878.html)

Nerissa's question ('shall we turn to men?' (78)) tropes physiology and sexual desire. Objections to theatricality argued that boy performers might literally become women (see Resources 4.b and 4.c), a fear based both on the effect of performance on the performer's body and on an Elizabethan and Jacobean physiological model in which women were physically described as inverted men (Resource 4.b). Nerissa's question foregrounds this fear as simultaneously possible and ridiculous, a doubled acknowledgement that allows an audience a frisson of fear and a delicious voyeurism into gender bending. Equally, the erotic double entendre (shall we use men for sex?) tropes possibilities of both hetero- and homoeroticism.

Resource 4.b: Helkiah Crooke, *Microcosmographia* (1615)

The Testicles in men are larger and of a hotter nature then in women; not so much by reason of their situation, as because of the temperament of the whole body, which in women is colder, in men hotter. Wherefore heat abounding in men thrusts them foorth of the body, whereas in women they remain within, because their dull and sluggish heate is not sufficient to thrust them out. The trueth of this appeareth by manifold stories of such women, whose more active and operative heate hath thrust out their Testicles, and of women made them men. (p. 204)

*

Wherefore a woman is so much lesse perfect then a man by how much her heate is lesse and weaker then his; yet as I saide is this imperfection turned unto perfection, because without the woman, mankinde could not have beene perfected by the perfecter sexe. (p. 216)

*

But this opinion of *Galen* and *Aristotle* we cannot approve. For we thinke that Nature aswell intendeth the generation of a female as of a male: and therefore it is vnworthily said that she is an Error or Monster in Nature. For the perfection of all naturall things is to be esteemed and measured by the end: now it was necessary that woman should be so formed or else Nature must have missed of her scope, because shee intended a perfect generation, which without a woman cannot be accomplished.

(p. 271)

All four feminist interpretative positions can provide illuminating insights and performance possibilities: Portia might be an independent woman using cross-dressing to enable her to speak out in the male world of the court room (simultaneously retrieving her husband), defying patriarchal norms about expectations surrounding women. Ellen Terry's Portia became a symbol of the women's suffrage movement's advocacy of votes for women (Grant Ferguson, 2019: 33). Equally, Portia's and Nerissa's self-conscious discussion of the erotic dynamics of cross-dressing might be playful expressions of the homoeroticism of boys playing women on stage. New Historicist readings might argue that the limitation of female-to-male cross-dressing to the court room, for the purposes of confirming racial and gender hierarchies in the court's judgement, explicitly shows non-normative gender identity or erotic desire should be closed down. Queer theory and fourth-wave feminist interpretations focus on the continued playfulness of gender and erotic expression, showing cross-dressing as the initial plot and performative trigger for such expressions and the ongoing problematization of binary gender and erotic identifications throughout the plot.

Resource 4.c: Philip Stubbes, *An Anatomy of Abuses* (1578)

Philoponus. The Women also there have dublets & Jerkins as men have here, buttoned up the brest, and made with wings, welts and pinions on the shoulder points, as mans apparel is, for all the world, & though this be a kinde of attire appropriate onely to man, yet they blush not to wear it, and if they could as wel chaunge their sex, & put on the kinde of man, as they can weare apparel assigned onely to man, I think they would as verely become men indeed as now they degenerat from godly sober women, in wearing this wanton lewd kinde of attire, proper onely to man. It is written in the 22. of *Deuteronomie,* that what man so ever weareth womans apparel is accursed, and what woman weareth mans apparel is accursed also. Now, whether they be within the hands and lymits of that cursse, let them see to it themselves. Our Apparell was given us as a signe distinctive to discern betwixt sex and sex, & therfore one to weare the Apparel of another sex, is to participate with the same, and to adulterate the veritie of his owne kinde. Wherefore these Women may not improperly be called *Hermaphroditi,* that is, Monsters of bothe kindes, half women, half men.

(fo.F5^{r-v})

Shakespeare and Gender

As You Like It (*c*. 1599) and *Twelfth Night* (*c*. 1601) were written in the last years of Elizabeth I's reign. The queen had refused to name an heir, she was old and visibly decaying, but the myth of the Virgin Queen played on, in which she was simultaneously old and young, living and reborn, masculine and feminine (see Resources 4.a, 4.f). *As You Like It*'s initial rationale for cross-dressing is physical safety, as Rosalind makes clear: 'what danger will it be to us, / Maids as we are, to travel forth so far! / Beauty provoketh thieves sooner than gold' (1.3.105–6). Celia's answer (to 'put myself in poor and mean attire … so shall we pass along' (107)) is countered by Rosalind's gender cross-dressing proposal:

> ROSALIND Were it not better,
> Because that I am more than common tall,
> That I did suit me all points like a man?
> A gallant curtal-axe upon my thigh,
> A boar-spear in my hand, and in my heart,
> Lie there what hidden woman's fear there will,
> We'll have a swashing and a martial outside,
> As many other mannish cowards have
> That do outface it with their semblances.
>
> (1.3.111–19)

Cross-dressing (here of class *and* gender) is protective covering for the dangers of travelling as unaccompanied gentry women: the performance ('swashing') and appearance ('outside' (l.117)) are key to 'mannish' (l.118) identity. Social identity and credibility is a successful 'outface [ing] … with … semblances' (l.119), and emphatically located in terms of freedom, 'Now go we in content / To liberty and not to banishment' (1.3.134–5).

Resource 4.d: Judith Butler, *Gender Trouble* (1992)

There is no gender identity behind the expressions of gender … identity is performatively constituted by the very 'expressions' that are said to be its results.

(p. 25)

Resource 4.e: Emmanuel le Roy Ladurie, *Carnival in Romans* (1979)

Carnival was not merely a satirical and purely temporary reversal of the dual social order, finally intended to justify the status quo in an 'objectively' conservative manner. It would be more accurate to say it was a satirical, lyrical, epic-learning experience for highly diversified groups. It was a way to action, perhaps modifying the society as a whole in the direction of social change and possible progress.

(p. 316)

Cross-dressing creates gender identity as credible: masculinity is all about the exterior and performance. Nevertheless, through the allocation of allegorical names, Shakespeare allows us to see these new identities as both sexualized and 'othered'. Rosalind's new name ('Ganymede') would have been instantly recognized by the educated in the audience as that of Jove's page in mythical stories, and coded as homoerotic in Elizabethan poetry. Celia's name ('Aliena') is an aptonym literally meaning 'other': both names connote non-normative identities. Otherness characterizes much of the forest experience. From the opening scene, Arden flaunts itself as a carnivalesque world in which conventional modes of behaviour, time, speech and love are disregarded. The exiled Duke's lifestyle is delineated as that of an outlaw ('in the Forest of Arden … many merry men with him, and there they live like the old Robin Hood of England' (1.1.109–10)), Jaques gives a star-struck account of the fool's wit and freedom ('O noble fool / A worthy fool. Motley's the only wear' (2.7.33–4)) and Oliver Martext queers the accepted, conventional readings of the Bible on marriage. There are, too, various disquisitions on how time moves strangely (Orlando's 'There is no clock in the forest' (3.2.319)). Mikhail Bakhtin's model of the Carnivalesque (Resource 4.e) models how liberatory such inversions could be in early modern society (see also Chapters 1 and 6). By reiterating the carnivalesque through setting, cross-dressing, characterization, misreadings of gender, and performative tableaux, the play deliberatively delivers a self-conscious campness. The most recent Globe production (dir. Michelle Terry, Shakespeare's Globe, 2018) drew inspiration from modern and early modern carnivals, to show the forest transcending conventional notions of time, gender and sexuality, celebrating not erasing difference.

Jaques' 'All the world's a stage, / And all the men and women merely players' speech (2.7.140–67) exemplifies the metaphor of life as performance. Life as playing, both in terms of performance and games, was a conceit used in Christian and other ethical discourse to suggest the transience of mortal life. Is the carnival we see and feel in the play merely a plangent reminder to us that life on earth is brief, the afterlife very long? Jaques' speech is certainly melancholic but in his equal address to men and women, alongside its suggestion that manliness is defined by age not biology ('his big manly voice, / Turning again toward childish treble' (3.3.162–3)), Jaques posits a radical connection between the plot's cross-dressing and wider explorations of performative and alternative identities. Donnellan's Cheek by Jowl (1992) production used all-male casting with festive design and costumes, to connect and connote carnivalesque freedoms with alternative sexual and gender identities.

One scene between Rosalind-as-Ganymede and Orlando in the forest functions as a climax to the plot's gender and sexual erotics: their mutual desire coincides, but only the audience, Rosalind and Celia know this. Their courtship is predicated on Orlando's agreement to suspend disbelief about gender, while the audience is 'reassured' that the fictional Ganymede is actually a woman, so the plot's explicit heterosexual love story is retained. Rosalind's conversation with Celia foregrounds her internal woman (although the original actor was male):

> ROSALIND
> Good my complexion! Dost thou think,
> though I am caparisoned like a man, I have a doublet
> and hose in my disposition? One inch of delay more is
> a South Sea of discovery. I prithee tell me who is it
> quickly and speak apace. I would thou couldst stammer,
> that thou mightst pour this concealed man out of thy
> mouth as wine comes out of a narrow-mouthed bottle
> – either too much at once or none at all. I prithee take
> the cork out of thy mouth that I may drink thy tidings.
> CELIA
> So you may put a man in your belly.
>
> (3.2.189–98)

Rosalind suggests there is a division between an inner and outer self, in which an intrinsic, essential femininity might be found. Yet the play

Cross-Dressing and Gender Transgression(s)

continually toys with ideas about cross-dressing, so how can we find credible Rosalind's assertion of essential femininity? The answer lies partly in Celia's caustic comment: she reminds us that the 'character' of Rosalind underlying her boy-disguise is a desiring heterosexual woman. Yet this leaves open queerer interpretations of the boy actor underneath the character who may also take a man into his belly (as Cheek by Jowl insinuated in their production).

This implicit engagement with alternative erotic relationships is made explicit in a slightly later conversation between Rosalind and Orlando, when masculinity in love is measured by the external markers of what she sees in Orlando:

> Then your hose should be ungartered, your bonnet
> unbanded, your sleeve unbuttoned, your shoe untied,
> and everything about you demonstrating a careless
> desolation. But you are no such man. You are rather
> point-device in your accoutrements, as loving yourself
> than seeming the lover of any other.
>
> (3.2.364–9)

When she insists 'I thank God I am not a woman, to be touched with so many giddy offences as ... hath generally taxed their whole sex ... every one fault seeming monstrous' (3.2.225–43), her cross-dressed status underlines the critique of gendered stereotyping. Her picture of an immaculate and composed Orlando is often forgotten in productions, although in Branagh's film (2006) Orlando's composure weakens Rosalind's role as master of ceremonies. This particular conversation initiates a shift in their relationship; Rosalind becomes knowing director of appropriate gendered appearance and behaviour, implying in her coming erotic lessons to him both the necessity of such knowledge and her expertise as boy/girl. However, the charged erotics in the scene depend on a dance between two intriguing non-standard gendered beings. Rosalind's plot to play out a mock courtship is explicitly between a man who doesn't look as if he is a man in love and a boy acting as a woman dressed as a man, acting a woman. What we *see* is a man wooing a man – a visual validation of homoeroticism – whilst the fictional plot maintains that this is a male character wooing a female character – and the reality of the two male bodies beneath the costumes can be forgotten and/or remembered through the performance.

> ROSALIND I set him every
> day to woo me. At which time would I – being but a
> moonish youth – grieve, be effeminate, changeable,
> longing and liking, proud, fantastical, apish, shallow,
> inconstant, full of tears, full of smiles; for every passion
> something and for no passion truly anything, as boys
> and women are for the most part cattle of this colour;
> would now like him, now loath him; then entertain
> him, then forswear him; now weep for him, then spit at
> him; that I drave my suitor from his mad humour of
> love to a living humour of madness, which was to
> forswear the full stream of the world and to live in a
> nook merely monastic. And thus I cured him, and this
> way will I take upon me to wash your liver as clean as a
> sound sheep's heart, that there shall not be one spot of
> love in't.
> ORLANDO
> I would not be cured, youth.
>
> (3.2.391–407)

Rosalind's self-characterization as a 'moonish' (393) youth who can 'be effeminate, changeable, longing and liking, proud, fantastical, apish, shallow, inconstant, full of tears, full of smiles' (393–5) parallels young men and women's biologies (both are 'moonish'). This physiology (or humour) produces exterior characteristics gendered 'effeminate' (393). Such labelling simultaneously produces gendering of behaviour and slippages between physiology and exterior gender (boys and women might appear to be the same), generating a fluid erotics between the characters. The lack of certain knowledge (is it a boy making love to a man, or a woman to a man, or a transwoman making love to a man?) is absolutely key to the deliciously deferred nature of erotic contact itself. By queering desire, Shakespeare dramatically posits desire itself as slippery, perverse and titillating.

The queer visual and representational erotics, implicit also in Sonnet 20 (see Introduction) but explicit in the play, are played out in the mock-marriage. Celia acts as a priest-substitute, the couple's words spoken by two men (one of whom is in double-drag):

> ROSALIND
> You must begin: 'Will you, Orlando –'

CELIA
　Go to. – Will you, Orlando, have to wife this Rosalind?
ORLANDO
　I will.
ROSALIND
　Ay, but when?
ORLANDO
　Why now, as fast as she can marry us.
ROSALIND
　Then you must say: 'I take thee, Rosalind, for wife.'
ORLANDO
　I take thee, Rosalind, for wife.
ROSALIND
　I might ask you for your commission. But I do take thee, Orlando, for my husband. There's a girl goes before the priest, and certainly a woman's thought runs before her actions.
ORLANDO
　So do all thoughts – they are winged.
ROSALIND
　Now tell me how long you would have her after you have possessed her?
ORLANDO
　For ever and a day.
ROSALIND
　Say 'a day' without the 'ever'. No, no, Orlando, men are April when they woo, December when they wed. Maids are May when they are maids, but the sky changes when they are wives. I will be more jealous of thee than a Barbary cock-pigeon over his hen, more clamorous than a parrot against rain, more new-fangled than an ape, more giddy in my desires than a monkey. I will weep for nothing, like Diana in the fountain, and I will do that when you are disposed to be merry.

(4.1.120–44)

Rosalind's actions perform 'her' identity as female lover – she accepts Orlando as husband – but the speeches' mode, delivery and content belie restrictions on conventional feminine conduct. Celia's comment (once Orlando departs) underlines this from within the play's fiction when she scolds, 'You have simply misused our sex in your love-prate! We must have your doublet and hose plucked over your head and show the world' (189–91): Rosalind's female physical 'parts' will out. Rosalind takes over the priest's role (125), *explicitly* ventriloquizing three voices at once (priest/Ganymede/Rosalind) within the fiction of the play and *implicitly* the fourth voice of the actor-boy. Rosalind continually draws attention to roles – to the 'parts' actors and genders play and to the 'parts' that sometimes distinguish men from women – a trope played out in Sonnet 20 ('she pricked thee out for women's pleasure', see Introduction).

The play decouples gender from physiology through cross-dressing and ventriloquism but also by misdirection: for example, Rosalind claims Phoebe's letter must be 'a man's invention and hand' (4.3.30), defamiliarizing our assumptions about linguistic style and gender. Clothes, voice, physical looks and words are all shifted from conventional gender attribution. Rosalind's response to Oliver's accusation that she lacks a 'man's heart' and should 'counterfeit to be a man' when she faints on hearing of Orlando's injury foregrounds her physical fluid doubleness: 'So I do. But i'faith, I should have been a woman by right' (4.3.163–75). When she claims to be able to 'do strange things' and that finding matching partners to the several mismatched lovers 'is not impossible to me' (5.2.55), her character takes on a fantastic, magical quality. Rosalind reiterates a choral counterpoint to competing claims on her love ('and I for no woman' (5.2.84, 89, 98)), underlining a set of impossible closures. For all the characters who 'see' her as a boy, her mantra connotes the potentiality of non-binary erotics and gender fluidity (while the plot reassures a heterosexual closure). 'Her' speaking position and physical presence on stage offer a queer interpretative view spoken on stage never completely obliterated by the play's formal closure (see the Practitioner Perspective with Lucy Phelps on playing Rosalind's gender).

Orlando's 'I sometimes believe and sometimes do not' (5.4.3) posits epistemological indeterminacy as a state of being, describing perfectly the suspension of disbelief any audience makes when watching a play. *As You Like It* suggests that this state of suspension – this theatrical being-ness – is epitomized by the crossing and re-crossing of gender, the endless deferral of closure and finality. The pairings of lovers, through the magical invocation of Hymen, the god of marriage, closes the play's plots in heterosexual unions. But there are three specific instances, in addition to the resonances of playful cross-dressing, which point to alternative unions and queer identities. Touchstone claims the song 'It was a lover and his lass' (5.3.13–36) is 'foolish', critiquing binary unions: Jaques resolutely refuses to participate in the finale, and Rosalind's Epilogue postpones erotic closure:

Cross-Dressing and Gender Transgression(s)

> It is not the fashion to see the lady the
> Epilogue, but it is no more unhandsome than to see the
> lord the Prologue. If it be true that good wine needs
> no bush, 'tis true that a good play needs no epilogue.
> Yet to good wine they do use good bushes, and good
> plays prove the better by the help of good epilogues.
> What a case am I in then, that am neither a good
> epilogue, nor cannot insinuate with you in the behalf
> of a good play. I am not furnished like a beggar,
> therefore to beg will not become me. My way is to
> conjure you, and I'll begin with the women. I charge
> you, O women, for the love you bear to men, to like as
> much of this play as please you. And I charge you, O
> men, for the love you bear to women (as I perceive by
> your simpering none of you hates them), that between
> you and the women the play may please. If I were a
> woman I would kiss as many of you as had beards that
> pleased me, complexions that liked me and breaths
> that I defied not. And I am sure as many as have good
> beards, or good faces, or sweet breaths will for my
> kind offer, when I make curtsy, bid me farewell.
>
> (Epilogue 1–21)

This is Shakespeare's only play to close on a female voice and Rosalind self-consciously plays on the gendering of voice and body through theatricality and cross-dressing. Her trope on 'case' (7) underlines this by reminding the audience simultaneously of her unusual status, her outer disguise, the physical (costumed) female body ('case' was bawdy for female genitalia) and of the fiction of all of these in the underlying 'truth' of the boy's body beneath. Yet this boy's body remains intangible, even as she/he apparently offers to 'uncase' themself. Theatrical selfhood ('my way is to conjure you' (10)) is defined by effective stage performance. Her final two sentences proclaim her ongoing and unchanged doubled gender: speaking as the boy actor ('If I were a woman' (16)) he hypothesizes future kisses to both the bearded and the non-gender specific audience (only those with good faces and sweet breaths).

Viola in *Twelfth Night* cross-dresses for self-protection but the trajectory of desire generated by the cross-dressing (unlike *As You Like It*) does not have a pre-story of heterosexual attraction (as in the story of Rosalind and Orlando). Other than the Captain in 1.2, who helps her disguise, no man in Illyria 'knows' Viola as a woman; instead, the erotics of the play's action are all predicated on a network of forbidden desires. From Orsino's love for Olivia, through Olivia's for Cesario (Viola), Viola's for Orsino and Antonio's for Sebastian, the plot suggests that love fixes on the impossible and that, in the majority of cases, this 'looks' like non-heterosexual desire. The plot's resolution shows the impossible *can* happen, but only if we invent twins who can split and offer both male and female versions of the beloved.

Here is Viola's first recognition that desire is a set of mis-cues. Queer female-to-female desire is simultaneously acknowledged and denied, both because Olivia believes she is in love with a boy and, underneath, the 'real' actor *is* a boy:

> ... What means this lady?
> Fortune forbid my outside have not charmed her.
> She made good view of me, indeed so much
> That methought her eyes had lost her tongue,
> For she did speak in starts, distractedly.
> She loves me sure. The cunning of her passion
> Invites me in this churlish messenger.
> None of my lord's ring? Why, he sent her none.
> I am the man. If it be so, as 'tis,
> Poor lady, she were better love a dream.
> Disguise, I see thou art a wickedness,
> Wherein the pregnant enemy does much.
> How easy is it for the proper false
> In women's waxen hearts to set their forms.
> Alas, our frailty is the cause, not we,
> For such as we are made of, such we be.
> How will this fadge? My master loves her dearly,
> And I, poor monster, fond as much on him,
> And she, mistaken, seems to dote on me.
> What will become of this? As I am man,
> My state is desperate for my master's love;
> As I am woman, now alas the day,
> What thriftless sighs shall poor Olivia breathe?
>
> (2.2.17–39)

Cross-Dressing and Gender Transgression(s)

There is an element of misogyny implicit in Viola's words. When spoken by a boy, acting as a woman in boys' clothes, what does this imply about femininity and theatricality? Viola's 'Such as we are made of, such we be' (32) implies an essential physiological female identity that is weaker than that of maleness but also a reversion to the 'boyness' of the actor beneath the clothes. Her assertion of disguise as a 'wickedness' (27) evokes Stubbes' diatribe against the confusions wrought by cross-dressing (Resource 4.c). Equally, although Viola's acknowledged doubled self ('as I am man ... as I am woman' (36–8)) draws erotic lines in two impossible but present contradictions: as a man she cannot love a man, as a woman Olivia cannot love her. Although echoing Stubbes' critical language of doubled or trans identity as monstrous, impossibility is central to the play's plot. This plot is triangular: both between three characters of opposite desires, and in transcending binaries of gender and sexuality. How does the play reconcile these strands? The 2016 National Theatre production utilized some of these questions in casting Malvolio as a woman, played by Tamsin Greig, renamed Malvolia, whose desiring of Olivia concretized this lesbian moment. Yet the lesbian gaze was explicitly demonized through Greig's delivery of her/him as a repressed lesbian, although the finale of her as a carnivalesque queen suggested moments beyond the play-world where liberation from heteronormative identities and restrictions might be possible.

Orsino and Viola's discussion of love was set in a homoerotic bath-house in the films by Trevor Nunn (1996) and Tim Supple (2003) and the RSC 2009 production, recognizing this scene's centrality to the play's debate about power within erotic relationships:

> ORSINO ... Let still the woman take
> An elder than herself; so wears she to him,
> So sways she level in her husband's heart.
> For, boy, however we do praise ourselves,
> Our fancies are more giddy and unfirm,
> More longing wavering, sooner lost and worn
> Than women's are.
> VIOLA   I think it well, my lord.
> ORSINO
> Then let thy love be younger than thyself,
> Or thy affection cannot hold the bent;
> For women are as roses, whose fair flower
> Being once displayed doth fall that very hour.

VIOLA
    And so they are. Alas that they are so,
    To die even when they to perfection grow.

(2.4.29–41)

Although Orsino demands that a woman should 'wear' (30) herself to a husband, and be much younger than him, he also claims that men are more 'giddy and unfirm' (33) than women: a physiological observation at odds with conventional discussions about masculinity and femininity (see Chapters 2 and 5). Orsino's version of masculinity incorporates early modern female physiological attributes. This sets up contradictory positions of interpretation; slippage of referents, a lack of clarity of any absolute gendered meaning (even whilst characters are talking about gender behaviour) makes the scene erotic and pleasurable. Although Feste's song ('Come away, come away death' (51–66)) and his departing apothegm ('pleasure will be paid, one time or another', 15–71) act as choral counterpoints to the erotic and fantastic possibilities of cross-dressing and cross-gendered attributes, the scene's sexual frissons resonate throughout the play.

Orsino continues:

ORSINO
    There is no woman's sides
    Can bide the beating of so strong a passion
    As love doth give my heart; no woman's heart
    So big to hold so much – they lack retention.
    Alas, their love may be called appetite,
    No motion of the liver but the palate,
    That suffer surfeit, cloyment and revolt.
    But mine is all as hungry as the sea,
    And can digest as much. Make no compare
    Between that love a woman can bear me
    And that I owe Olivia.
VIOLA   Ay, but I know –
ORSINO
    What dost thou know?
VIOLA
    Too well what love women to men may owe.
    In faith, they are as true of heart as we.

Cross-Dressing and Gender Transgression(s)

> My father had a daughter loved a man,
> As it might be, perhaps, were I a woman,
> I should your lordship.
> ORSINO   And what's her history?
> VIOLA
> A blank, my lord. She never told her love,
> But let concealment like a worm i'th' bud
> Feed on her damask cheek. She pined in thought,
> And with a green and yellow melancholy
> She sat like Patience on a monument,
> Smiling at grief. Was not this love indeed?
> We men may say more, swear more, but indeed
> Our shows are more than will, for still we prove
> Much in our vows, but little in our love.
>
> (2.4.93–118)

Viola's broken off 'ah but I know …' (103) is a theatrically coded gap suggesting (hidden) female knowledge, a gap in which different possibilities reside. Various productions use this gap to indicate, diversely: Orsino's growing suspicion that Viola is a woman, Orsino's feeling that homoerotic attachments might be stronger than heteronormative ones, Viola's almost-confession of her own feelings, or Viola's impatience with Orsino's strict demarcations of gender (contrast Trevor Nunn's 1996 film version with Luscombe's 2017–18 RSC production; see Figure 4.1). Knowledge and not-quite-knowledge are essential to Viola's cross-dressed passage in-between the two houses of Orsino and Olivia and to her in-between ambiguous status as servant and confidante, as man and woman. The liminal state of not-knowing, the tantalizing possibilities suggested by cross-dressed youths are playfully 'queoried' in staging and delivery.

Throughout the play, Viola uses paradoxes and asides to strengthen the audience's awareness of her doubleness, an effect that can be performed and interpreted as either an assertion of the character's essential femininity or a continuous reminder of the erotic charge of such doubleness. Such self-consciousness is particularly evident in her conversations with Feste, explicitly associating discussions of liminal identity with the character of the fool who is free to speak the non-conventional ('there's no slander in an allowed fool' (1.5.89–90)). Cross-dressing situates her character as 'allowed' to cross streets, walking between the male household of Orsino and the female one of Olivia, and to speak almost equally (but not fully truthfully)

Figure 4.1 *The Valorous Acts Perform'd at Gaunt, by the Brave Bonny Lass Mary Ambree* (c. 1674, with kind permission of the National Library of Scotland).

to both. Cross-dressing liberates the character from all gender expectations, rather than confining character to the one he / she is dressed as.

Doubleness allows Viola to situate her own identity as a set of negatives, a denial situating identity as deferred (not dependent only on biological essence) and open, and a rejection of how others try to construct her. This openness makes explicit a lesbian gaze in Olivia's declaration of love, for she is also called out as being 'not what you are':

Cross-Dressing and Gender Transgression(s)

OLIVIA

... I prithee tell me what thou think'st of me.

VIOLA

That you do think you are not what you are.

OLIVIA

If I think so, I think the same of you.

VIOLA

Then think you right: I am not what I am.

OLIVIA

I would you were as I would have you be.

(3.1.136–40)

Verbal and iconic imagery used by poets and painters often played on Elizabeth I's transcendence of dualities: until her death in 1603, a model of how gender conventions could be exceeded, transported and played with through the application of masculine images to a female figure, and vice versa (Resource 4.f, below). In the popular *Ballad of Mary Ambree* (first cited in 1600, see Figure 4.1) the heroine cross-dresses as a soldier to revenge her husband's death, proving both her womanly love and her manly courage, but ending on a heteronormative betrothal (Dugaw, 1989: 35). The appearance of the twins on stage at the end of the play mirrors the doubled ('most wonderful!') nature of the cross-dressing conundrum, a wonder spoken only by Orsino and Antonio. Orsino's 'One face, one voice,

Figure 4.2 Imogen Stubbs as Viola and Stephen Mackintosh as Sebastian, *Twelfth Night* (Trevor Nunn, 1996, UK).

one habit and two persons: / A natural perspective, that is and is not' is supplemented by Antonio's 'How have you made division of yourself?' (5.1.212, 218; see Figure 4.2). The 'natural perspective, that is and is not' posits the simultaneous reality of the two twins: they are the same and not the same (setting aside the biological impossibility of a boy and girl being identical twins). Just as cross-dressed Viola is and is not a woman, she is and is not a man. The responses of other characters to this revelation retains the explicit nature of tripled erotic attraction: Antonio, Orsino and Olivia are all in love with a different 'version' of this creature that was/is Viola/Cesario.

Resource 4.f: Sir Walter Raleigh, 'If Cynthia Be a Queen, a Princess, and Supreme' (c. 1595)

If Cynthia be a queen, a princess, and supreme,
Keep these among the rest, or say it was a dream,
For those that like, expound, and those that loathe express
Meanings according as their minds are moved more or less;
For writing what thou art, or showing what thou were,
Adds to the one disdain, to the other but despair,
 Thy mind of neither needs, in both seeing it exceeds.

When Orsino switches from Olivia as his love object to Viola ('Give me thy hand, / And let me see thee in thy woman's weeds' (5.1.268–9)), the visual encounter remains one between two men: Viola does not leave to change into women's clothes. Visual codes work in juxtaposition to the textual plot's narrative closure on heteronormative marriage promises, echoing Antonio's homoerotic love for Sebastian as partially encoded in other near-forbidden loves and identities the play performs. The term 'queer heterosexuality' (Chess, 2016: 9) usefully connotes the divergent endings and viewpoints an audience may take from these juxtapositions.

Conclusions

1. Cross-dressing is a material practice in early modern theatre and thematized as a plot device. Shakespeare's sole play where a male character dresses as a woman (*The Merry Wives of Windsor* c. 1597) uses cross-dressing to parody and belittle Falstaff's sexual

Cross-Dressing and Gender Transgression(s)

voraciousness. The comedies playing with sexual and gender fluidities are those of his middle period (1597–1602): perhaps the context of Elizabeth I's final years momentarily enabled Shakespeare to use cross-dressing as a theatrical code and practice to explore and play with non-binary erotics and identities.

2. Elizabethan and Jacobean cross-dressing stories played with cross-gender and cross-sexualized identification in narratives that firmly re-established the 'correct' gender and sexual order, by returning characters to their original identities. *As You Like It* and *Twelfth Night* conform to this plot model, modelling a carnivalesque gender topsy-turvydom, but closing on heteronormative marriage and returns to original identities. Nevertheless both plays problematize such endings through dramatic structure: *As You Like It* uses a meta-theatrical epilogue, while *Twelfth Night* twins male and female identities. Rosalind speaks her epilogue as a woman / boy, possibly in women's clothes as girl character and boy actor – and Viola retains her boy's clothes while promising marriage to Orsino.

3. These plays depend upon a knowing audience whose 'gaze' is titillated and explicitly evoked through meta-theatrical and self-conscious references to the doubling and tripling erotic effect of cross-dressing as performance and by homoerotic and heteroerotic physical and verbal play. This self-consciousness is an exuberant response to the anti-theatrical debates of the 1590s, when theatre was lambasted by Puritans and others for its supposed immorality. Shakespeare's contribution to this anti-theatricality suggests that performance, cross-dressing, gender-bending and erotic fluidity are central to his notion of drama and politics.

4. Concepts of gender in the early modern period are fluid, and cross-dressed heroines draw on two early modern discourses that support this: first, that in which exterior attributes perform gendered identity; and second, a physiological explanation of gender, positing the female sex is already part-male (sometimes called 'the one-sex model'), and that expression of identity is through the balance of humours (male dry and hot, female moist and cold), which can cross over and contradict those of biological sex (see also Chapters 5 and 8).

5. There remains a political gender hierarchy in early modern England in which patriarchal identity and function concur with social and divine order (see Chapters 2 and 6), where boys and women are

alike subject to men. Thus, cross-dressing by female characters merely replicates and underlines this supposedly 'natural' order in which men have more power and status, and in which boy actors dressing as women is not representationally or erotically problematic because both are equally subject to male adults (sexually and politically).

6. Female-to-male cross-dressing as integral to the plot (as opposed to the initial boy actor crossing to be a female character) opens up possibilities of trans and queer identities to contemporary readers, performers and viewers that allow us to re-inhabit characters, pasts and identities with new stories and new histories.

Further Work

As You Like It and *Twelfth Night*

The plays' titles posit a carnivalesque time or place – how do plot, dress and character develop this trajectory? What happens when the Blazon (see Introduction) is spoken by a cross-dressed man and how does this problematize the discourse (*As You Like It*, 3.2.135–54; and *Twelfth Night*, 1.5.231–70)? How have different performances visualized the gender and erotic possibilities of the characters through costume?

Cymbeline

How is Innogen's descriptions of her cross-dressing in Act 4 a political rather than an erotic motif? Why does tragedy nearly ensue through that cross-dressing?

The Merry Wives of Windsor

The 2018 RSC production (Laird) sets this in a 'the only way is Essex' mode, appearing to empower women as agents of their own sexual freedom. How does Shakespeare's original 'shaming' of Falstaff by the women's plots suggest that male-to-female cross-dressing demonizes and belittles femininity as against masculinity?

Further Reading

Simone Chess, *Male to Female Cross-Dressing in Early Modern Literature* (Routledge, 2016). **First comprehensive discussion of male characters dressing as women.**

Lisa Jardine, 'Twins and Travesties: Gender, Dependency, and Sexual Availability in *Twelfth Night*' in Susan Zimmerman (ed.), *Erotic Politics* (Routledge, 1992), 27–38. **Key discussion of the parallels between women and boys in sexual and erotic hierarchy and in sexual relations.**

Natasha Korda, *Labor's Lost: Women's Work and the Early Modern Stage* (University of Pennsylvania Press, 2011). **Rediscovery of the presence and impact of women's work on early modern stage.**

Laura Levine, *Men in Women's Clothes: Anti-Theatricality and Effeminization 1579–1652* (Cambridge University Press, 1994). **Classic discussion of the gendered and erotic fears underlying the Elizabethan and Jacobean antitheatrical debates.**

Steven Orgel, *Impersonations: The Performance of Gender in Shakespeare's England* (Cambridge University Press, 1996). **Brilliant discussion of both gender and erotics as performed, embedded in material history of theatre.**

Phyllis Rackin, *Shakespeare and Women* (Oxford University Press, 2005). **See chapter four on cross-dressing.**

Michael Shapiro, *Gender in Play on the Shakespearean Stage: Boy Heroines and Female Pages* (University of Michigan Press, 1996). **Classic discussion of plays.**

Bruce Smith, *Shakespeare and Masculinity* (Oxford University Press, 2000). **Useful discussion of divergent notions of masculinity, including fluid sexual identities.**

Valerie Traub, 'The Homoerotics of Shakespearean Comedy', in her *Desire and Anxiety: Circulations of Sexuality in Shakespearean Drama* (Routledge, 1992). **Excellent discussion of the fluidity and possible non-binary economies of sexual desire in these plays.**

PRACTITIONER PERSPECTIVE: LUCY PHELPS

Actor Lucy Phelps reflects on her performances as Rosalind in *As You Like It* (Figure 4.3) and Isabella in *Measure for Measure* (2019–20), both with the Royal Shakespeare Company. The interview was held at the Royal Shakespeare Theatre, Stratford-upon-Avon, 30 May 2019.

Figure 4.3 Lucy Phelps as Rosalind, *As You Like It* (Kimberley Sykes, Royal Shakespeare Company, 2019). Live From Stratford-Upon-Avon broadcast, 2019 © RSC.

Practitioner Perspective: Lucy Phelps

What is your approach, in terms of performing gender, to embodying Rosalind on stage in this production?

For her scenes in the forest I wanted to explore the limits of my physicality, how high can I jump, how fast can I run, how noisy can I be, how much space can I take up? I wanted to focus more on exploring the boundaries of my 'body' and my 'humanness' rather than adopting any stereotypical 'masculine' movements. The forest is a space of play and performance and in our production we wanted to explore different forms of theatricality. Pop music is a big love of mine so I went there for inspiration for some of the greatest artists who've blurred the lines of gender and deconstructed it through their performances – Mick Jagger, David Bowie, Prince, Annie Lennox and Christine and the Queens. For me, Rosalind becomes a rock star in the forest. She takes that stage and says 'this is my story and this is our story as humans'.

I found it very helpful to identify the differences of Rosalind's physicality in the Court once we had rehearsed the Forest. I had all of that freedom and experience inside my body but now I had to hold it back: I couldn't move as fast as I was constrained by my tight dress and high heels, I couldn't be as loud, as I had to wait for permission to speak, and I couldn't take up as much space, as in our production the playing space in the early part of the play is reduced to a small section of grass in the centre of the stage. In the court Rosalind is constrained by what that society expects of her; 'you are a woman and therefore you must wear a dress, you must wear heels, you must wear make up, you must wait to be spoken to, you are not in a position of power'.

Rosalind has a strong potential within her that she knows is there but isn't allowed to exercise in the Court. When she steps into the forest, whilst putting on what I have chosen in our production to be a more androgynous disguise, she sees the benefits that are afforded to men in society: she can buy property, she has money, power, and doesn't have to apologize anymore. Here are two women that have run away together and are now suddenly in control of their own lives. Rosalind's full potential is unleashed in the forest – she can explore the limits of her brain, her sexuality, and transgress without fear. Arden is this liminal space in which you can be whoever you want to be. You might look at her and think 'that is a masculine trait' or 'that is a feminine trait'. I didn't want it to be that when she is in the forest she is suddenly doing 'masculine' things and when she's in the court she is doing 'feminine' things, I wanted a clash, a blurring of the two throughout the play and in any one moment they are both present but are more 'HD' in Arden.

I think she is trying to smash the social construct of gender and challenge all our preconceptions about gender and of course, love.

What are your thoughts on the gender-swapping of characters in the RSC production of *As You Like It*?

On a basic level, the RSC have committed to a 50:50 casting goal; they have set themselves that bar and I think that is so important and much needed. What we want is a balance. Too many of any one group or the lack of representation of a group means a conversation isn't being had, a conversation is being lost and the potential for all these different experiences to come together and create something ground breaking and explosive is also lost. It's the responsibilities of theatre-makers to reflect society and enable everyone to see their stories being told on stage.

It's so exciting to see women taking on Shakespearean roles not previously afforded to them and playing them as women, providing a different prism through which to view the narrative. And it is even more exciting, for me personally, to see women taking on the male roles but not playing them as female, necessarily. Hamlet is Hamlet.

In our production, Jaques is played by Sophie Stanton. She has had a huge response from women who are identifying with Jaques' narrative as we are presenting it – a single woman, who hasn't chosen to have a family, who doesn't have a long-term partner and who is having potent and challenging conversations about life. She throws the uncomfortable statement or idea into the room that no one wants to talk about and says let's talk about it. It's wonderful to see a woman in Shakespeare exploring philosophical ideas and possessing such verbal wit – this is more often than not the privilege of the male characters in the canon and the women provide the emotional charge.

What was your experience of working with a female director on *As You Like It*?

Right now, with all the important conversations that are being had about gender equality and knowing there is still a long journey ahead, I couldn't have imagined doing this production with anyone else other than Kim Sykes, a person of huge intelligence, heart, passion, openness and plugged in to the conversation.

I would never want to be quoted as saying that female stories must only be told by women and vice versa, but the balance has tipped too far one way for too long. So yes, in our production it was very special to have so many more female voices leading the rehearsal room, in both the acting company and the creative team.

How can a contemporary production deal with the models of femininity in *Measure for Measure*?

I think in *Measure for Measure*, for instance, Isabella is in some ways totally revolutionary because she says 'I will not conform'. Everyone else in her society is being boxed in as wife, whore, virgin, which is how, one could argue, women are still seen today. Isabella says: 'I will have autonomy over my body. I won't be anyone's property. I will debate with you on your level without my gender being a part of it at all. I will debate with you about philosophical ideas and greater principles and I will hold onto my principle despite how many times you try to push me off centre.' You may have some quibbles with her subsequent behaviour but, from start to finish, she says 'these are my principles and they are bigger than any individual person and that might pain me and that might hurt you but that is how it is.' And I think that is incredible. Even if a boy did play it in 1604!

With new approaches and positive moves forward such as 50:50 casting, how does understanding the original context balance that in which it is being performed and viewed today?

When we rehearse, we start with when it was written, and we talk about what ideas are shared with today. You always have to start with the text – what are the ideas that Shakespeare is presenting? Half the time they are pretty revolutionary for his era and are equally revolutionary for now, which is both brilliant and sad in my mind as it begs the question how far have we come really? In *As You Like It* we looked at proto-feminism in the sixteenth and seventeenth centuries and found there was a huge amount present – more than you might think. It is always important to analyse, what was Shakespeare talking about? What was he fighting for? What are the questions being asked? And then, how does that relate to us today?

Shakespeare and Gender

These plays are not going to survive if we don't shake them up a little bit. The core ideas are so strong and they are so well written they can more than withstand the narrative being presented through different prisms to see what that opens up. But if we continue to play them as faithful history projects, they won't survive. They do hold old ideas about society too: they are politically incorrect at times; misogynistic at times and often reflect a world that we don't want to see represented as much anymore unless we are making a comment on that in some sort of way. If you keep putting different gender representation on the stage, people will become more accustomed to it. Through this we are saying 'this is what a reflection of society actually is': it is not an absence of women or anyone.

CHAPTER 5
GENDERING MADNESS
Key Text: *Hamlet*, with *The Two Noble Kinsmen*

In Act 2, Scene 2, Polonius muses on Hamlet's bizarre speech and behaviour, 'Though this may be madness yet there is method in't' (203–4), attributing to Hamlet some vestiges of rationality. Much later, Laertes identifies significance in Ophelia's fragmented speech, 'this nothing's more than matter' (4.5.168). These moments reveal the problem of how we read 'madness' written for the stage, which is a rational construction of irrationality, and how we understand the gendered language of madness in this play. While male 'method' is still traced in Hamlet's cryptic words, Ophelia's 'speech is nothing' yet, for Laertes, carries deep emotional meaning. Hamlet's 'antic disposition' is explained early on as play-acting, underpinning the metatheatricality of the play throughout; it is a performed persona and narrative within the play world. Ophelia, though, is what Laertes describes as a 'document in madness' (4.5.172), a textbook case. Yet, both characters perform their madness – Hamlet literally by acting it and Ophelia via song– and both can be read more literally as textbook cases, drawing on early modern gendered ideas on the nature of madness.

Hamlet has much to answer for in how we understand, write and perform madness in literature and culture. Indeed, Carol Thomas Neely credits Shakespeare with 'inventing[ing] a new language through which madness can be voiced' from the mulitple discourses of medical, spiritual and supernatural explanations of insanity that surrounded his cultural moment (Neely, 2004: 46). *Hamlet*'s gendered presentation of insanity has provided the quintessential dramatic template of tragic and visceral female madness, in Ophelia, and the troubled intellectual male, in the melancholic Hamlet. It has filtered deep into critical and popular perceptions. We are likely, on seeing the title of this chapter, to picture Hamlet dressed in mourning black, his 'antic disposition' 'put on' (1.5.170) to forward his agenda. We might contrast this mental picture with one of the distraught Ophelia, distributing flowers or singing her songs of grief and bawdy. Hamlet's active 'put[ting] ... on' of madness, his playing of a mad part, is thus established as a binary opposite to Ophelia's subjection both to the calamities of her environment and to the fragility of her mind. In this model, the male is active, choosing his own level of sanity; the female is passive, abject, a victim of her weaker mind. Yet is Ophelia's mental collapse 'a feminine echo of Hamlet's madness' (Berry, 1999: 71) or are there quite different types and presentations of madness in these characters? This chapter explores and interrogates gendered ideas of madness in the play and how the language of madness might be gendered.

When Hamlet entreats Horatio and the watchmen to be silent witnesses to his father's ghostly visitation in 1.5, he appears to make a snap decision on his course of action. Having so far simply requested that they must 'Swear by my sword / Never to speak of this that you have heard' (158–9), he then emphasizes that the secret must be kept regardless of how 'odd' he may subsequently appear, however 'strange' his behaviour may be:

Here as before: never – so help you mercy,
How strange or odd some'er I bear myself
(As I perchance hereafter shall think meet
To put an antic disposition on) –
That you at such times seeing me never shall
With arms encumbered thus, or this headshake,
Or by pronouncing of some doubtful phrase
As 'Well, well, we know', or 'We could an if we would',
Or 'If we list to speak', or 'There be an if they might',
Or such ambiguous giving out to note
That you know aught of me.

(1.5.167–77)

Shakespeare provides the audience with a preface to Hamlet's puzzling, sometimes contradictory, ensuing behaviour. Hamlet's clear, stated intention to behave 'odd[ly]' and 'strange[ly]' introduces his manipulation of others' predictable responses to perceived mad behaviour. While Hamlet shortly later bemoans the weight of the duty he now feels, 'O cursed spite / That ever I was born to set it right' (1.5.186–7), Shakespeare assigns him at least one clear intention: to *act* his way to success. A logical resolution is made here, in which Hamlet 'think[s] meet / To put an antic disposition on', creating the duality that continues to haunt the play. Hamlet's rational decision (he 'thinks meet') to act *ir*rationally blurs boundaries between play-acting and the 'real' world, on and off the stage. *Hamlet*'s metatheatrical nature is established when Hamlet's audience within the play (Horatio and the watchmen) are asked to go along with whatever his subsequent performance may be and not be tempted to display knowingness, 'by pronouncing of some doubtful phrase / As "Well, well, we know"'. They must be, in other words, a good audience and not spoil the show.

What exactly madness *was*, though, in the early modern period, was contentious. A discourse emerged that strove to define, and offer treatments for, various types of madness. The roots and the cures of mental maladies (physical [medical], spiritual, social or philosophical) were under constant discussion. Defining madness relies on establishing a sense of behavioural and social normalcy against which the 'mad' can be measured. This normalcy, in the early modern period, reflected the contemporary sociopolitical hegemony, producing a gendered (and class-based) definition of what it was to be mad – and to be sane. The fundamentally gendered discourse of madness would become paradigmatic of early modern intersections of the medical and the theological, the supernatural and the natural, the political and the personal. Emerging at the epicentre of this sociocultural moment, *Hamlet*'s afterlife has allowed early modern perceptions to permeate how we view madness, at least in literary and dramatic texts, to this day.

Resource 5.a: From Thomas Bright, *A Treatise on Melancholie* (1586)

Of all other practise of phisick, that parte most commendeth the excellency of the noble facultie, which not only releeveth the bodily infirmity, but after a sort even also correcteth the infirmities of the mind. For the instrument of reason, the braine, being either not of well tempered substance: or disordered in his parts: all exercise of wisedome is hindred: and where once understanding lodged, wit, memorie, & quick conceit, kept residence, and the excellencie of man appeareth above all other creatures: there unconsiderate judgement, simplicitie, & foolishnes make their seat, and as it were dispossessing reason, of her watch tower, subjecteth the nature of man vnto the annoyance of infinite calamities, that force vpon vs in the course of this fraile life, & baseth it farre under the condition of brute beasts. The heart the seate of affection (and neither immoderate in temper, nor in figure or quantitie otherwise disposed then is expedient for good action) the seate of temperancie, of justice, of fortitude and liberalitie, dayly practice of phisicke sheweth how much it is disposed and framed to mediocritie of affection wherin vertue consisteth, by such meanes as nature ministreth, & the phisitian hir great steward according to her will, dispenseth where need requireth: in so much that what reason bringeth to passe by perswasion and counsell, that medicine and other helpes of that kinde seeme to worke by instinct of nature. The dayly experience of phrensies, madnesse, lunasies, and melancholy cured by this heauenly gift of God, make manifest demonstration hereof. The notable fruit & successe of which art in that kinde, hath caused some to judge more basely of the soule, then agreeth with pietie or nature, & have accompted all maner affection thereof, to be subiect to the phisicians hand, not considering herein any thing divine, and above the ordinarie euents, and naturall course of thinges: but have esteemed the vertues them selves, yea religion, no other thing but as the body hath ben tempered, and on the other side, vice, prophanenesse, & neglect of religion and honestie, to have bene nought else but a fault of humour. For correcting the judgement of such as so greatly mistake the matter, and partly for the use of many that may neede instruction and counsel, in the state of melancholy, & affection of braine and hart, & wold have both to satisfie their owne doubts, and to answer the prophane objections of others, I have taken this paines to confute the absurde errour of the one, & to satisfie the reasonable and modest inquiry of the other that seek to be enformed. I have layd open howe the bodie, and corporall things affect the soule, & how the body is affected of it againe: what the difference is betwixt natural melancholie, and that heavy hande of God upon the afflicted conscience, tormented with remorse of sinne, & feare of his judgement: with a Christian resolution according to my skill for such as faint vnder that heauie burthen. And that I might to the uttermost of my endevor (as other businesse wold permit me) comfort them in that estate most comfortles, I have added mine advise of phisicke helpe: what diet, what medicine, and what other remedie is meete for persons, oppressed with melancholie feare, & that kind of heavinesse of hart. I have enterlaced my treatise besides with disputes of Philosophie that the learned sort of them, and such as are of quicke conceit, & delited in discourse of reason in naturall things, may find to passe their time with, and knowe the grounds and reasons of their passions, without which they might receave more discomfort, and greater cause of error.

(pp. ij–iiij)

Gendering Madness

Hamlet's first performance (likely to be between the late 1590s and 1601; Thompson and Taylor, 2019: 44) triangulates its position in relation to specific viewpoints on madness, written during the same period. The most influential work on the subject for late Elizabethans was Thomas Bright's *A Treatise on Melancholy* (Resource 5.a, first published 1586, reprinted several times over the following years). Robert Burton's seminal *Anatomy of Melancholy*, published in 1621, partially supplanted Bright's approach and became the age's enduring study of mental malady. In 1603, Edward Jorden's *A Brief Discourse of the Disease of the Suffocation of the Mother* ('the Mother' meaning the womb and referring to hysteria), cemented the gendered nature of madness in early modern discourse (see Resource 5.b). These two books are arguably products of the same historical attitudes to madness as those manifested in *Hamlet* and act as direct contexts for the play's gendered ideas of madness. However, by the time another play, with striking echoes of Ophelia's plot, appeared, Jorden's book and its suggestions of symptoms and cures was well established. Co-authored by Shakespeare and his friend, John Fletcher, a later play, *Two Noble Kinsmen*, features a subplot focusing on the Jailer's Daughter (a nameless character) and her mental collapse. She runs mad following thwarted love and physical disorientation and, like Ophelia, then communicates via fragmented, proverbial speech and song. Events take a different turn, however, when the Daughter is saved from a near identical fate of drowning. Instead, attempts are made to bring about a cure through sex, revealing much on how female madness was perceived, as we will explore later. This tangible similarity between the characters, jarred by a crucial moment of narrative difference, helps us understand the changing approaches to female madness during the period but also the class difference between the response to Ophelia's madness among the nobility and the visceral attempts to cure the lower class Daughter.

By the late sixteenth century, the dominant understanding of mental illness as we now see it and, in particular, the affliction known as 'melancholy', was that it arose from the melancholic humour becoming dominant over the the body (see also Chapter 9 and Arikha, 2007: IV). Early modern melancholy, as it was viewed, cannot neatly be defined in terms of our modern vocabulary of mental health, though many continue to be tempted broadly to equate it to what we might now identify as depression; as Hamlet tells Rosencrantz and Guildenstern, he has 'of late, but wherefore I know not, lost all my mirth' (2.2.261–2). While it cannot be claimed that melancholy was viewed exclusively as a male condition, the spiritual or intellectual struggles that characterize Bright's two main roots for melancholy are consistently portrayed as masculine afflictions. They are implicitly male because of the *absence* of the female: and the idea that the female is defined by absence, a 'nothing' to the male 'something', figures endemically through early modern culture, from sexual and anatomical euphemism to the silence expected of women versus the speech of men. In *Hamlet*, the spectre of mental and verbal nothingness follows Ophelia through the text; her assertion to Hamlet 'I think nothing, my lord' is echoed later in the male response to her madness, 'her speech is nothing' (4.4.7). Later seventeenth-century texts addressing female madness certainly admitted the idea of a melancholy woman, though both the nature and root of the malady is seen as far more related to lovesickness, reproductive dysfunction and abstinence than it is to intellectual or spiritual turmoil (Dawson, 2008).

Hamlet echoes Bright's *Melancholy* at various points, including Hamlet's description of his own state of mind and the strategies adopted by those around him as they attempt to counter his melancholy. Bright resonates in Hamlet's most famous soliloquy, when he questions the purpose of suffering through a life that appears punishing, relentless and revolting to him, 'that makes calamity of so long a life', through which we must, animal-like, 'grunt and sweat' (3.1.68–76). Hamlet's view of the human condition reflects a melancholic attitude, in which the mind is disordered and reason is no longer supreme, which 'subjecteth the nature of man unto the annoyance of infinite calamities, that force upon us in the course of this fraile life' (Resource 5.a) such that we are repositioned below the condition of animals. Melancholy represents, then, a contemplative mental affliction, in which a tragic disorder of the brain leads great minds to fall to despair, 'a noble mind … o'erthrown' (3.1.149). Simply put, melancholy is perceived as broadly masculine precisely *because* it is intellectual, contemplative and relies upon the assumption that the afflicted mind was once entirely governed by reason, the male archetype (see Shepard, 2006: 9–10).

Act 2, Scene 2 is chiefly concerned with how Hamlet's family and friends respond to his conduct. The range of this behaviour, though, remains somewhat ambiguous for the audience. We know that he is displaying extreme grief, as made clear in 1.2, but we also know that he has stated that he will deliberately enact an 'antic disposition' (an odd personality), implying that he will *feign* madness or distraction. Scene 2 begins with the King discussing Hamlet's state of mind with the prince's friends, Rosencrantz and Guildenstern, whom he has summoned to help bring his errant stepson/nephew under control:

> Something have you heard
> Of Hamlet's transformation – so call it
> Sith nor th'exterior nor the inward man
> Resembles that it was. What it should be
> More than his father's death, that thus hath put him
> So much from th'understanding of himself
> I cannot dream of.
>
> (2.2.4–10)

The King has clearly seen Hamlet's mental condition suddenly worsen, which he finds both mysterious and troubling. The audience knows that this change derives, either by Hamlet's own design or through the shock it engendered, from the prince's encounter with his father's Ghost. Claudius's assessment of Hamlet is that he is 'transform[ed]': no longer himself in appearance or behaviour. The King's earlier language clearly gendered Hamlet's 'unmanly grief' (1.2.94), yet here Claudius is less critical, describing, rather, a man who is confused, changed, who no longer 'understand[s] ... himself', as a man should.

Claudius proceeds to explain his summons of Rosencrantz and Guildenstern, representing it as an attempt to find ways to help Hamlet to recover himself:

> I entreat you both,
> That, being of so young days brought up with him,
> And sith so neighbour'd to his youth and havior,
> That you vouchsafe your rest here in our court
> Some little time: so by your companies
> To draw him on to pleasures, and to gather,
> So much as from occasion you may glean,
> Whether aught, to us unknown, afflicts him thus,
> That, open'd, lies within our remedy.
>
> (2.2.10–18)

Framing his entreaty in apparent fatherly (or at least kingly) concern for Hamlet, at the heart of Claudius's speech is another agenda: that these friends might act as his spies, reporting back on Hamlet's actions and state of mind. Claudius wishes to 'remedy' Hamlet's disorder (in every sense of that word) by knowing the root of the malady, bringing him thus back under the King's control. Bright's *Melancholy* recommends the company of good male friends as a treatment. Claudius also notes the friends' connection to Hamlet's past, 'being of so young days brought up with him', attempting to circumnavigate the present changes that have taken place in the court and return Hamlet to the 'pleasures' he found distracting in his younger days.

Later in the scene, Rosencrantz and Guildenstern attempt to put Claudius' request into practice. Hamlet immediately suspects their arrival is no coincidence, interrogating them, 'Were you not sent for? Is it your own inclining? Is it a free visitation?' (2.2.240-1). Though he seems aware that his friends have been engaged to report back to the King (259-60), he immediately embarks on a lengthy speech apparently describing his feelings. This speech is so indicative of core symptoms and ideas of melancholy, that it could just as easily be read as a deliberate posture, for the benefit of the King's proxy ears, as a genuine description of his feelings:

> I have of late, but wherefore I know not, lost all my mirth, forgone all custom of exercises and, indeed, it goes so heavily with my disposition that this goodly frame the earth seems to me a sterile promontory, this most excellent canopy, the air, look you, this brave o'erhanging firmament, this majestical roof fretted with golden fire, why it appeareth nothing to me than a foul and pestilent congregation of vapours. What piece of work is a man – how noble in reason; how infinite in faculties, in form and moving; how express and admirable in action; how like an angel in apprehension; how like a god; the beauty of the world; the paragon of animals. And yet, to me, what is this quintessence of dust?
>
> (2.2.261-74)

Hamlet begins here with a fairly standard and accessible complaint of melancholy, that he has 'lost all [his] mirth', unable to find happiness or contentment, but equally that *why* he feels this way is unclear ('wherefore I know not'), specifically *not* linking his melancholy to 'unmanly grief' and concealing the devastating shock of his father's ghostly visitation. He then expresses that his 'disposition' is so negative as to lose all joy in the qualities either of man or nature. This extract could describe Bright's 'natural' melancholy, a mortal affliction: the slightly dangerous 'how like a God' not only compares man to the divine but the use of the indefinite article ('*a* God') suggests an unspecified polytheistic philosophical underpinning. There is no clearly defined relationship with a single God here, nor the spiritual doubt nor fear of sin that characterizes the pious melancholy that Bright describes, one that could be treated through theological study and dedication to faith in God. Here is a mortal problem: Hamlet is describing himself as deeply unhappy, enduring a joyless existence impervious to solace from external wonders.

Whether the wily Hamlet is deliberately 'put[ting] ... on' a textbook melancholy, complete with its appearance of having no clear root in events, or whether Shakespeare is presenting us with the model of a melancholic man is ambiguous. Indeed, the reflexive reference to 'this majestical roof fretted with golden fire' elides the physical reality of the Globe playhouse's decorated ceiling with the figurative presentation of the sky as 'roof' to the world below. This is a complex moment, first blurring performance and reality, then reversing them (the actuality of the theatre, the sky made figurative); it draws attention to Hamlet as player of madness as well as Hamlet the player on the Globe stage. His melancholy, too, must literally be acted; yet, it is never clear *within* the play world quite whether to believe in it. Hamlet's performance of melancholy is potentially deliberate. He has a choice in it. This contrasts starkly with Ophelia's later presentation. Ophelia's distraction appears to be considered satisfactorily explained as an affliction caused by grief, when Claudius identifies it as 'conceit upon her father' (4.5.45), the root cause he discredits in Hamlet's supposedly 'unmanly' behaviour. He does however see it as gender-appropriate, if tragic, in 'pretty' Ophelia (4.5.41).

Hamlet's description of his disengagement from the world and its wonders (as well as other characters' responses to his state of mind) reflect Bright's first descriptions of melancholy. Bright explains how the disorder of the brain through the affliction of melancholy (caused here by physical imbalance), destroys the reason that characterizes man and that places him above animals. Bright's 'man' represents mankind: throughout his treatise Bright addresses melancholy as affecting men. He genders Reason as female, yet never admits women as afflicted. We can read in Hamlet's 'paragon of animals' the same rhetoric as Bright's 'excellencie of man appeareth above all other creatures', in which it is the loss of reason, through melancholic derangement, that leaves a man in danger of losing his supremacy. Although

Hamlet proclaims his loss of mortal wonder, he spends much of his time presenting his rationality, until the turning point of Polonius's murder, when the audience might baulk at his crass amorality as he 'lug[s] the guts into the neighbour room' (3.4.210). Only moments earlier Hamlet emphatically counter-asserts his sanity to his mother's 'O! He is mad!', 3.4.102), when he confidently avows, 'It is not madness / That I have uttered' (3.4.139–42). Yet here, when he is most confident of his sanity is when he obsessively attacks his mother, kills a man while showing little conscience and sees a ghost. In other words, in the very scene in which the prince discards his acted madness, Shakespeare presents the maddest Hamlet of all.

By the time Ophelia enters 'mad' in 4.5, the audience has been prepared to witness the change to a new, disarrayed, afflicted Ophelia. Her description, through an anonymized third party, readies us for her transformed state:

> GENTLEMAN
> She speaks much of her father; says she hears
> There's tricks i' th'world; and hems, and beats her heart,
> Spurns enviously at straws, speaks things in doubt
> That carry but half sense. Her speech is nothing,
> Yet the unshaped use of it doth move
> The hearers to collection. They yawn at it
> And botch the words up fit to their own thoughts
> Which, as her winks, and nods, and gestures yield them,
> Indeed would make one think there might be thought,
> Though nothing sure, yet much unhappily.
>
> (4.5.4–13)

Critical analyses of Ophelia's changed voice explore every word and phrase to discover coded meaning in her fraught discourse. Is Ophelia's 'speech ... nothing'? Is female madness, by contrast to Hamlet's 'method', presented merely as chaotic? In analysing Ophelia's songs and speech in 4. 2, we should ourselves not 'botch the words up fit to [our] own thoughts'; Ophelia's fragmented discourse represents the difficulty of interpreting the language of madness onstage. However, Ophelia's altered modes of speech do present some clues to the gendered understanding of madness in Shakespeare's age that seeps into today's readings and portrayals of Ophelia, as well as broader cultural expectations of female irrationality, proximity to nature and weakness.

Gendering Madness

In Kenneth Branagh's film production of *Hamlet* (1996), a broad nineteenth-century aesthetic characterizes the production's visual style, re-historicizing Ophelia's madness into Victorian representations of, and responses to, perceived insanity, depicting her wearing a straitjacket in a padded cell. Other productions have used Ophelia's madness to present a general disconnection with reality via use of film and photographs, such as Michael Almereyda's (2000) film and Lindsey Turner's (2015) production at the Barbican, both of which replace Ophelia's flowers with scattered photographs. Ophelia's onstage presentation during her madness is paradigmatic of each generation's approach to female identity and to the idea of mental disconnection and unrest.

Horatio's response to the report is that Ophelia's madness is dangerous: her loose tongue will bring disrepute in 'ill-breeding minds' (4.5.16). Despite being the rightful heir to the throne, Hamlet's madness is not met with this same concern. Rather, it is the threat to stability that troubles those around him; madness so near the 'head' of state is dangerous to order itself, not simply to reputation. Male madness is taken seriously politically; the woman's madness remains a private tragedy. Arguably, contrasting the control Hamlet applies over his own behaviour, Ophelia's reappearance in Act 4 represents her disconnection from the play's internal politics. Expressing herself largely through song and proverb, Ophelia de-classes herself, leaving behind the conduct codes of the court, ordering the queen repeatedly, 'pray you, mark', demanding to be heard. After her songs, to which we shall return shortly, Ophelia appears briefly to return to the reality of her immediate situation:

> I hope all will be well. We must be patient. But I cannot choose but weep to think they should lay him i' the cold ground. My brother shall know of it. And so I thank you for your good counsel. Come, my coach! Goodnight, ladies, good night. Sweet ladies, goodnight, goodnight.
>
> (4.5.68–73)

Here, Ophelia swerves back into courtly language, 'and so I thank you for your good counsel' and 'Come, my coach!'. Her parting words, in the polite, formal mode of speech, gender the assembled company female: 'sweet ladies'. The ironic *lack* of 'ladies' in Elsinore's court is highlighted by her pronouncement. She either ignores or feminizes the King, or perhaps multiplies the Queen, to create a female audience for her preceding singing. The male, patriarchal court is rejected in favour of an audience of women and the theatre audience itself.

Women of Ophelia's social position would certainly not be expected to sing spontaneously in public, let alone to perform bawdy songs. Her first song relates a tale of men's fickleness and what we now recognize as an enduring sexual double standard:

> OPHELIA   *Sings*
> Tomorrow is Saint Valentine's Day
> All in the morning betime,
> And I a maid at your window
> To be your valentine.
> Then up he rose and donned his clothes
> And dupped the chamber door –
> Let in the maid that out a maid
> Never departed more.
> CLAUDIUS
> Pretty Ophelia!
> OPHELIA
> Indeed, la, without an oath, I'll make an end on't:
>   *Sings*
> By Gis and by Saint Charity,
> Alack, and fie for shame!
> Young men will do't, if they come to't;
> By Cock, they are to blame.
> Quoth she, 'Before you tumbled me,
> You promised me to wed.'
> He answers:
> 'So would I ha' done, by yonder sun,
> An thou hadst not come to my bed.'
>   (4.5.48–66)

Ophelia's language no longer reflects her high, courtly politeness of earlier in the play, nor the taciturn attempt to communicate safely with Hamlet in 3.2. Using euphemism to sing 'without an oath', she adopts 'Gis' for Jesus and 'Cock' for God, which produces an ironic effect: she refuses to use the Lord's name in vain yet sings openly about sex, intensifying the obscenity with the semantic doubling of 'Cock'. This language compromises the play's former emphasis on her chastity of speech, mind and body. While the freedom of speech attained through her mad state could be read as effecting liberation from patriarchal control, ultimately she still expresses those constraints through song. The paradox of the maid's position in Ophelia's song deepens her articulation of a sense of entrapment under a patriarchal system that polices female sexuality and behaviour via unattainable or paradoxical expectations.

Throughout *Hamlet*, the audience has experienced its hero's misogynistic pronouncements on women's weakness and deceitfulness, from his mother's perceived betrayal – 'Frailty, thy name is woman' (1.2.146) – to the bawdy brutality of the nunnery scene with Ophelia. Hamlet frequently uses gendered metaphor or philosophizes on women's falseness. In 2.2, Hamlet's self-chastisement is gendered, cursing his own lack of action by feminizing and sexualizing his reliance on words, not deeds, foreshadowing Ophelia's metamorphosed language: 'That I … / Must like a whore unpack my heart with words / and fall a-cursing like a very drab' (2.2.518–21). The idea of women as words and men as deeds underpins Hamlet's gendered language here (Thompson and Taylor, 2019: 307). The looseness of the female tongue is a perpetual source of fear and mistrust in early modern discourses of gender. Ophelia's tight adherence to gendered codes of speech before her madness, answering as opposed to addressing the men around her, endures to the last of her appearances on stage before her metamorphosis. Hamlet goads her as they share a space in the audience of his *Mousetrap*; she is the passive audience member, he, director-like, controls the action:

HAMLET
    Lady, shall I lie in your lap?
OPHELIA
    No, my lord.
HAMLET
    I mean, my head upon your lap?
OPHELIA
    Ay, my lord.
HAMLET
    Do you think I meant country matters?
OPHELIA
    I think nothing, my lord.
HAMLET
    That's a fair thought to lie between maids' legs.
OPHELIA
    What is, my lord?

HAMLET
    Nothing.
OPHELIA
    You are merry, my lord.
HAMLET
    Who, I?
OPHELIA
    Ay, my lord.

(3.2.109–17)[1]

The audience has just shared Hamlet's elation and hopes for the play gambit to move his purpose forwards, to 'catch the conscience of the king' (2.2.540). They are therefore complicit co-conspirators in Hamlet's plot, which fast becomes as Machiavellian as any laid by Claudius. Yet, when he seats himself with Ophelia, Hamlet proceeds to goad her with bawdy innuendo that is entirely unnecessary to his cause. Suggesting the obvious double meaning of lying in Ophelia's 'lap', Ophelia objects: 'No, my lord'. In the Folio version, an extra two lines (italicized in extract) provide more ambiguity with her 'Ay my lord' variously interpreted in performance as Ophelia giving her consent for Hamlet's head to lie in her lap (which would be extremely unlikely in the context) or simply agreeing that, 'ay', she understands his meaning. She maintains a strict adherence to linguistic hierarchy, repeating the epithet 'my lord' in every single utterance. This effects a sense of distance and formality between herself and the 'antic' prince, albeit with palpable subservience.

This exchange, stichomythic and effectively prose, does not follow the metrical patterns of the play's dominating verse. Yet Ophelia's monosyllabic utterances present a blunt and sparse rhythmic voice; only twice does she use a duosyllabic word, 'nothing' and 'merry'. In production (such as Gregory Doran's, RSC, 2008), this uncharacteristic bluntness is interpreted both as unease and as a response to other business around the pair precluding conversation. Ophelia's speech could also represent the awkwardness of an audience member aware of the inappropriate speech of their neighbour, reconfiguring the audience outside the play world to ally with Ophelia, embarrassed by Hamlet's crass behaviour. However, Ophelia's stunted

---

[1] Line numbers from Arden 3rd Series, which uses the Second Quarto; italicized lines are additions in Folio.

speech is also a precursor of the linguistic fragmentation found when we next meet her. Hamlet's bawdy punning throws the blame onto Ophelia, inferring her unchaste mind makes unspeakable connections: 'did you think I meant country matters?' Ophelia's attempt to escape this assault manifests in her self-subjugation and self-effacement, 'I think nothing, my lord', but is met with further harassment. Hamlet adopts the common euphemism of 'nothing' to represent the vagina with sharp, skilful punning and tricks Ophelia into drawing the joke in upon herself: 'That's a fair thought to lie between maids' legs.' / 'What is my lord?' / 'Nothing'. Claudius's judgement of Ophelia's madness as purely based on grief for her father is, therefore, undermined by preceding scenes in which she suffers misogynistic verbal abuse from Hamlet. In production, this abuse is sometimes presented as physical, such as in the presentation of the nunnery scene (3.1) in Branagh's 1996 film adaptation. As we have seen in Chapter 3, where a popular heart-throb is cast in the main role (David Tennant, Jude Law, Benedict Cumberbatch, Keanu Reeves), the audience is drawn further into sympathy with the troubles of its protagonist. In this context, Hamlet's subsequent abuse of Ophelia, whether mental or interpreted as physical, runs the risk of appearing justified, or at least forgivable, especially if we accept Hamlet as melancholic and not to be held accountable for his actions. Indeed, Hamlet's abusive, systematic undermining of Ophelia, including the deconstruction and reconfiguration of her language in the play scene, anticipates the transformation of Ophelia's speech.

Yet Hamlet's goading eventually draws at least some slight resistance from Ophelia, in that she dares to correct him: 'Nay, 'tis twice two months, my lord' (3.2.121). Ophelia's madness might be read as a kind of liberty, a breaking free from the restrictions of patriarchal authority, particularly in the change from her emphatically minimalist and subservient language of these earlier scenes to her later utterances when, freed from the restrictions of 'my lord' she entirely feminizes her audience ('sweet ladies'). In her mad state, Ophelia's obedience to patriarchal structures of language unravels. Where she earlier speaks only when spoken to, she now controls the stage space via her language and the sound of her singing voice. Through song, Ophelia transgresses her social boundaries into a more popular mode both of expression and performance. Hamlet's performance of madness has been calculated, purposeful and, almost literally, by the book. He displays the symptoms of melancholy at some points, lovesickness at others and presents a general mania that convinces those around him of his mental collapse as a tragic, intellectual madness ('a noble mind ... o'erthrown'

3.1.149). Yet he remains, for the audience, coherent and *compos mentis* in his soliloquies as well as his interactions with his confidant, Horatio. He also frequently reminds his audience, both on the stage and off, that he is merely acting madness, that he is 'but mad north-north-west. When the wind is southerly I know a hawk from a handsaw' (2.2.315–16). Even the obtuse Polonius is not entirely taken in, noticing from Hamlet's speech that 'though this be madness, yet there is method in't' (2.2.203). Ophelia, by contrast, metamorphoses into a new structure of expression and the presentation of her mental state, once changed, does not falter. Ophelia is never onstage alone during her madness; she never soliloquizes and she is without a confidant. We are only to see her madness as witnessed by others. We can choose, as Elaine Showalter has identified as the project of some feminist critics, to become that missing confidant, her 'Horatia', and bear witness to her story (1985: 78). Yet, as Showalter identifies, the problem with this approach is that there is so little story to tell. Shakespeare gives us only glimpses of Ophelia, and always framed by others. Hamlet's madness – or performance of it – takes centre stage.

Hamlet predates Jorden's treatise on hysteria, *The Suffocation of the Mother* (Resource 5.b), and the play's melancholic characters seem to echo the earlier Bright. Yet Shakespeare's later collaboration with Fletcher, *The Two Noble Kinsmen*, was written a decade or so after the publication of Jorden's influential text on the physical and mental state of women suffering from 'the Mother'. *The Two Noble Kinsmen* retells Chaucer's *Knight's Tale* of rivalry between two male friends, Palamon and Arcite, adding a significant subplot in the form of the passionate love developed by a Jailer's daughter for her noble prisoner, Palamon, for whom she risks everything to free and pursue, only to find herself lost and alone, descending into a lovesick madness. The Jailer's Daughter has no name, yet significantly more lines to speak than Ophelia. Ophelia's governance by her brother and father appears completely established; by contrast, the Daughter, in name defined entirely by her father, defies that father to act independently and lawlessly. The presentation of her madness closely echoes Ophelia's at first but the plots diverge. In *Hamlet*, the woman's descent is lamented rather than addressed with pragmatism and her death is viewed by the other characters as an inevitable end to her narrative. The Jailer's Daughter's madness, by contrast, is met with attempts to treat or cure her malady: she is saved from drowning and a Doctor is summoned, medicalizing her condition.

Resource 5.b: From Edward Jorden, *A Briefe Discourse of the Disease Called the Suffocation of the Mother* (1603)

As in this disease the want of due and monethly evacuation, or the want of the benefit of marriage in such as have beene accustomed or are apt there unto, breeds a congestion of humors about that part, which increasing or corrupting in the place, causeth this disease. And therefore we do observe that maidens and widowes are most subject thereunto. Motion and rest being well ordered do preserve health, but being disordered do breed diseases, especially to much rest and slothfulnesse is a meanes of this griefe, by ingendering crudities and obstructions in womens bodies, by dulling the spirits and cooling naturall heate, &c. So likewise sleepe and watching, the one by benumming, the other by dissipation of the spirits and natural heate, may occasion this griefe.

Lastly the perturbations of the minde are oftentimes to blame both for this and many other diseases. For seeing we are not maisters of our owne affections, wee are like battered Citties without walles, or shippes tossed in the Sea, exposed to all maner of assults and daungers, even to the overthrow of our owne bodies.

We have infinite examples among our Historiographers, and Phisitions of such as have dyed vppon ioy, griefe, loue, feare, shame, and such like perturbations of the mind: and of others that upon the same causes have fallen into grievous diseases: as women delivered of their children before their time, upon feare, anger, griefe, &c. others taken with the Falling sickenesse, Apoplexies, Madnesse, Swounding, Palsies, and diverse such like infirmities upon the like causes.

(pp. G2^r–G3)

Let us begin by reading the presentation of the cause and manifestation of the Jailer's Daughter's sudden distraction. Her increasing realization that she will not be able to find Palamon, the object of her desire, is located in an external disorientation, in which she finds herself lost and cold in the woods:

> I am moped.
> Food took I none these two days;
> Sipped some water. I have not closed mine eyes,
> Save when my lids scoured off their brine. Alas,

> Dissolve, my life! Let not my sense unsettle,
> Lest I should drown, or stab, or hang myself.
> Oh, state of nature, fail together in me,
> Since thy best props are warped! – So, which way now?
> The best way is the next way to a grave:
> Each errant step beside is torment. Lo,
> The moon is down, the crickets chirp, the screech – owl
> Calls in the dawn; all offices are done
> Save what I fail in. But the point is this:
> An end, and that is all.
>
> (3.2.25–37)

Unlike Ophelia, whose mental deterioration is finally triggered by her father's death, the Jailer's Daughter is more clearly presented as becoming lost, both in love and in an unfamiliar world. She has risked the life and liberty of herself and her father in releasing Palamon yet, as well as grief and ensuing melancholy, she appears to suffer lovesickness. The brutality of her dry eyes, whose 'lids scoured off their brine' is reminiscent of the cold dryness associated with melancholy. Echoing Hamlet's wish that his 'flesh would melt, / Thaw and resolve itself into a dew' (1.2.129–30), the Daughter exclaims, 'dissolve, my life', drawing a watery image for her despair. In *Hamlet*, it is Ophelia who becomes at one with water, viewed as the feminine element (Long, 2016: 77), dragged down into a brook, 'like a creature native and endued / Unto that element' (4.7.177–8). Hamlet dies a hot death of poison in the midst of the masculine exertion of a fight. Both conform, in death, to their archetypal gendered elements. The Daughter, though, will survive to be presented not with a gender-appropriate death but the prospect of a troubling 'cure'.

The Daughter presents the audience with her fear of losing her faculties and committing an unwitting suicide; she is *compos mentis* and fearful of losing her sanity, 'Let not my sense unsettle, / Lest I should drown, or stab, or hang myself'. Yet she expands this terror beyond the pragmatic fear of death into an apparently unstoppable nihilistic onward movement toward either mental nothingness or death, 'But the point is this – / An end, and that is all'. Her contemplation of her own sanity, as well as of suicide, is far from the *fait accompli* with which *Hamlet*'s audience is presented when it comes to Ophelia's madness. Ophelia has mourned Hamlet's sanity ('O! What a noble mind is here o'erthrown' (3.1.149)), watches *The Mousetrap* with Hamlet (3.2) and then is not seen on stage until her entrance, mad (4.5). The precise journey of Ophelia from rationality to distraction is hidden from *Hamlet*'s audience and, while Claudius immediately settles blame on 'the poison of deep grief' (4.5.75), this is the same character whom Shakespeare has presented as entirely failing to understand Hamlet's true state of mind. Therefore, how much Hamlet's own apparent distraction, or his cruel treatment of Ophelia in Act 3, Scenes 1 (the nunnery scene) and 2 (*The Mousetrap*), has contributed to her ultimate mental collapse is open to speculation. Claudius's assumption that her ultimate disintegration into madness is entirely due to grief at her father's loss presents Ophelia either as an extremely doting daughter or as unable to function alone outside her patriarchally governed sphere.

The Jailer's Daughter's descent is much more visible; the audience sees, but is powerless to stop, her fall into distraction. Its romantic root is repeatedly suggested, with later diagnoses clearly designating a kind of combination of greensickness (a supposedly virginal complaint), lovesickness and melancholy. When we next encounter the Daughter, it is in a pastoral setting, her madness seen as adding to the merriment of a rustic dance. Male strangers to the plot, like the nameless Gentlemen that heralds Ophelia, assess and discuss the Daughter's madness. Here, there is a sinister sense that she is a commodity for the entertainment of others:

3 COUNTRYMAN
>There's a dainty madwoman, Master,
>Comes i' th' nick, as mad as a March hare.
>If we can get her dance, we are made again;
>I warrant her, she'll do the rarest gambols.

1 COUNTRYMAN
>A madwoman? We are made, boys.

(3.5.73–7)

The Daughter has wandered into a pastoral scene, where she is assigned an archetypal role immediately, one useful to the men around her. When found by the Wooer later on, she attempts to return to her original, urban environment, 'presently / She slipped away and to the city made' (4.1.97). In the pastoral setting, she is lost and bewildered: she finds an unwelcome niche as a 'madwoman' in this mode of pastoral performance, where her songs and proverbs fit as perfectly as Ophelia's similar performances jar in the public political court of Elsinore. Despite her fear that madness might lead her to suicide ('Let not my sense unsettle, / Lest I should drown, or stab, or hang myself'), the Daughter would have completed her journey in madness back to nature as Ophelia did: by drowning. The Wooer recounts how he witnessed the Daughter about to drown but, unlike Gertrude (or her witness), he was able to intervene:

> WOOER
> I'll tell you quickly. As I late was angling
> In the great lake that lies behind the palace,
> From the far shore, thick set with reeds and sedges,
> As patiently I was attending sport
> I heard a voice, a shrill one, and attentive
> I gave my ear, when I might well perceive
> 'Twas one that sung and, by the smallness of it
> A boy or woman.
>   (4.1.52–9)

The Wooer first hears the Daughter's voice, before seeing her among the water plants. Unlike Ophelia, whose death report scarcely mentions her own voice (Gertrude only notes that Ophelia 'chanted snatches of old lauds', or 'tunes' in Q1/Folio (4.7.175)), the Wooer goes into some detail about the sound and matter of the Daughter's voice. The 'shrill[ness]' of it carries through the environment, despite its 'smallness'. It is de-gendered as belonging to 'a boy or a woman', self-reflexively referencing the boy-actor who would have played the Daughter, emphasizing the tonal and aural androgyny.

The Wooer does not gloss over the content of the woman's words, as Gertrude does, but recounts the Daughter's songs of love and loss in direct speech. This ventriloquizing of the female voice, is not, however, merely an 'impersonation' (Callahan, 2002: 7, see Chapter 1). The Wooer recounts:

> I'll bring a bevy,
> A hundred black-eyed maids that love as I do,
> With chaplets on their heads of daffadillies,
> With cherry lips and cheeks of damask roses,
> And all we'll dance an antic 'fore the Duke
> And beg his pardon.' Then she talked of you, sir:
> That you must lose your head tomorrow morning,
> And she must gather flowers to bury you,
> And see the house made handsome. Then she sung

> Nothing but 'Willow, willow, willow,' and, between,
> Ever was 'Palamon, fair Palamon'
> And 'Palamon was a tall young man.' The place
> Was knee-deep where she sat; her careless tresses
> A wreath of bullrush rounded; about her stuck
> Thousand freshwater flowers of several colours,
>
> (4.1.71-90)

The songs recall Desdemona's portentous performance of the Willow Song in *Othello* (4.3.39-56) and Ophelia's gathering of flowers before her death and distributing them to her audience. Like Ophelia, the Daughter reconfigures established songs and proverbs, common knowledge, via which she speaks. 'She must gather flowers to bury you,' suggests that the Daughter's guilt at endangering her father is manifested in grief for his imagined death; and that linearity of time, cause and effect, is beginning to slip away from her. While Ophelia more rationally laments, 'I would give you some violets, but they withered all when my father died' (4.5.177), the Daughter seeks flowers to lay at an imagined paternal grave.

As both the Daughter and Ophelia edge closer to absorption by nature, the further they drift from sanity. Ophelia's bawdy songs remove her from the court in her behaviour; her distribution of flowers locates her within a pastoral world, further from any awareness of her surroundings. The Daughter's displacement into the woods and the subsequent rustic dance literalizes through dramaturgy this connection between female madness and the natural environment. Ophelia's flowers are symbolic of emotions; her language of flowers – 'there's rosemary, that's for remembrance' (4.5.169) invites the other flowers to be read (rue for repentance, daisies for unrequited love and so on). By contrast, the Daughter's flowers are to decorate imagined women in love, who are then described using highly conventional conceits drawn from the conventional blazon, in which women were described using specific metaphors drawn from nature, 'cherry lips and cheeks of damask roses' (see Introduction and Chapter 1 on Shakespeare's critique of these conventions). The women conjured by the Daughter (apparently) are constructions of the male sonneteer's gaze, not drawn from reality, which highlights her isolation, like Ophelia, from genuine female society.

Saved from drowning, the Daughter has now outlived her template, Ophelia. No attempts are made to 'cure' Ophelia: were it a textbook case study, perhaps due to her rank and class, the idea of the sex cure jars with the play's earlier emphasis on her chastity by her father and brother. Where

Two Noble Kinsmen displays, with some dark comic effect, the later wider use of such cures for the madness of 'the Mother', Shakespeare's other most enduring portrayal of female mental collapse, the sleepwalking Lady Macbeth, is met with abortive attempts to cure her via medical intervention. Faced with the sinister ramifications of her unconscious outpourings, *Macbeth*'s Doctor is convinced that Lady Macbeth's malady is more spiritual than physical, immediately fearing 'this disease is beyond my practice' and suggesting, 'more needs she the divine than the physician' (5.1.71). Lady Macbeth is presented throughout as transgressing the boundaries of her own gender and into the masculine ('unsex me' (1.5.41)). The Doctor sees similar division between physical and spiritual madness to that which Bright had identified in the male melancholic. Alternatively, in the context of the play's presentation of witchcraft, his fear may rather be of darker supernatural sources, which were frequently interpreted as behind women's 'mad' behaviour: Jorden's *Suffocation of the Mother* was originally designed to counter the idea that witchcraft is to blame for madness in women. However, unlike *Macbeth*'s despondent doctor, who, faced with Lady Macbeth's sinister somnambulatory behaviour, suggests only spiritual assistance can help her, the Doctor in *Two Noble Kinsmen* takes a much more pragmatic approach reminiscent of Jorden's ideas that the wandering womb (the Mother) and reproductive blockages caused mental distraction.

While Ophelia is reported to have drowned without any kind of intervening action either in this catastrophe or in terms of any suggestion of treatment beforehand, the Jailer's Daughter is subjected to medical intervention. A Doctor is consulted by the men who still surround her and suggests a practical, if disturbing, solution. While *Hamlet*'s Elizabethan Ophelia seems destined to remain mad until inevitable death claims her, the Jacobean Jailer's Daughter is subjected to more modern attempts at a cure:

DOCTOR
    That's all one, if ye make a noise.
    If she entreat again, do anything.
    Lie with her if she ask you.
JAILER   Whoa there, Doctor!
DOCTOR
    Yes, in the way of cure.
JAILER   But first, by your leave,
    I' th' way of honesty.

DOCTOR   That's but a niceness.
Ne'er cast your child away for honesty.
Cure her first this way; then if she will be honest,
She has the path before her.

...

Whate'er her father says, if you perceive
Her mood inclining that way that I spoke of,
Videlicet, 'the way of flesh' – you have me?
WOOER
Yes, very well, sir.
DOCTOR   Please her appetite,
And do it home, it cures her, *ipso facto*,
The melancholy humour that infects her.

(5.2.16–38)

Nowhere here is the attempt to use Bright's good friends or spiritual study to cure the Daughter's lovesick melancholy. Instead, the cure is sex – more specifically, good sex – to disperse the 'melancholy humour that infects her'. In Blanche McIntyre's 2016 RSC production, this scene was played for its humour but the Wooer (Patrick Knowles), who had been portrayed as a simply comic character earlier, was transformed into a conscientious suitor, as uncomfortable with the Doctor's proposal as the twenty-first-century audience. While at first her father objects, he is quickly silenced by the Doctor, who urges the cure be effected first while problems this will produce for her 'honesty' can be addressed later. This specific cure can be found in Jorden's treatise, when he diagnoses some 'hysterical' behaviours as due to 'the want of the benefit of marriage', or sex: abstinence creates 'a congestion of humors' resulting in the perceived mad behaviour (Resource 5.b). This cure is based on a fundamentally gendered perception of mental unrest in the first place, especially lovesickness and melancholy. As Lesel Dawson writes:

> Whereas lovesickness in men is defined as a form of melancholia, in women it is associated with diseases of the reproductive tract: women's illnesses are thus constructed as bodily and passionate rather than intellectual and creative.
>
> (Dawson, 2008: 93)

Shakespeare and Gender

Hamlet's melancholy is consistently presented as either deliberately feigned or a result of intellectual suffering, while both Ophelia's and the Daughter's are visceral and dangerous.

Conclusions

1. Shakespeare's presentation of madness in *Hamlet* is gendered in several ways: via the responses of those around Hamlet and Ophelia; by the characters' language; and by references to or hints at contemporary sources on the diagnosis and treatment of madness in men and women. *Hamlet*'s iconic status has entrenched these gendered presentations of madness beyond their early modern medical, social and political context and created archetypes of madness that endure and influence Western society today.
2. Contemporary physicians' ideas on the rational, intellectual male as more often afflicted by melancholy seep through Hamlet's performance of madness and making it more convincing to both his onstage audience and to his audience in the theatre.
3. Ophelia's madness, juxtaposed with Hamlet's, presents contrasting ideas of women's mental illness as tied not to the intellectual or spiritual confusion often attributed to Hamlet, but to their reproductive, sexual organs, via her bawdy songs – an idea made darkly humorous in the later *Two Noble Kinsmen* when the Doctor instructs that the Daughter's similar madness must be cured by sex. However, Ophelia is not simply an archetype: her shift into 'mad' language can be read as a shift of her status in the play world, in which she moves outside her sociopolitical sphere and into a hinterland beyond the court/stage's restrictive space.

Further Work

Hamlet

What is the effect of either gender-blind, flipped gender or all-female/all-male productions of *Hamlet* on how the audience views madness in the play? Look up some recent productions, such as the Globe's 2018 production directed by Michelle Terry, that have played with conventional gendered casting. How do these affect our perceptions of madness as gendered in performance contexts?

The Two Noble Kinsmen

Look again at the Jailer's Daughter among the rustics in 3.5. When asked if she is mad, why does she reply, 'I would be sorry else'? Compare her interactions with others to Ophelia's.

Macbeth

How do we read Lady Macbeth's sleepwalking compared to her husband's guilt-ridden hallucinations or supernatural visitations? How are their different behaviours treated by those around them? How does the presence of the witches affect the gendering of madness in the play?

King Lear

Look at the portrayal of 'madness' in the titular king and how Edgar feigns madness in constructing his alter ego, Poor Tom. How do the real and feigned insanities compare to the presentation of the actions of Lear's two oldest daughters, Goneril and Regan? How is their apparent cruelty portrayed in terms of their mental states? Is Goneril's sudden reported suicide anticipated in her behaviour earlier in the play?

Further Reading

Philippa Berry, *Shakespeare's Feminine Endings* (Routledge, 1999). **A seminal work applying feminist, queer and postmodern theory and ideas to how we read and view Shakespeare's tragedies.**

Douglas Bruster, 'The Jailor's Daughter and the politics of madwomen's language', *Shakespeare Quarterly*, Vol. 46, No. 3 (Autumn, 1995), 277–300. **A good starting point for reading about the gendered configuration of madness, particularly the way the Daughter's isolation and 'mad' language is Shakespeare's addition to the original source materials.**

Lesel Dawson, *Lovesickness and Gender in Early Modern English Literature*, (Oxford University Press, 2008). **A crucial book examining the early modern gendering of medical discourses through accounts of lovesickness, melancholy and 'female' maladies such as greensickness.**

Shakespeare and Gender

Carol Thomas Neely, *Distracted Subjects: Madness and Gender in Shakespeare and Early Modern Culture* (Cornell University Press, 2004). **Essential reading for approaching the gendering of madness in the cultural moment of Shakespeare's work.**

Carol Thomas Neely, Gayle Greene and Carolyn Ruth S. Lenz (eds), *The Woman's Part: Feminist Criticism of Shakespeare* (University of Illinois Press, 1980). **Offers a window into feminist criticism in the early days of feminist approaches to Shakespeare: particularly interesting for work on madness.**

Elaine Showalter, 'Representing Ophelia: Women, Madness and the Responsibilities of Feminist Criticism', in Patricia Parker and Geoffrey Hartmen *Shakespeare and the Question of Theory* (Routledge, 1985). **An influential voice in the development of feminist literary criticism, Showalter explores how feminist critics up to 1985 had viewed Ophelia, interrogating the various arguments on her madness from a range of feminist perspectives.**

CHAPTER 6
PATERNITY AND PATRIARCHY
Key Text: *King Lear*, with *The Tempest*

How does Shakespeare present the state of paternity and its relationship with patriarchal power? The very word, 'patriarchy', describes a sociopolitical ideology based on the father as ruler. As such, exploring fathers in Shakespeare can help to unpick how Shakespeare presents what we now identify as the mechanisms of patriarchy in his plays. In *King Lear*, Shakespeare deconstructs the father-ruler, revealing the mechanics of the patriarch by exploring what happens when this masculine 'head' of the body politic is disordered. The chapter will examine a gendered hierarchy of parent and child as both a domestic and a public phenomenon and explore male patrilineage and legitimacy as crucial patriarchal political structures. In *King Lear*, the king-father's judgement is compromised by a figurative blindness, in which the patriarchal power Lear yields is waning, while the actual blindness of another father mirrors the swift and catastrophic collapse of order. In both *Lear* and *The Tempest*, a geography of patriarchy can be traced, mapped from domestic to political tyranny, from the bodies of daughters to the nation itself. Both these fathers lack wives and their children are thus motherless. This absence of motherhood exposes both the tyranny and the fragility of paternal power.

From the outset of the play, *King Lear* presents the king's possession of his daughters and his kingdom as inextricably linked. Lear maps his power onto the land and, in dividing it, deconstructs his kingship into three smaller powers:

> Give me the map there. Know that we have divided
> In three our kingdom; and 'tis our fast intent
> To shake all cares and business from our age'
> Conferring them on younger strengths, while we
> Unburdened crawl toward death.
>
> (1.1.36–40)

However, these 'younger strengths' in two cases become strengths that oppose him and, as Lear himself descends into a chaotic state of mind, his kingdom, too, enters a state of havoc. Lear's egotism as patriarch both of family and of nation catalyses, and is reiterated by, the ensuing chaos. His possession of the map demonstrates his ability to have complete political control over both his kingdom and his daughters, and enacts the crucial significance of the map as emblem of power and possession in Jacobean England (Gordon and Klein, 2001). Lear's devolution of power to his daughters itself is, in early modern terms, a fundamentally wrong principle. He avoids the proper system of heredity and, indeed, redirects it to women, disrupting a patrilineal continuum beyond simple sonlessness and into a deliberate act of delegation to daughters. Yet Lear's obstinate paternal (domestic) and patriarchal (public) arrogance itself could equally be read as the catalyst for tragedy.

Ultimately, though, *Lear* presents a sustained parallel in which the loss of parental – specifically paternal – authority is analogous with the loss of monarchic, patriarchal control of the nation. Lear decides to divide his kingdom because of both his own ageing and his daughters' married (or likely to be married) status, and take an effective retirement. This part of Act 1 scene 1 of *Lear* begins the cycle of tragedy that will drive the entire play. Having appeared to have decided already on the allocation of land, the King reveals his 'darker purpose': he will first subject each daughter to a trial of their love for him, demanding,

> ... Tell me, my daughters –
> Since now we will divest us both of rule,
> Interest of territory, cares of state –
> Which of you shall we say doth love us most,
> That we our largest bounty may extend
> Where nature doth with merit challenge.
>
> (1.1.48–53)

This is a trial of rhetoric and courtly flattery. In demanding declarations of love from his daughters, Lear essentially asks them to reaffirm, despite their married or betrothed state, that he retains his patriarchal autocracy in his domestic affairs, even as he relinquishes his official duties. By weighing their 'love' with their 'bounty', Lear indentures them not to legal succession but a continual filial duty. Thus, if he passes his kingdom on to his daughters but his daughters nevertheless retain their fundamentally inferior position in the family hierarchy, he really does not relinquish power at all, on either a philosophical or a practical level. His fatherhood, and the love, duty and obedience he perceives that state commands, assures his continuing power despite delegations of pragmatic duties.

Shakespeare's plays, especially the Histories, frequently return to the vexed notion of a meritocratic, as opposed to a hereditary, monarchic succession and Lear's demand initially appears to champion this, 'challeng[ing]' birth right with 'merit' (see Chapter 2). Indeed, shortly after, the audience is party to Cordelia's asides and is predisposed to establish her as the worthiest, wisest and, by meritocratic model, therefore most deserving daughter. Yet Lear in fact seeks not merit but flattery, demanding 'Which of you shall we say doth love us most'; like Richard II, Lear is a victim of his own vanity. Cordelia is shunned where she should, by his own pronouncement, be rewarded and Lear, for the first time, is branded 'mad' by an outraged Kent (1.1.147). Cordelia's logical approach responds to Lear's growing rage and indignation at her declaration of having 'nothing' to say in the love trial. 'Nothing will come of nothing' (1.1.89), he declares, and thus invokes a feminine line of heredity as null, where 'nothing', the common euphemism for vagina, becomes a wider referent for the female. Critical discourse tends not to identify the 'nothing' of *Lear* as carrying the gendered weight of the 'nothing' in *Much Ado About Nothing*'s title, or in *Hamlet*'s punning attack on Ophelia (3.2.114–17) (see Chapters 1 and 5). Yet the gendered nuances of 'nothing' in the context of the foregrounding of female heredity here remind us that Cordelia, however favoured, can never be a son.

Cordelia rationalizes her refusal to take part in the love trial exercise in terms of her own daughter- and wifehood. She explicitly identifies herself in her specified female roles within a patriarchal model of domestic hierarchy as daughter and future wife. Yet it is love, rather than obedience, that is her currency:

> CORDELIA
> Unhappy that I am, I cannot heave
> My heart into my mouth. I love your majesty
> According to my bond, nor more nor less.
> LEAR
> How, how, Cordelia? Mend your speech a little,
> Lest it may mar your fortunes.
> CORDELIA   Good my lord,
> You have begot me, bred me, loved me. I
> Return those duties back as are right fit,
> Obey you, love you, and most honour you.

> Why have my sisters husbands, if they say
> They love you all? Haply when I shall wed,
> That lord whose hand must take my plight shall carry
> Half my love with him, half my care and duty.
> Sure I shall never marry like my sisters
> To love my father all.
>
> (1.1.90–102)

One of the core premises for Cordelia's assertion here is doubled; while she 'cannot heave her heart into her mouth', she cannot flatter and must be honest. She also shows acute understanding of the divided duty she will owe to father and husband on the occasion of her marriage, directing 'half [her] love' to her husband. Her direct criticism of Regan and Goneril – rhetorically interrogating 'why have my sisters husbands, if they say / They love you all?' – presents them as erroneously assigning precedence to father *over* husband in the patriarchal familial order. Thus, Cordelia, in speaking out to her father the King, at once both exposes and reinforces traditional patriarchy. In its public setting, Cordelia's speech is even more challenging. In this patriarchal space she ought to be silent; yet she has been ordered to speak and instead pleads to be silent. With this plea, though, she challenges the King, her father. In this sense, too, then, Cordelia exposes the paradoxes inherent in patriarchal control over women's voices.

The daughters' speeches are all in public. They take place in the presence of Lear's sons-in-law, Albany and Cornwall, who both have enormous vested interests in the proceedings, as well as Kent, Edmund, Gloucester and an unspecified number of 'attendants'. Only Cordelia is free of the rule of a husband here. In production, there is flexibility in how far the sisters may be portrayed as behaving specifically under the eye of their husbands. In Richard Eyre's (2018) BBC production (to which we will return later), for instance, exchanges of nervous glances between Goneril and Regan and their respective husbands, as well as Albany and Cornwall's clear distaste at their shares of the kingdom, all serve to highlight the sisters' lack of autonomy in speaking. In any production though, with potential husbands Burgundy and the King of France unequivocally not present in this scene, Cordelia may risk her father's wrath, but no husband's, when she states that love must be divided. Like *Much Ado About Nothing*'s Beatrice and *The Winter's Tale*'s Paulina, Cordelia uses her voice publicly to speak truth to power (see Chapter 1). She neither modestly stays silent nor ends at her declaration that she cannot express her emotion. Rather, she establishes the inappropriate and unwise nature of Lear's gambit and, as such, risks humiliating him with her comparative wisdom in the presence of many powerful men.

Cordelia's understanding of her duty to father and husband resembles a Christian patriarchal model. The female relationship with God was understood through a discourse of sister-, daughter- and wifehood, through which, at various stages of the development of faith, the woman would pass (see Resource 6.a). These states being mutually exclusive, once a woman becomes a wife, daughterhood is deprioritized: 'She forsaketh hir old father, and all the goods that he giueth hir, for hir husbands sake'. In this context, Cordelia's pronouncement adheres to a patriarchal order, both sociopolitical and religious, in her refusal to declare her love as worship and idolatry. Her shocked response is not radical resistance to patriarchy, but to Lear's deviant expectations. The audience is, from the first, complicit in – and presumably, then, expected to sympathize with – her confusion and distress at what is being asked of her:

> [*Aside*] What shall Cordelia do? Love, and be silent.
> ...
> [*Aside*]   Then poor Cordelia,
> And yet not so, since, I am sure my love's
> More ponderous than my tongue.
>
> (1.1.62–78)

Here, Cordelia conforms to the early modern ideal of silence. Shakespeare establishes for the audience that her failure to respond is a result of active decision. Her love for her father is not in question but her sense of order, of proper behaviour, is demonstrated.

Lear's desire for his daughters' love goes hand in hand with their obedience and Cordelia's protestations fall on deaf ears. Lear has disrupted a clear order of hierarchy and duty, one that is the foundation of the female place in the family, society and church, as Kent rushes to point out:

> KENT   Royal Lear,
> Whom I have ever honoured as my king,
> Loved as my father, as my master followed
> As my great patron thought on in my prayers, –
> LEAR
> The bow is bent and drawn; make from the shaft.

KENT
> Let it fall rather, though the fork invade
> The region of my heart: be Kent unmannerly
> When Lear is mad. What wilt thou do, old man?
> Think'st thou that duty shall have dread to speak,
> When power to flattery bows?
>
> (1.1.140–9)

Daughter-, sister- and wifehood were also expressed as distinct states in early modern Protestant doctrine; they functioned as persistent analogies with the relationship a woman could have with God (Resource 6.a). Lear constructs a dangerous space in which a mortal man attempts to command such obedience and disorders a supposedly natural political and familial hierarchy. He flouts the natural progression of womanhood from daughter to wife that was reflected in the states of piety. Lear's disruption of patriarchal mechanisms creates a sense of complete disorder, in which Lear has set in motion a deconstruction of the very processes that have given him power. He has cast his daughters out of their patriarchal positions himself and the result is self-deposition.

Resource 6.a: Extract from Thomas Bentley, *The monument of matrones conteining seven severall lamps of virginitie* (1582)

Now sith my soule may saie of hir selfe, that shee is the sister of God, ought she not to have hir selfe assured in him? Yes trulie. For thou doest declare with great love, that hir creation was onlie of thy good wil, which it pleaseth thee alwaies to have towards hir, giving assurance, that before hir first daie, or time of being provided for hir, thou thorough love hast made hir, as thou of power alone canst well doo it, and also didst put hir within this bodie, not for to slacke with sloth, but that both of them should have none other exercise, but only to thinke how to doo some service unto thee. Then this truth maketh hir to feele that there is in thee true paternitie. O what honor, what sweetnesse, and what glorie hath the soule, which doeth alwaies remember that she is thy daughter, and that in calling thee father, shee doth thy commandement! What is there more? Is that all? No, it doth please thee to give hir another name,

> to call hir thy wife, and that she againe doo call thee husband, declaring therby how thou hast freelie manifested the mariage of hir. By baptisme hast thou made a promise, to give hir thy goods and riches, and to take on thee hir sinnes: for she hath nothing by heritage but sinne of hir first father Adam. All hir treasures that she hath of nature, are nothing else but sinnes, which thou hast tied upon the Crosse, and paid all hir debts with thy goodes & lands. Thou hast made hir so rich, and with so great a jointure endued hir, that she knowing hir selfe to be thy wedded wife, doth beleeve to be quit of all that she oweth, esteeming verie little that shee hath heere beneath. She forsaketh hir old father, and all the goods that he giveth hir, for hir husbands sake.
>
> (pp. 6–7)

Fatherhood, in early modern contexts, is not only a state of power over children in life but a crucial element of patriarchal power, in which offspring embody a visible line of heredity. Anxiety around the legitimacy of this line rears its ugly head in many of Shakespeare's fathers and husbands (see Chapters 8 and 9). In Chapter 2, we have explored the problems of heredity versus a nascent meritocracy in *Richard II*, in which the king's refusal to acknowledge Bolingbroke's rights of heredity, while asserting his own divine right to rule, is presented as the catalyst, if not cause, for the disorderly end to his reign and the change of the royal line. In *King Lear*, legitimacy and illegitimacy of male lines recurs throughout the play, even though the central daughters' legitimacy is never in question. At the very outset, Kent and Gloucester have a conversation about the illegitimacy of Gloucester's son, Edmund. Gloucester appears to relish the opportunity to boast of his younger sexual exploits and reduce Edmund's mother to 'sport' and a womb, despite Kent's apparent discomfort and attempt to compliment Edmund:

> KENT
> Is not this your son, my lord?
> GLOUCESTER
> His breeding, sir, hath been at my charge.
> I have so often blushed to acknowledge him that now I am brazed t'it.
> KENT
> I cannot conceive you.

GLOUCESTER
> Sir, this young fellow's mother could;
> whereupon she grew round-wombed, and had, indeed,
> sir, a son for her cradle ere she had a husband for her
> bed. Do you smell a fault?

KENT
> I cannot wish the fault undone, the issue of it being
> so proper.

GLOUCESTER
> But I have a son, sir, by order of law, some
> year elder than this, who yet is no dearer in my account.
> Though this knave came something saucily into the world
> before he was sent for, yet was his mother fair, there was
> good sport at his making, and the whoreson must be
> acknowledged. Do you know this noble gentleman,
> Edmund?
>
> (1.1.7–24)

Gloucester's attitude to paternity is skewed by the circumstances of Edmund's birth. While he 'blush[es] to acknowledge' Edmund, Gloucester goes on unnecessarily to eroticize the conception, positing Edmund as the product of both sin and glorious youth. In identifying Edmund as the younger son, Gloucester admits adultery and shamelessly labels Edmund a 'whoreson', the common insult gleefully becoming literal. He denegrates Edmund and his mother before even introducing Kent to him. Gloucester clearly establishes Edmund's lack of power and precarious position outside legitimate lines of succession. Edmund resides in a liminal space both within and without the upper levels of the social hierarchy. This conversation takes place in front of Edmund, speaking as if he were not present, until Gloucester addresses him 'Do you know this noble gentleman, Edmund?' Edmund is thus clearly established as excluded from that family structure and hierarchy that would mirror the patriarchal order of the state; he is, by virtue of his illegitimate birth, a challenge to order.

Just as the 'John the Bastard' identifies as a villain and seeks to wreak havoc for its own sake in *Much Ado About Nothing* (see Chapter 1), Edmund, as Gloucester's illegitimate son, is a symbol of the embittered state of bastardy, in which his entire identity is centred on the circumstances of his conception and birth. The language of illegitimacy is gendered throughout *King Lear*. The mother (both woman and womb) is the author of the bastardy. Edmund, who has contained his rage in the presence of his father and Kent, bursts out with his first soliloquy once free of their company:

> Thou, Nature, art my goddess; to thy law
> My services are bound. Wherefore should I
> Stand in the plague of custom, and permit
> The curiosity of nations to deprive me?
> For that I am some twelve or fourteen moonshines
> Lag of a brother? Why bastard? Wherefore base?
> When my dimensions are as well compact,
> My mind as generous and my shape as true
> As honest madam's issue? Why brand they us
> With base? With baseness, bastardy? Base, base?
> Who in the lusty stealth of nature take
> More composition and fierce quality
> Than doth within a dull stale tired bed
> Go to the creating of a whole tribe of fops
> Got 'tween a sleep and wake.
>
> (1.2.1–15)

Edmund here invokes Nature as 'my goddess' (as Lear will do later), in which he chooses, in this theistically unspecific play world, to align himself with this female deity. Distinct from the 'plagues of custom', Nature is outside the sociopolitical ideologies that constrict Edmund in his 'bastardy'. Edmund challenges the ideology in which privilege is based on the legal and religious union (or lack of it) of parents when their child was conceived: a challenge which proleptically foreshadows Lear's disruption of lineage. Yet he still genders the illegitimacy of his conception, comparing himself bitterly (though favourably) with 'honest madam's issue'. As in Gloucester's version of events, it is the mother of the illegitimate child, rather than the father, that bears label and responsibility. Lear will echo Edmund's soliloquy on the illogical nature of legitimacy later, raging, 'Let copulation thrive; for Gloucester's bastard son / Was kinder to his father than my daughters / Got 'tween the lawful sheets' (4.6.112–14). The dramatic irony here lies in the audience's already established knowledge of Edmund's treachery. However, it is clear from Edmund's soliloquies that society's restrictions placed on him as 'bastard' have led to a solipsistic pattern of behaviour in which, stripped of a place in the patriarchal order of heredity, his self-interest leads to amorality.

Edmund's various last utterances, however, focus on contrition based on emotion rather than the politics of succession that have driven his actions through the play: 'Let sorrow split my heart, if ever I / Did hate thee or thy father' (5.3.176-7). Yet, he blames innate sin for his actions, rebelling against this in his final act of attempted redemption: 'some good I mean to do / Despite of mine own nature' (5.3.242-3). Whether this is because his baseness is innate, as Edmund hints, or as a result of his father's attitude (representative of a broader ideology) to his illegitimacy, is debatable. Nevertheless, in the finale, it is Gloucester, the father, who is denounced for conceiving an illegitimate child, while the mother's sin is erased, when Edgar argues 'The dark and vicious place where thee he got / Cost him his eyes' (5.3.170-1) and, Edmund agrees, 'the wheel is come full circle' (5.3.173).

Resource 6.b: Extract from John Dod and Robert Cleaver, *A Godlie Form of Household Government* (1598)

Parents also have to remember, that they shall commit an act very unnaturall, injurious, and ungodly if they should undeseruedly disinherit their eldest sonne. For as nature in all her workes· for the most part, seemeth to make some one thing to bee chiefe before all the rest, whereby the same is and the rather continueth: so reason in the order of a familie, which is an imitation of a state civill, or bodie politike, perswadeth of experience and necessitie, that there be one before the rest as chiefe.

(pp. 338-9)

Lear presents a pattern of the disorder that results when father–child hierarchies unravel causing both domestic and public chaos, just as civil war ensues after the king blocks Bolingbroke's rightful inheritance in *Richard II* (see Chapter 2). Both Lear's own misjudgement in rejecting Cordelia and Gloucester's mistake in trusting his illegitimate son over his legitimate lead to fatal chaos. Gloucester falls to superstition in attempting to explain the disorder that the audience knows is about to lay waste to his world:

> These late eclipses in the sun and moon
> portend no good to us. Though the wisdom of Nature
> can reason it thus and thus, yet nature finds itself
> scourged by the sequent effects. Love cools, friendship
> falls off, brothers divide: in cities, mutinies; in

Paternity and Patriarchy

countries, discord; in palaces, treason; and the bond
cracked 'twixt son and father. This villain of mine
comes under the prediction – there's son against father.
The king falls from bias of nature; – there's father
against child. We have seen the best of our time.
Machinations, hollowness, treachery and all ruinous
disorders follow us disquietly to our graves.

(1.2.103–17)

For the audience, also deeply ironic, given his speech is directed to Edmund, whom we know to be the villain; the chaos is not in the stars but very much manmade. Disorder (or specifically civil war) is characterized here by disruption to familial order and specifically fathers against sons.

Gloucester's rejection of Edgar is an unnatural act, such that to an early modern audience he may have been seen as the author of his own downfall. Dod and Cleaver's influential manual, *A Godlie Forme of Household Government*, demonstrates the extent to which such behaviour does not fit with ideals of fatherhood: it extends dangerously beyond the domestic into the public sphere (Resource 6.b). Gloucester's effective banishment of his eldest son, then, is against both God and society. Dod and Cleaver demonstrate the mutual interdependence of public and private patriarchy where the family must be 'an imitation of a state civill, or body politike' and vice versa. In their model, representative of the pervasive patriarchal sociopolitical model of the time, the father must be the head of the household as the monarch is head of the body politic of the nation. Those that form the hierarchy that support this head must stay in place to prevent chaotic and 'ungodly' consequences.

This is enacted in Gloucester's lack of wisdom and failure to fulfil his duty as father and as 'chiefe'. By trusting the word of Edmund over Edgar, he reverses their positions in the family hierarchy: Edgar, the eldest and legitimate son, is demoted 'unnaturall[y]' beneath his younger, illegitimate brother, Edmund. The latter weaves his deceit precisely *via* invoking the sanctity of father–son hierarchy and 'bond':

But that I told him the revenging gods
'Gainst parricides did all their thunders bend,
Spoke with how manifold and strong a bond
The child was bound to the father.

(2.1.45–8)

Edmund establishes parricide as the worst of abominations, and his attack on filial 'bond[age]' takes aim at Gloucester's emotional, rather than rational link to his sons, ensnaring Gloucester – and chaos ensues.

The lasting threat to paternal authority inherent in the carnivalesque reversal of father and son disrupts the patrilineal basis of patriarchal order itself. However, Gloucester's metaphorical and physical blindness means he cannot see the reversal of power and, in contrast to his sociopolitical framework of legitimacy and illegitimacy in 1.1, he turns instead to an emotional outlook on the father–child relationship, telling Edgar (believing him a stranger):

> Thou say'st the king grows mad; I'll tell thee, friend,
> I am almost mad myself. I had a son,
> Now outlaw'd from my blood; he sought my life,
> But lately, very late. I loved him, friend,
> No father his son dearer.
>
> (3.4.161–5)

A male bond of love ties father and son, here, rather than Edgar being the manifestation of Gloucester's conformity to an ideal of producing a legitimate male heir. Gloucester's figurative blindness in being led by Edmund is actualized in physical blindness and instead Edgar must literally lead him. In both scenarios, the increasing inversion of Lear's paternal (*qua* patriarchal) authority is mirrored in the image of the father led by the son. This is keenly evident in the emblematic presentation of the blind Gloucester led to the imaginary precipice by Edgar, only to be reborn, wiser after his spiritual death. In parallel, Lear's reversal of paternal/patriarchal power is followed by spiritual death, in which, as the Doctor explains 'the great rage, / You see, is kill'd in him' (4.7.78). Lear awakes to a new awareness, with his favour for Cordelia restored and his foolishness clear to him:

> CORDELIA   O look upon me, Sir,
> And hold your hands in benediction o'er me!
> No, sir, you must not kneel.
> LEAR   Pray, do not mock me.
> I am a very foolish fond old man,

Paternity and Patriarchy

> Fourscore and upward, not an hour more nor less;
> And, to deal plainly,
> I fear I am not in my perfect mind.
>
> (4.7.57–63)

In this scene, the reversal of father and daughter roles is no longer horrifying to Lear; instead, he reaches a state of humility, embodied onstage in kneeling to Cordelia. Casting off his monarchic identity, Lear sees himself in human terms, a 'very foolish, fond old man', outside the sociopolitical hierarchy to which he has so adamantly clung, both paternal and patriarchal. The kneeling king is the culmination of carnivalesque reversal, in which Lear has increasingly become not the true but the carnival king, a temporary and chaotic version of monarchy.

As the (wise) fool clearly identifies early in the action, carnivalesque reversals permeate the play world: 'the cart draws the horse' (1.4.221). However, the whole play's inversions of authority and hierarchy create a sense not of simple chaos or comic reversal but of a dangerous overturning of the structures of patriarchal power. Michael Bakhtin's definition of the carnivalesque is apposite:

> One of the indispensible elements of the folk festival was travesty, that is, the renewal of clothes and of the social image. Another essential element was a reversal of the hierarchic levels: the jester was proclaimed king.
>
> (Bakhtin, 1984: 81)

Lear is a carnivalesque text in its various 'reversal[s] of the hierarchic levels' in every plotline. The fool is wise, children rule their parents and the place- and timelessness of the storm provide a suspension of the usual rules that define the sociopolitical world. Cordelia, with a gentler tone, notes her father's mental disruption as the generational inversion when she refers to her 'child-changed father' (4.7.17), recalling Jaques's identification of old age as 'second childishness and mere oblivion' in *As You Like It* (2.7.166). Even Goneril warns her father of the growing disruption of a deconstructed and inverted hierarchy when she complains of his rowdy entourage, 'your disorder'd rabble / Make servants of their betters' (1.4.254). Gender difference compounds *King Lear*'s parent–child reversal trope. Lear's rejection of Cordelia and disintegration in the face of his other two daughters' increasing power produces a heightened carnivalesque inversion, forcing political questions about such inversions onto the audience.

In Dod and Cleaver's ideal, and the broader political model of patriarchal social order, what happens to the father of daughters? Without a male heir to whom the mantle of patriarchal authority can be passed, Lear is already on what we might recognize as a 'faultline' in Cultural Materialist terms. The father–daughter power relationship may be just such an 'awkward, unresolved' issue that Alan Sinfield identifies as exposing the paradoxes and problems of the ideology in which the text was created (1992: 47). Applying feminist discourse and transposing the term 'patriarchy' onto *King Lear* (rather than viewing the play as a family or individual crisis), we can read the father–daughter power distribution problem as one rooted in the fact there is no clear solution to the father-without-sons in the simplified patriarchal model offered by such influential commentators as Dod and Cleaver. When the father–daughter relationship (as opposed to the father–son in Gloucester's case) is inverted, the carnivalesque upheaval is more acute and chaotic. The power structure is multi-layered when the male–female hierarchy overlays and aggravates the parent–child one; the reversal creates a double disruption.

Moreover, the sonless King is, in the first place, in a precarious position in terms of his place in the patriarchal lineage. The Fool loses no opportunity throughout the text to remind Lear of both situations, by remarking upon the king being ruled by his own female offspring, who make him 'an obedient father' (1.4.232). The fool establishes the redoubled inversion by noting that, in reversing the power structure of father over child, Lear's daughters do not become fathers but mothers, when 'thou mad'st thy daughters thy mothers; … thou gav'st them the rod, and putt'st down thine own breeches' (1.4.168–70). The fool's crass *double entendre* layers the toilet humour of 'putt[ing] down … breeches' over Lear effectively putting aside his masculinity ('rod', 'breeches') to be ruled by women *and* his paternal/patriarchal authority to be ruled by his own daughters as 'mothers'. This fear of being 'mother[ed]', or female authority and power more generally, fuels repulsion of motherhood in this motherless text. Lear invokes images of motherhood with horror, particularly in his curse on Goneril following her rebellion against his autocratic rule:

Hear, Nature, hear, dear goddess, hear:
Suspend thy purpose if thou didst intend
To make this creature fruitful.
Into her womb convey sterility,

Paternity and Patriarchy

Dry up in her the organs of increase,
And from her derogate body never spring
A babe to honour her. If she must teem,
Create her child of spleen, that it may live
And be a thwart disnatured torment to her.

(1.4.273–81)

Gendered female according to convention, Nature is called upon to turn upon her fellow female and render Goneril barren, stripping her of the maternal purpose that is central to her place in the patriarchal model both of home and state. Apostrophizing Nature (echoing Edmund, 1.2.1), Lear addresses a female deity and calls upon her to render Goneril functionally *un*female in the eyes of the patriarchal society. Childless, Goneril not only loses her socially endorsed female purpose but, recalling Lear's designation of land and property in 1.1, strips both her and Albany of a crucial element of the legacy earlier bestowed: the honour of their rule being not only a life interest as Lear's daughter but in perpetuity for their offspring and descendants (1.1.65–6). Lear thus attacks both Goneril's domestic *and* her potential public power as a woman but, in so doing, thwarts his own lineage.

Lear's savage attack on Goneril's reproductive potential is brutally gendered, and in production can serve to evoke sympathy for Goneril on stage. While in its own time the play would have been performed by an all-male company, in modern production we may here see a man attack a female body, either figuratively or literally. In Eyre's film production, Lear (Anthony

Figure 6.1 Anthony Hopkins as Lear and Emma Thompson as Goneril, *King Lear* (Richard Eyre, 2018).

Hopkins) takes violent aim at Goneril's (Emma Thompson) abdomen at this point, his brutal words and physical assault causing her to shrink and protect her stomach, appearing to enter into a state of traumatic shock (Figure 6.1). The casting of a woman of late middle age delivers a different meaning here, in which Lear's curse perhaps may seem all the more cruel (see 'Production in Focus' section). Lear's verbal attack on his daughter's womb attacks her physical gender identity both within the patriarchal notion of female purpose and in physiological terms of her femaleness. While the speech's proverbial conclusion figures most prominently in the popular imagination, Lear's preferred curse is to render Goneril childless, verbally amputating the organ perceived as defining femininity and denying his daughter's potential maternal authority and existence.

Lear also feminizes his own mental breakdown when he later invokes the womb as organ not only of reproduction but of feminine physiological weakness:

> O, how this mother swells up toward my heart!
> *Hysterica passio*, down, thou climbing sorrow,
> Thy element's below. Where is this daughter?
>
> (2.2.246–8)

The 'mother' here is the womb, or the trouble it causes to the mind and body of its possessor. This was a frequently used term in early modern medical and general parlance, in which, often with a definite article attached, '*the* mother' is used to mean the womb itself or the condition of 'hysteria', differentiated from 'mother' meaning maternal parent. Madness of certain kinds was frequently gendered female; in particular, 'hysteria' was contrasted with the masculine intellectuality of melancholy (see Chapter 5). Here, Lear attempts to order the figurative womb back into position, apostrophizing 'down, thou climbing sorrow!', asserting his masculine power over the feminine madness he feels creeping upwards from the femaleness of the belly to the heart, threatening the masculine mind. This idea of a body in which organs move reflects the dynamic model of anatomy found in some early modern medical discourses and is foreshadowed in Cordelia's aside 'I cannot heave my heart into my mouth' (1.1.91). Cordelia's organized, moral fortitude is reflected in the soundness of her bodily cohesion. Lear's outburst suggests a rebellious body, in which the emotional attacks the rational and this dichotomy is gendered. Lear's image of 'the mother' creeping upwards to overtake male courage or rationality is not an image isolated to *Lear* but a common conceit, as, for example, in Exeter's apology to Henry V for the fact that 'all my mother came into mine eyes / And gave me up to tears' (4.6.31; see Chapter 2). Yet in *Henry V*, as in *Richard II*, sadness rather than madness is feminized. In *Lear*, the King genders both states and, recognizing his own sorrow and instability, blames an unruly womb 'climbing' out of its place 'below' and attacking upwards. His following interrogative, 'where is this daughter?' juxtaposed with his outburst on 'the mother' accentuates the link between his state and his female offspring, highlighting a manifest terror of maternity.

Throughout *King Lear* there are references to the symbiotic relationship between parent and child, a sense of the child as the flesh of the parent. In 1.1, Cordelia posits herself pragmatically in relation to her father, stating 'You have begot me, bred me, loved me: I / Return those duties back as are right fit' (95–6), establishing a physical as well as an emotional heredity to be honoured. This contrasts with Goneril's love declaration, in which her father is 'Dearer than eye-sight, space, and liberty' (56), an ominous foreshadowing of those precious articles that will be lost to the play's fathers, Gloucester and Lear, both literally (in Gloucester's blinding) or figuratively, such as in Lear's loss of his kingdom's 'space'. Lear's later rage at Goneril's refusal to accommodate his entourage of knights regurgitates Cordelia's identification of the parental bond, in horrific terms:

> I prithee, daughter, do not make me mad:
> I will not trouble thee, my child. Farewell:
> We'll no more meet, no more see one another.
> But yet thou art my flesh, my blood, my daughter,
> Or rather a disease that's in my flesh,
> Which I must needs call mine. Thou art a boil,
> A plague-sore, or embossed carbuncle,
> In my corrupted blood.
>
> (2.2.407–14)

From 'my flesh, my blood, my daughter', Lear moves quickly to a visceral analogy of his child as a 'disease that's in my flesh'; her rebellion is physically dangerous to his parental, as well as kingly, person. This scene contains practically the only acknowledgement of the women's mother, when he threatens that he 'would divorce me from thy mother's tomb, / Sepulchring an adultress' if Regan should not meet him with 'glad[ness]' (2.2.319–21). Lear thus presents the power of fatherhood as so unequivocal that to deny its love and authority is to render oneself illegitimate.

Lear's fury at his 'thankless' children merges with the political and natural chaos surrounding him. *Lear*'s storm is frequently identified as exemplifying the pathetic fallacy, in which the weather reflects the inner world of the character. However, Lear directly addresses the storm in moments of apostrophe. Here he compares it with what he sees as his daughters' unnatural rejection of his authority:

> Rumble thy bellyful! Spit fire! spout rain!
> Nor rain, wind, thunder, fire are my daughters;
> I tax not you, you elements, with unkindness.
> I never gave you kingdom, call'd you children;
> You owe me no subscription.
>
> (3.2.14–18)

What we see here is, in eco-theoretical terms, the collapse of Lear's anthropocentric notion of power and hierarchy: nature is now pre-eminent. Lear relinquishes claim over the elements, since they 'owe' him nothing. Lear begins by ordering the elements, assuming his characteristic imperative in apostrophe, 'spit, fire! Spout, rain!', yet he moves quickly to explaining this is his way of giving the elements licence, freeing them from any claim of his authority. The freedom of the wind and rain to hurl their injurious actions upon the king is contrasted with the debt ('subscription') he considers his daughters to owe him. The women's particular disobedience is rooted in their failure, as he sees it, to pay their debt to him, in return for being 'call[ed] daughters' and their pre-emptive inheritance of the kingdom. Lear thus shifts blame onto his daughters for his own decision to relinquish political power.

For Lear, then, fatherhood is understood in commercial terms; a debt is owed, for the parenthood he has bestowed, and his daughters' independence is shirking the due payment. This is a pervasive conceit in Shakespeare's drama, and in early modern discourse of the fatherhood of daughters. In *Much Ado About Nothing*, for instance, Claudio refers to Hero as a 'jewel' in the play's opening scene (1.1.171) but in the abortive wedding scene sarcastically asks her father 'And what have I to give you back whose worth / May counterpoise this rich and precious gift?' (4.1.26), establishing the expectation of marriage of a daughter as a commercial exchange. In

Hamlet, too, Polonius uses an extended pecuniary metaphor to assert his greater authority over Ophelia: 'Tender yourself more dearly / Or – not to crack the wind of the poor phrase, / Running it thus – you'll tender me a fool'(1.3.105–9). The idea that Ophelia has been defrauded by Hamlet's attentions segues into asserting Polonius's own interest in her honour and potential for marriage. He will be the 'fool' who is tricked out of his valuable daughter, whose worth is measured in her chastity. This is evident, too, in *Lear*'s opening scene in which Lear focuses on 'our daughters' several dowers' (43) and the renegotiation with Burgundy, who has expected a certain 'portion' to be attached to Cordelia's marriage:

> BURGUNDY Most royal majesty,
> I crave no more than what your highness offer'd –
> Nor will you tender less?
> LEAR   Right noble Burgundy,
> When she was dear to us, we did hold her so,
> But now her price is fallen.
>
>   (1.1.194–8)

Cordelia is for sale here, the men negotiate between themselves over her worth (or otherwise). France's opposing opinion, that 'she is herself a dowry' (243) attaches more worth to Cordelia's virtues than the money with which she has previously been offered. Cordelia herself seeks to clear her good name and, in begging her father to admit she has committed 'no vicious blot, murder or foulness, / No unchaste action or dishonour'd step' (1.1.229–30), she foreshadows the many crimes her sisters are soon to commit. Ironically, Cordelia's adherence to the expectations of her gender – to 'obey' her father, to be chaste and *not* to speak – have left her cast out. However, in France's offer of marriage, she gains her own place in another monarchy, disowned as a princess only to become a queen. This finally makes a mockery of Burgundy's haggling; the woman voices her own defence and is recognized as possessing her own value.

The Tempest also presents us with an obedient, motherless daughter. Paralleling Lear mapping his kingdom onto his daughters, Miranda provides a site for her Father's kingly authority over the island, since he has enslaved the only other beings in his miniature dominion. While Cordelia is clear on her history and lineage (1.1), Prospero has, the play informs us, parented Miranda without revealing her history: 'You have often', accuses Miranda, 'Begun to tell me what I am, but stopp'd / And left me to a bootless inquisition, / Concluding "Stay, not yet"' (1.2.33-6). Her history, here, elides with her very identity via the layered meaning in Prospero's paternal power to 'tell me what I am'. This presents a stark contrast to masculine individualist proclamations of identity, such Richard III's 'I am I' (5.3.183) or Lear's sarcastic 'Who is it that can tell me who I am?' (1.4.221), when patrilineal and gender hierarchies are disrupted by daughter (Goneril) attempting to influence father. In *The Tempest*, too, we see a lucid example of a daughter's position as bound to listen to her father. In *Lear*, the daughters repeatedly refuse to listen to and obey their father, frustrating his dictatorial patriarchal approach to rule and sending him into a rage that turns to madness; he has no means by which to understand a world in which he is no longer in possession of autocratic paternity. Prospero, too, displays an almost comic paranoia that his daughter is paying attention to him:

> PROSPERO
>   Dost thou attend me?
> MIRANDA   Sir, most heedfully.
> PROSPERO
>   Being once perfected how to grant suits,
>   How to deny them, …
>   And sucked my verdure out on't. Thou attend'st not!
> MIRANDA
>   O, good sir, I do.
> PROSPERO   I pray thee, mark me.
>   …
>   With all prerogative: hence his ambition growing –
>   Dost thou hear?
> MIRANDA   Your tale, sir, would cure deafness.
>
>   (1.2.78–106)

Throughout this exchange, Prospero interrupts his tale to ensure his daughter is listening. In performative terms, this can be read as a stage direction telling us that Miranda must seem in some sense *not* to be listening to her father. However, this is not unequivocal. Prospero's obsession with control over the island, its inhabitants and his daughter could manifest in this frantic series of demands that he be heard and 'attend[ed]' by his daughter, as he constructs for her the history he has for so long withheld.

Miranda's idea of 'what I am' relates directly to legitimacy and lineage. Miranda's innocent 'Sir, are you not my father?' (1.2.55), spoken in disbelief or confusion that he is suddenly revealing his identity as Duke of Milan, is met with a wry response from Prospero that assumes Miranda understands the basic notion of legitimacy despite her having no memory of general society: 'Thy mother was a piece of virtue, and / She said thou wast my daughter' (1.2.56-7). Moreover, Miranda does indeed seem to understand the concept of legitimate birth, when she responds to Prospero's tale of his villainous brother, with 'I should sin / To think but nobly of my grandmother: / Good wombs have borne bad sons' (1.2.118-20). Unlike the female gendering of the fault of illegitimacy throughout *Lear*, Miranda here sees her female ancestor as blameless for her son's ill deeds, gendering villainy male and innocence female in her heritage. Miranda's only independent memory, too, is that of feminine presence in her infanthood. In these ways, Miranda constructs a matrilineality that threatens Prospero's carefully constructed, exclusive paternal claim:

PROSPERO
...Of any thing the image, tell me, that
Hath kept with thy remembrance.
MIRANDA   'Tis far off
And rather like a dream than an assurance
That my remembrance warrants. Had I not
Four or five women once, that tended me?
PROSPERO
Thou hadst, and more, Miranda. But how is it
That this lives in thy mind? What seest thou else
In the dark backward and abysm of time?
(1.2.43-9)

Prospero has begged of Miranda, here, to open up her memory to him but she remembers only the women of her past. The journey with her father that he so fervently recalls has left no impression upon her, yet she feels the loss of the female company by which she was once surrounded. Prospero's 'How is it this lives in thy mind?' declares his disbelief that it is a feminine past and heritage Miranda's memory has preserved.

In *Lear*, the three daughters' motherlessness is rarely mentioned, other than Lear's rhetorical threat to divorce their mother posthumously, and that the daughters are definitively motherless, womanless, in the play world. In both plays, however, maternal absence lays bare the specific power wielded by paternity, whilst exposing patriarchal anxiety in which loss of autocracy over daughters elides loss of control over land. In both plays, too, feminine Nature rages with storms. Prospero's enslavement of Ariel allows him to control the elements, retaining an anthropocentric patriarchy on the island but *Lear* shows us a Nature goddess that can be ruled by neither father nor king.

Production in Focus: Richard Eyre's Film, *King Lear*, 2018

Richard Eyre's 2018 film adaptation of *King Lear* sets the play in a militarized version of modern London and Kent, using locations that range from royal meetings in the stone belly of an ancient building to a dingy concrete shopping mall, where the mad Lear pushes a trolley past dubious pedestrians. Deploying some of the most highly respected British actors, the film presents *Lear* as a British crisis of identity, made in the tumultuous political atmosphere immediately following the Brexit referendum of 2016. Here, we focus particularly on how casting choices impact on the politics of a production.

Played by Florence Pugh, only 22 years old at the film's release, the Cordelia of Eyre's production is generationally distinct from her sisters, played by Emily Watson (51) and Emma Thompson (59). Hopkins' Lear is an octogenarian, whose age had been accentuated for the film, skin age-spotted and gait stooping. These casting decisions risk demonizing the older woman, where fresh-faced Pugh presents as victim to these two childless women of late middle age. This is not Eyre's original gambit by any means. It is common to cast Goneril and Regan as far older than their younger sister, such as in Trevor Nunn's 2007 RSC production starring Ian McKellen, who was in his late sixties, compared to Romola Garai as Cordelia in her mid-twenties, while her sisters were played by Frances Barber (50) and Monica Dolan (38). In Shakespeare's own time, there is no reason whatever to believe this designation of Goneril and Regan as materially – generationally – older would or could have been effected. All three played by boys, the sisters could be viewed as roughly the same age. Both married sisters are, after all, as yet childless and the text does not age them. Therefore Eyre's production, like so many others, chooses to present two brutal older women in direct contrast to the innocence of youth, which remains troublingly critically unchallenged.

This production, too, confronts the question of legitimacy as a core theme. By cutting the play extensively, Eyre foregrounds Edmund's story and centralizes the relationship between the two brothers and their father.

Paternity and Patriarchy

In this context, the film's casting of an actor of colour, John Macmillan, as Edmund surely cannot be read as race-blind casting. In the opening scene, two powerful white men discuss Edmund, a uniformed soldier, in the third person, which posits his illegitimacy as racialized and in which Gloucester's 'good sport' in his youth has been with a woman of colour. Edmund is in this way othered beyond his illegitimacy but as a racial other in the white world of the production. The film casts actors of colour, too, as Burgundy (Simon Manyonda) and France (Chuck Iwuji), who speak with Francophone accents and are clearly demarcated as foreign to the white British milieu. The self-destructive arrogance of Lear's patriarchal privilege is thus compounded with white male privilege, which complicates the troubling racialization of Edmund's illegitimacy in this production. This casting choice creates a hidden woman of colour in the play's past and compounds the significance of Edmund's subjection in a court of white men.

Produced precisely as the #MeToo movement, challenging the endemic nature of sexual assault and harassment, went viral in late 2017 and released as the movement gained further global notice in 2018, Eyre's film presents Lear's treatment of one of his daughters, Goneril (Thompson), as abusive. As we have seen earlier in this chapter, when hurling his curse of infertility upon his daughter, Lear physically attacks her abdomen (Figure 6.1). However, at another time during this sequence, he kisses her sexually on the mouth – as well as at another point kissing her husband – establishing a sexually abusive, incestuous implication to his rage, recalling Jane Smiley's rewriting of *Lear* into the American Midwest in *A Thousand Acres* (1991), in which two women clash with their younger sister when she refuses to acknowledge their father's early sexual abuse. By framing patriarchal abuse as sexual abuse, both texts present a physical embodiment of the gendered oppression suffered by the daughters of Lear. The film, too, cuts some of Goneril's lines including, crucially, her plot to have her husband killed, and Hopkins and Thompson's portrayals of Lear and Goneril in 1.4 establish some justification for the daughter's later behaviour. Her complicity in Regan's heinous assault on Gloucester is downplayed, too, when her line 'pluck out his eyes' (3.7.5) is pronounced in a throwaway, joking tone, not to be taken literally. Goneril is thus established in part as a victim of her father's abuse, rather than as a sadist, distancing her from traditional portrayals as an epitome of the woman corrupted by power: unstable or evil. In the case of Goneril, we find the casting of a British national treasure and the truncating of the text allows this much more sympathetic (if still sinister) Goneril to emerge.

Conclusions

1. The line between domestic paternity and public patriarchal power is by definition blurred in any society that subscribes to a patriarchal model. In *Lear*, fatherhood and kingship are deconstructed and the mechanisms of power are laid bare, exposed as fragile and contestable.
2. The carnivalesque reversal of parent and child, played out in the parallels between Lear's and Gloucester's narratives, is dangerous to order both privately and publicly. In presenting sons and daughters leading their fathers, Shakespeare presents the upending and inversion of fundamental power structures that purport to keep order. Two plot reversals – the location of political power, from father to Lear's two eldest daughters, and of wisdom between father and daughter in the case of Cordelia – redoubles and intensifies the carnivalesque inversions, gendering the deconstruction of sociopolitical assumptions.
3. Lear attacks his daughters' reputations and female bodily identities. These attacks expose the faultlines on which women dwell, such as when female silence is socially dictated, yet in speaking to declare the aptness of her silence, Cordelia is cast out by both family and state.
4. The catastrophic collapse of order in *King Lear*'s world is created by fathers and sons and blamed upon mothers and daughters. By positioning the audience to be party to the true architects of destruction from the start, Shakespeare exposes the fragility of paternal and patriarchal order.

Further Work

Hamlet

Consider the father–child relationships. Hamlet obeys his father even in his ghostly form, and consistently idolizes his memory; Ophelia and Polonius are a study in a father–daughter relationship. Where *King Lear* is filled with references to legitimacy and heredity, in *Hamlet* questions of legitimacy are absent. Are the play's parent–child relationships rooted in domestic or public discourses?

Romeo and Juliet

Consider 3.5 in which Capulet's fury configures Juliet's filial disobedience in refusing to marry Paris as effectively unchaste, in which her assertion of autonomy is tantamount to sexual misconduct. This is a scene worth exploring in production – some portray Capulet as physically abusive towards his daughter. Shakespeare is presenting paternal tyranny here, but what place does this have in the play as a whole and its presentation of patriarchal order?

Titus Andronicus

The mutilated body of Titus's daughter, Lavinia, becomes a living symbol of male sexual brutality. How far does Shakespeare present Titus's response as indicating a sense of property damage? What is Lavinia's function as 'daughter' and how does it change through the play? Is she an emblem of female abjection or resilience?

Further Reading

Diane Elizabeth Dreyer, *Defiance and Domination: Fathers and Daughters in Shakespeare* (University Press of Kentucky, 1986). **An approach based on early modern contexts and modern critical approaches of the gendered relationship between fathers and daughters, including gender transgressions and character transformations. This is a useful book to explore in combination with feminist critical approaches to the plays in the 1980s and today.**

Gabriel Egan, *Green Shakespeare: From Ecopolitics to Ecocriticsm* (Routledge, 2006). **A path-leading book applying new ecocritical theories to how we interpret Shakespeare. This is useful for pursuing the ideas raised here on anthropocentrism.**

Oliver Ford Davies, *Shakespeare's Fathers and Daughters* (Bloomsbury, The Arden Shakespeare, 2017). **Takes a chronological approach to Shakespeare's fathers and daughters, offering both reflective insight from the point of view of the performer and critical ideas, including ideas on Shakespeare's own daughters – an approach worth interrogating.**

CHAPTER 7
SEXUAL EXCESS: SPACE, SEX AND GENDER

Key Texts: *The Comedy of Errors, Measure for Measure, Antony and Cleopatra, Pericles*

Gayle Rubin argues that 'the "exchange of women"... places the oppression of women within social systems, rather than in biology [and] suggests that we look for the ultimate locus of women's oppression within the traffic in women rather than the traffic in merchandise' (Rubin, 1975: 37). Female sexuality and female bodies are valued according to local ideological and social prescriptions and must be exchanged for something (money, sex, place, status). As objects in that exchange system, women become part of an actual and a metaphorical marketplace. Space, economics and gender intersect. Early modern London saw the growth of nascent capitalism and global colonization: how did these emergent economic and spatial practices impact notions of sexuality and gender and how are these explored in Shakespeare's plays? This chapter will consider how the drama uses space as setting and metaphor to investigate and nuance notions of gender and sexuality.

> ### Resource 7.a: Stephen Gosson, *The Schoole of Abuse* (1579)
>
> Compare *London* to *Rome*, & *England* to *Italy* you shall finde the Theaters of the one, the abuses of the other, to be rife among us ... In our assemblies at playes in *London*, you shall see suche heaving, and shoving, suche itching and shouldring, too sitte by women; Suche care for their garments, that they bee not trode on: Such eyes to their lappes, that no chippes light in them: Such pillowes to ther backes, that they take no hurte: Such masking in their eares, I knowe not what: Such giving them Pippins to passe the time ...: Such ticking, such toying, such smiling, such winking, and such manning them home, when the sportes are ended, ...

> For they that lack Customers al the weeke, either because their haunte is unknowen, or the Constables and Officers of their Parishe, watch them so narrowly, that they dare not queatche; To celebrate the Sabboth, flock to Theaters, and there keepe a generall Market of Bawdrie: Not that any filthynesse in deede, is committed within the compasse of that grounde, as was doone in *Rome*, but that every wanton and his Paramour, every man and his Mistresse, every John and his Joan, every knaue and his queane, are there first acquainted & cheapen the Merchandise in that place, which they pay for elsewhere as they can agree. (pp. 16–18)

During Shakespeare's lifetime, London grew exponentially from about 50,000 people to well over 200,000 – an astonishing 400 per cent rise driven predominantly by internal migration since death registrations always exceeded births in London (Finlay, 1981). The social, economic and political pressures attendant upon such growth can be experienced via the drama and social texts of the day; notions and practices of gender and sexuality were often flash-points for such pressures. Stephen Gosson inveighed against theatres as a place for sexualized and gendered (female) freedoms (Resource 7.a), reiterating issues about gender and space: mass 'assemblies' of people involve too much physical contact between men and women; prostitutes will use such occasions to gain customers; theatres as 'a general market of bawdry' offer explicit knowledge and experience of sex. The novel phenomenon of an urban theatre that men and women attend in daytime was viewed as politically and socially threatening, signalled through language that blamed female sexuality for this perceived urban chaos. Theatres are spaces where dangerous social and economic activities and meetings can happen, where disease spreads, where 'masterless' men engage in non-policed (by Church, State or City) activities, and where 'unchaste matters and lascivious devices' of both audience and fiction are matters for political and legal concern. In 1597 the Lord Mayor demanded that plays be banned within the City (see Resource 7.b).

Resource 7.b: *Letter from the Lord Mayor of London and the Aldermen to the Privy Council* (1598)

The inconveniences that grow by stage-plays about the City of London

1. They are a special cause of corrupting their youth, containing nothing but unchaste matters, lascivious devices, shifts of cozenage, and other lewd and ungodly practices, being so as that they impress the very quality and corruption of manners which they represent, contrary to the rules and art prescribed for the making of comedies even among the heathen, who used them seldom, and at certain set times, and not all the year long, as our manner is. Whereby such as frequent them, being of the base and refuse sort of people, or such young gentlemen as have small regard of credit or conscience, draw the same into imitation and not the avoiding the like vices which they represent.

2. They are the ordinary place for vagrant persons, masterless men, thieves, horse-stealers, whoremongers, cozeners, coney-catchers, contrivers of treason, and other idle and dangerous persons to meet together and to make their matches to the great displeasure of Almighty God and the hurt and annoyance of her Majesty's people…

3. They maintain idleness in such persons as have no vocation, and draw apprentices and other servants from their ordinary works and all sorts of people from the resort unto sermons and other Christian exercises to the great hindrance of trades and profanation of religion…

4. In the time of sickness it is found by experience that many, having sores and not yet heart-sick, take occasion hereby to walk abroad and to recreate themselves by hearing a play. Whereby others are infected, and themselves also many things miscarry.

(Transcribed in Blakemore Evans (ed.), *Elizabeth-Jacobean Drama*, pp. 5–6)

The early modern imaginary, amongst theatre-goers and their detractors, conceived of theatres, theatricality and the public spaces around them as places for sexualized and gender-exceeding behaviours. Such an imaginary coincided and conflicted with newly reiterated protestant codes on female conduct, which also linked space and appropriate gendered behaviour. Robert Cleaver's views on appropriate feminine conduct (see also Chapters 1 and 6) connoted notions of space: interpreting Proverbs 10–12, he reiterates the Biblical notion that a loud woman not 'in her house' and 'in the streets' is a whore (Resource 7.c).

Resource 7.c: Robert Cleaver, *A briefe explanation of the whole booke of the Prouerbs of Salomon* (1615)

Verse 10. *And behold, there met him a woman, with the attire of an harlot, and subtill in heart.*
Verse 11. *She is loud and stubborne, and her feete abide not in her house.*
Verse 12. *Now she is without, now in the streetes, and she lieth in waite at euery corner.*
...the wise man noteth both what a one she is, in the whole course of her behaviour... And one thing whereof hee taketh notice, and whereby hee describeth her, is her apparell, wherein she was tricked, and trimmed, unbeseeming the modestie of a sober Matrone, or the honestie of a chast woman. The second is, her inward deceit, and guilefulnes, in that she was of *a subtill heart*. The third is, her unwomanly disposition, and properties· she is a babler, and full of tattle, she is *stubborne*, perverse, and rebellious to God, and her husband, she is a gadder abroad, and everywhere given to allure, and corrupt all those whom she can intice into her companie.

(pp. 115–16)

Jonson, Middleton and Marston all located comedies on the streets and homes of Londoners. Such plays (for example, Marston's *The Dutch Courtesan* or Jonson's *The Alchemist*) figure successful masculinity as an urban trickster-like ability to con marks out of money, and the public female body as a dangerous threat to political and social stability. Chaste female bodies are absent from the streets: space and place become proxy markers of moral status. Shakespeare's plays do not use early modern London settings but they do debate space, gender and sexuality using historical, European or other settings to trouble and reinforce gender and sexual stereotypes.

The Comedy of Errors (1594) circles around the homes and streets of the Greek city of Ephesus. Most scenes occur in public fora: a street, a public square or space or *outside* a domestic house or shop. Political, personal and economic activities are transacted between men in public spaces, while the five female characters (Luciana, Adriana, Luce, Emilia and the 'Courtesan') mainly converse indoors or at their front door. A double set of twins (Antipholus and Dromio of Syracuse, twins to Antipholus and Dromio of Ephesus) generates a plot where norms and conventions of identity, recognition, and location are challenged by the doubled potentials of farce and mis-cognition. This challenge to urban identity is delivered through

Sexual Excess: Space, Sex and Gender

debates about and by women and by farce and action centred on setting. Adriana, Antipholus of Ephesus's wife, and her unmarried sister debate appropriate gendered behaviour:

> LUCIANA
> ... A man is master of his liberty;
> Time is their master, and when they see time,
> They'll go or come; if so, be patient, sister.
> ADRIANA
> Why should their liberty than ours be more?
> LUCIANA
> Because their business still lies out o'door.
> ADRIANA
> Look, when I serve him so, he takes it ill.
> LUCIANA
> O, know he is the bridle of your will.
> ADRIANA
> There's none but asses will be bridled so.
> LUCIANA
> Why, headstrong liberty is lash'd with woe.
> There's nothing situate under heaven's eye
> But hath his bound in earth, in sea, in sky.
> The beasts, the fishes, and the winged fowls
> Are their males' subjects, and at their controls;
> Man, more divine, the master of all these,
> Lord of the wide world and wild wat'ry seas,
> Indued with intellectual sense and souls,
> Of more pre-eminence than fish and fowls,
> Are masters to their females, and their lords:
> Then let your will attend on their accords.
> ADRIANA
> This servitude makes you to keep unwed.
> LUCIANA
> Not this, but troubles of the marriage bed.
> ADRIANA
> But were you wedded you would bear some sway.
> LUCIANA
> Ere I learn love, I'll practise to obey.
>
> (2.1.5–31)

Male liberty is defined by business beyond the home ('out o'door' (9)) while female conduct is placed inside the house, within a patriarchal framework of behaviour ('obey'; 'male's subjects' (16–24)), normalized as a natural part of a hierarchical model of human, natural and divine ecology (see Chapters 1 and 6). Adriana's resistance to this ideology as a knowing married woman suggests her lived reality is more valid than her sister's ideological conventionalism.

The central farcical dramatization of mistaken identities occurs outside the home of Adriana and Antipholus of Ephesus, explicitly staged as a conflict between the two unknowing Dromios through a door, with one group of characters off-stage and unseen. Adriana's refusal to allow her husband into her home is facilitated by the two Dromios' presence on either side of the locked door, so marital resistance is staged within the 'safe' plot envelope of mistaken identity, in which the indoors Dromio can claim that Antipholus is 'really' home. Shakespeare plays out fantasies of female power over a husband and male anxieties about the spaces his wife inhabits. Antipholus's control – over his business dealings, his servants, and wife – is tossed aside in his wife's refusal to let him enter his home.

EPH. ANTIPHOLUS
...But soft, my door is lock'd; go bid them let us in.
EPH. DROMIO
Maud, Bridget, Marian, Cicely, Gillian, Ginn!
SYR. DROMIO
(*within*) Mome, malthorse, capon, coxcomb, idiot, patch,
Either get thee from the door or sit down at the hatch:
Dost thou conjure for wenches, that thou call'st for such store
When one is too many? Go, get thee from the door.
EPH. DROMIO
What patch is made our porter? my master stays in the street.
SYR. DROMIO
Let him walk from whence he came, lest he catch cold on's feet.
EPH. ANTIPHOLUS
Who talks within there? ho, open the door.
SYR. DROMIO
Right, sir, I'll tell you when, and you'll tell me wherefore.
EPH. ANTIPHOLUS
Wherefore? for my dinner; I have not din'd to-day.
SYR. DROMIO
Nor to-day here you must not; come again when you may.

Sexual Excess: Space, Sex and Gender

EPH. ANTIPHOLUS
What art thou that keep'st me out from the house I owe?
SYR. DROMIO
The porter for this time, sir, and my name is Dromio.
EPH. DROMIO
O villain, thou hast stol'n both mine office and my name.
(3.1.30–44)

The stichomythic exchange of rhymed one-liners simultaneously emphasizes sameness *and* difference, in the two identical Dromios, physically and linguistically patterning the motif of inside/outside as space and concept (Dromio of Syracuse inside and Dromio of Ephesus outside). This reversal of belonging destabilizes notions of who belongs where. Dromio of Ephesus's calls to female maids to let them in ('Maud, Bridget, Marian, Cicely, Gillian, Ginn!' (31)) is opposed to Syracusan Dromio's masculinized slurs (32): domestic space is coded as feminine, the street as masculine. The farce of doubled identities across the closed door establishes the liminal line between outer and inner spaces as, momentarily, absolute. Adriana's immediate entrance to the street after this extract signals women's physical and verbal power over the liminal space of the home's entrance. Equally, at the finale the abbess's memory (of lost twins) enables the resolution of everyone's rightful relationships. Her arrival from the private retreat of the nunnery into the public space of the political square models female knowledge and action as necessarily crossing such binaries. This blurring of spatial boundaries through language, action and plot dissolves Luciana's absolute notions of binary gendered spaces and behaviours.

Dromio of Syracuse's description of the woman who claims him as her lover (fat, greasy, black-haired) conversely speaks a choral alternative to that radical testing. When he linguistically anatomizes her body as land in stereotypes associated with different nationalities his reverse blazon can be heard as either absolute misogyny or farce (see Introduction and Chapter 1). When he claims 'she is spherical, like a globe; I could find out countries in her', the variety of nationalist stereotypes is predictable (Ireland is in her buttocks, the chalky cliffs of England in her chin, the heat of Spain in her breath, and so on (3.2.115–38)). His *contreblason*, his inverted eulogic misogyny contrasts the play's other testings of stereotypes of body, place and gender: slapstick arguably negates such serious engagements. McIntyre's 2014 production (Shakespeare's Globe) interpreted this as a clowning interval on the main action. Dromio's '[I] ran from her as a witch' (143) is a choral undercurrent that femininity as delusive witchcraft shadows experience. *The Comedy* of *Errors* plays out human fears of losing one's identity, of being lost in a familiar place and of woman being monstrous, albeit resolving such fears with a reassuringly happy ending. Antipholus's dalliance with the courtesan, Dromio's abjectification of Nell, the threat of a wife shutting out a husband, are all fears about excessive public female sexuality. The comic resolution allows such fears to be both fantastically explored, and finally resolved.

Earlier performative histories of the Shakespearean stage (Brook, 1968; Weimann, 1978) and Mullaney's *The Place of the Stage* (1988) foregrounded the liminal location of theatres built in the suburbs, linking theatricality with excess and its social and political control, but tended to omit accounts of sexuality and gender. Second-wave feminism's critique of the bourgeois notion of an ideology of 'separate spheres', included recognition of its pre-history in the early modern period, implicitly associating femininity with domesticity and the indoors, and masculinity with public spaces. Elite, theological and conduct-prescriptive literature advocating a spatially-delimited female life through sexualized and gendered policing of behaviour have informed readings of early modern plays (Jardine, 1983; Woodbridge, 1984).

Four overlapping critical and theoretical influences help conceptualize gender and sexuality in space on stage and in performance. The first, underpinned by de Certeau's *Practice of Everyday Life* (1984) and Lefebvre's *Production of Space* (1974) on gendered space as an ideological formation, have shown how actual space on stage is used by female characters within the fiction to critique and/or reinforce gendered notions of space (Howard, 2007; Newman, 1991; Schwartz, 2011). The second is the influence of feminist geography (Grosz, 1995; Massey, 1994), which shows how space and place are always gendered by ideology and practice and how feminist activism can use concepts of, and actual, spaces to achieve change. The third critical influence has been feminist post-colonial theories arguing that space and place are ideologically construed and constructive of hierarchical identities (Moss, 2007). Finally, material feminist history uses local history, court cases and localized maps to show where women worked and spoke (Calaresu and Van den Heuvel, 2018; Gowing, 1999) and has mapped out nuanced versions of how space was conceived and used in early modern London (de Sousa, 1999; Korda, 2002; Richardson, 2011). All four influences have informed performances over the past twenty years by re-figuring the space of the stage and the fictional places it represents as a vibrant and contemporary arena in which the geography of gender and sexuality is explored (for example, via cross-casting). Yachnin's (2017) argument that early modern theatre's creation of a physical and metaphorical public space (on stage and in the

Sexual Excess: Space, Sex and Gender

audience) enabled the first 'call-out' culture is compelling. Theatre's actual and metaphorical spaces are thus political, open-ended and democratic.

Scenic organization can be indicative of experiments with space on stage and narrative mimetic space. Looking at the location of scenes and people in a schematic way in *Twelfth Night* (see Table 7.1) makes this immediately tangible (shaded according to location).

Table 7.1 *Twelfth Night's* **Locations**

Act/scene	Location	Characters
1.1	Orsino's court	Orsino, male courtiers
1.2	Seashore	Viola, sea captain, sailors
1.3	Olivia's house	Sir Toby, Maria, Sir Andrew
1.4	Orsino's court	Viola (as Cesario), Orsino, Valentine
1.5	Olivia's house	Olivia, Feste, Maria, Malvolio, Sir Toby, Viola (as Cesario)
2.1	Street	Antonio and Sebastian
2.2	Street	Malvolio and Viola (as Cesario)
2.3	Olivia's house	Sir Toby, Sir Andrew, Feste, Maria, Malvolio
2.4	Orsino's court	Orsino, Viola (as Cesario), Valentine, Fool
2.5	Olivia's house	Sir Toby, Sir Andrew, Maria, Fabian, Malvolio
3.1	Street	Viola (as Cesario), and Feste
3.2	Olivia's house	Sir Toby, Sir Andrew, Fabian, Maria
3.3	Street	Sebastian and Antonio
3.4	Olivia's house	Olivia, Maria, Malvolio, Sir Toby, Fabian, Sir Andrew, Viola (as Cesario)
4.1	Street near Olivia's house	Feste, Sebastian, Sir Toby, Sir Andrew, Olivia
4.2	Olivia's house/ estate	Maria, Feste, Malvolio
4.3	Olivia's garden? Front of her house?	Sebastian, Olivia, Priest
5.1	Olivia's house	Feste, Fabian, Orsino, Olivia, Sebastian, Antonio, Officers, Viola (as Cesario), Sir Toby, Sir Andrew, Malvolio

The location column immediately shows how place and action are gendered: the first act see-saws between an all-male and a female-led household, while Olivia's house draws successively more of the action as the narrative proceeds, including the resolution. Feste, Viola (as Cesario), Sebastian and Antonio traverse space and streets (men or cross-dressed women); Feste and Viola (as Cesario) alone enter both the masculine and feminine house spaces; finally, Orsino remains in his domestic space until the final act, when he demands union with a cross-dressed man/woman. Setting thus offers up experiential challenges to a simple gendered divide between domestic and public spaces: space, setting and plot self-consciously echo the festive crossing of binaries, which Viola's cross-dressing symbolizes and celebrates (see Chapter 4). Many productions blur these binaries of space and location (such as Trevor Nunn's 1996 film and Simon Godwin's 2016 version, National Theatre), which can undermine Viola's radical control over space in the text.

Measure for Measure (first performed in 1604) uses street scenes to problematize how we see sexuality. The second scene is set on a street where conversation and action successively display people at work: Lucio and two gentlemen debate politics, war and sex and trade insults; Mistress Overdone, the owner of a bawdy house, notes Claudio has been arrested; her partner Pompey explains this as part of a political action against illegal sexuality, including a proclamation ordering bawdy houses be pulled down; Claudio and Juliet are paraded across the stage on the way to prison, while Claudio manages a conversation with Lucio (1.2.1–100). The public street is a space for masculine jostling for place and gossip; a female and male place of discoursing about and practising business; a space associated with state legislative control over sexual behaviour; and a space for the visible correction of perceived social ills (in the public parade of Claudio and Juliet's 'crime'). Mistress Overdone's 'Why, here's a change indeed in the commonwealth! / What shall become of me? (1.2.96–7) establishes public female labour as a comic butt for top-down political decisions simultaneously establishing Pompey's authority over selling female sexuality on the streets.

However, the 'change in the commonwealth' is actually an experiment in leadership: the Duke goes undercover to observe his people and his substitute Angelo. The streets of Vienna, epitomized by Lucio, Mistress Overdone, Pompey and Constable Elbow, are vibrantly imagined with colourful characterization, the language of sex and popular political views. Claudio's imprisonment because of 'too much liberty', which 'Our natures do pursue, / Like rats that ravin down their proper bane, / A thirsty evil; and when we drink, we die' (1.2.117–22), posits this bleak opposition between

Sexual Excess: Space, Sex and Gender

political authority and excess sexuality: the rat-like nature of humans can only be cured by curbing of 'liberty' (licentiousness). Yet 'liberty' has two additional resonances. The first is to the geographic areas of London outside the City's political authority (known as 'liberties') where bawdy houses and theatres thrived and the second to its political connotations. The Duke's subsequent incognito traversing of his streets to check on such liberty shows power as an invisible surveillance of the streets and public spaces of a state, and of private lives and spaces too, since the Duke performs as a friar taking confessions. Perhaps more than in any other Shakespeare play, public and private sexuality is figured as dangerous to political order and starkly associated with the public shaming of female bodies.

This simple model of the control of (female) sexual excess as political praxis is complicated by the plot and, in particular, by Angelo's actions. When Claudio's sister Isabella (a novitiate) pleads for her brother's life, Angelo demands sexual favours in return; Gregory Doran's 2019 production (RSC) openly associated this with its contemporary #MeToo movement in its programme and marketing and presented the harassment scene as, for Isabella (Lucy Phelps), deeply traumatic. The narrative arc disrupts the simple binaries of the play's opening premise (disruptive and dangerous sexuality = female) by suggesting that (male) sexuality protected by power, name and status is more dangerous. The play's finale offers to paper over these fissures. The Duke enters the city through the streets of Vienna, accepting petitions as he walks through the streets. The urban street becomes a metonymy of both the stage and throne of (patriarchal) power. Shakespeare actually stages this for us through repetition. There are three moments where the Duke deliberately stages power as generous beneficence: but in each case, the audience are shown that such generosity is fake. The first is his enacted disbelief of Isabella's accusation of Angelo's attempted rape in order (arguably) to force Angelo to perjure himself in public. The second is the delayed revelation that Claudio was not executed. The third is the Duke's insistence that Isabella kneel to plead with Mariana for Angelo's life, after finally accepting their accusations of his double guilt (the sexual propositioning of Isabella and abandonment of Mariana). The performative effect of these successive revelations to the public (on stage and in the audience) re-play the Duke as ultimate arbiter and judge with the street setting emblematically reinforcing the patriarchal authority as all-seeing, and explicitly about sexuality. Questioning Mariana on her status, the Duke laughingly judges: 'Why, you are nothing then: neither maid, widow, nor wife!' (5.2.178–9). Patriarchal nomenclature reiterates female status as essentially allied to a man (father/husband) and sexual status consequent upon that: otherwise 'you are nothing', troping female identity as both absent and a vagina (see also Chapters 2, 5 and 6).

The Duke's final speeches are a set of instructions, orders and judgements given publicly and successively to Claudio, Isabella, Angelo, Lucio, Mariana and Escalus. In three cases those instructions demand marriage: to Isabella ('Give me your hand and say you will be mine' (490)); to Angelo ('Look that you love your wife: her worth, worth yours' (495)); to Lucio ('If any woman wrong'd by this lewd fellow, / ... / Whom he begot with child – let her appear, / And he shall marry her. The nuptial finish'd, / Let him be whipp'd and hang'd' (507–11)). Lucio alone verbally resists his punitive closure ('Marrying a punk, my lord, is pressing to death, (520)) but the Duke's 'Slandering a prince deserves it' (521) suggests that absolute political authority over speech and sex as essential to good government. The Duke's final words ('we'll show / What's yet behind that's meet you all should know' (533–5)) posit leadership as essential withholding of truths. Yet the Duke's quickly successive demands are all strangely unresolved here. The Duke's demand for Isabella's 'hand' uncannily echoes Angelo's proposition in 2.1. Isabella does not respond directly (5.1.379–97), and many contemporary performances resist the impulse physically to show a conjoining of hands, using silence to represent resistance; in Doran's 2019 production, Isabella (Phelps) slumps in anguish as the lights go down. The 2012 performance (Yuri Butusov) at Shakespeare's Globe cast the same actor as both the Duke and Claudio, and ended with Isabella curled in a ball of physical resistance. Equally, the pardoning of Angelo's sexual harassment of Isabella by insisting on his marriage to Mariana is a jarring mis-match between offence and outcome that puzzles an audience. Finally, Lucio's critique of excessive force remains standing as the play ends. The resolution of sexual betrayal, un-regulated sex and broken sexual promises alongside a political restoration of a rightful ruler and three hetero-patriarchal marriages imposed from top-down posits a world in which political leadership extends to control over minds, bodies and sexualities. The Duke's insistence on 'care and secrecy' (5.1.527) and the withholding of information as ultimate political tools, echo James I's political ideology in *The True Law of Free Monarchies* (reissued on his coronation in 1603, Resource 7.d). Here paternal, monarchical and divine authority intersect and are coterminous: patriarchalism is an explicit political ideology that defines paternalist authority as familial, political and religious. The Duke's tripled display of performed authority plays out this masculinist ideology, where the public street represents the world of his people and his authority over them.

Sexual Excess: Space, Sex and Gender

Resource 7.d: James Stuart, *The True Law of Free Monarchies* (1603)

By the law of nature the King becomes a naturall father to all his lieges at his Coronation. And as the father of his fatherly dutie is bound to care for the nourishing, education and vertuous government of his children: even so is the king bound to care for all his subjects. As all the toyle and paine that the father can take for his children, will bee thought light and well bestowed by him; so that the effect thereof redounde to their profit and weale: so ought the Prince to do towards his people. As the kindly father ought to see all inconvenients and daungers that may arise towards his children, and though with the hazard of his owne person presse to prevent the same: so ought the King towardes his people. As the father's wrath and correction upon any of his children that offendeth ought to be by a fatherly chastisement seasoned with pittie, as long as there is any hope of amendment in them: so ought the King towards any of his Lieges that offends in that measure ...

And as ye see it manifest that the king is overlord of the whole land, so is he maister over every person that inhabiteth the same, having power over the life and death of every one of them ... For albeit it be true that I have at length prooved that the king is above the law, as both the author and giver of strength thereto, yet a good king will not onely delight to rule his subjects by the lawe, but even will conforme himself in his own actions thereunto, alwaies keeping that ground that the health of the commonwealth be his chiefe law.

(fo. A8^v–B1 C5$^{r\text{-}v}$)

This is the crux of Shakespeare's finale: the street is a fine and public place and, because of that, the Duke's ordering of events is itself put under scrutiny by the people. Female sexuality and agency, problematic to both the state and to individual men, are finally subordinated to his authority. But do we believe it? The public arena invoked by the street scenes and the binary of female agency/masculine power allows the audience to debate these issues as open-ended.

Antony and Cleopatra (*c*. 1608) uses setting and notions of space to problematize cultural and historical assumptions about gender, sexuality and power. The forty-two scenes (some as short as three or four lines) parade swiftly changing characters, time and space, creating a dramatic world of sensation and visual effect, rooting us in specific locations ranging from Rome to Alexandria, Sicily to Syria. The central political and military opposition between Rome and Egypt is also gendered as masculine and feminine. Cleopatra and Antony's defeat at the battle of Actium is often described as the origin of the Roman Empire, when the values of Roman militarism defeated the seductiveness (and supposed weakness) of Egyptian culture, particularly epitomized in Cleopatra's dangerous femininity (Loomba, 1998). The play's opening speech states this in stark portentous terms:

PHILO
    Nay, but this dotage of our general's
    O'erflows the measure. Those his goodly eyes,
    That o'er the files and musters of the war
    Have glowed like plated Mars, now bend, now turn
    The office and devotion of their view
    Upon a tawny front. His captain's heart,
    Which in the scuffles of great fights hath burst
    The buckles on his breast, reneges all temper
    And is become the bellows and the fan
    To cool a gipsy's lust.
                                              (1.1.1–10)

Mars, the Roman god of war, is opposed ('now bend, now turn', (4)) to the 'gypsy's lust' of the 'tawny' (10, 6) Cleopatra. The iconography of Mars (4) opposed to Venus was conventionally used to suggest that martial, public masculinity could be undone by the soft seductiveness of femininity: the Greek and Roman equivalent of the Christian story of the Fall. Mars and Venus are associated with Antony and Cleopatra respectively by other characters throughout the play, connoting place and power to gendered notions of agency and effectiveness. Rome is connotatively associated with authoritative white rule and masculinity, Egypt with luxury, tawny skin and femininity. Early modern oppositions between Rome (or Europe) and Egypt simplify notions of power as a naturalized defeat of the 'other' as characterized by colour, place and gender, as part of an emergent colonialist ideology (Loomba, 1998).

A schematic diagram of the play's structure and setting represents how space and setting are used ideologically (Table 7.2). Here, the dark shading represents scenes set in Egypt, or amongst Egyptian forces; no shading, in Rome or with the Roman army; and light grey shading, the scenes in which this is ambiguous (4.3) or both armies appear (3.10; 4.7). The play begins and ends in Egypt, Act 1 predominantly set in Egypt, with just one scene in Rome; whilst Act 2 is its mirror image, with all scenes but one set in Italy. Act 3 alternates between the Egyptian and Roman camps, with more set amongst the Egyptians after their defeat at Actium. Acts 4 and 5 are predominantly set amongst Egyptian protagonists, with the battles occuring off and around Alexandria. The final act is all set in Alexandria, with Caesar's Roman camp juxtaposed against Cleopatra's monument in Alexandria.

Table 7.2 *Antony and Cleopatra*'s Locations

Act/scene	Place
1.1	Alexandria
1.2	Alexandria
1.3	Alexandria
1.4	Rome
1.5	Alexandria
2.1	Sicily
2.2	Rome
2.3	Rome
2.4	Rome
2.5	Alexandria
2.6	Italy
2.7	Pompey's ship, Italy
3.1	Parthia
3.2	Rome
3.3	Alexandria
3.4	Athens
3.5	Athens, Egyptian army
3.6	Rome
3.7	Alexandria
3.8	Toryne (Greece)
3.9	Actium, Antony
3.10	Actium: both armies
3.11	Retreating from Actium
3.12	Actium, Roman army
3.13	Actium, Egyptians
4.1	Roman army

Table 7.2 *Antony and Cleopatra*'s Locations *(continued)*

Act/scene	Place
4.2	Alexandria
4.3	One or other of armies
4.4	Egypt
4.5	Egypt
4.6	Roman army, Egypt
4.7	Roman army/Egyptian army
4.8	Egyptian army
4.90	Roman army
4.10	Egyptian army
4.11	Roman army
4.12	Egyptian army
4.13	Alexandria
4.14	Alexandria
4.15	Monument, Alexandria
5.1	Roman army
5.2	Monument, Alexandria

Dramatic structure replicates the spatial progress of Rome's empire from the opening's free Alexandria to the finale of a conquered Africa. Rome's sovereignty by conquest of lands from Greece, across Syria to Egypt triumphantly represented by the stage's and play's diegetic swamping of Egypt's spaces by the invading Roman army. Yet, conversely, the diegetic setting, starkly displayed in Table 7.2, still suggests that Egyptian stories and setting dominate. What might this mean for our analysis of space and gender?

When Caesar explicitly hands over his sister in marriage to Antony as part of a political arrangement to ensure a political military allegiance against Pompey, even the opening stage direction (*'Enter Antony, Caesar; Octavia between them'*, 2.3.0) visually signals Octavia as a passive object of exchange. Roman masculinity is construed as, simultaneously, the conquering of both land and women. John Donne's *Elegy* XIX (Resource 7.e) associates masculine ownership and rights over a woman's body with colonial conquest ('O my America, my newfoundland' (27)), connoting a discourse of colonial power and ideology where military occupation is equated with a supposedly naturalized patriarchal authority. In this particular scene Shakespeare makes this explicitly constitutive of Roman military identity and power. More broadly the play shows Roman military colonial identity is based on this ideological model of power, particularly through Cleopatra's characterization as a foil to Antony, Caesar and Octavia.

Resource 7.e: John Donne, '*Elegy* XIX: To His Mistress Going to Bed' (1654)

COME, madam, come, all rest my powers defy;
Until I labour, I in labour lie.
The foe ofttimes, having the foe in sight,
Is tired with standing, though he never fight.
Off with that girdle, like heaven's zone glittering,
But a far fairer world encompassing.
Unpin that spangled breast-plate, which you wear,
That th' eyes of busy fools may be stopp'd there.
Unlace yourself, for that harmonious chime
Tells me from you that now it is bed-time.
Off with that happy busk, which I envy,
That still can be, and still can stand so nigh.
Your gown going off such beauteous state reveals,
As when from flowery meads th' hill's shadow steals.
Off with your wiry coronet, and show
The hairy diadems which on you do grow.
Off with your hose and shoes; then softly tread
In this love's hallow'd temple, this soft bed.
In such white robes heaven's angels used to be
Revealed to men; thou, angel, bring'st with thee
A heaven-like Mahomet's paradise; and though
Ill spirits walk in white, we easily know
By this these angels from an evil sprite;
Those set our hairs, but these our flesh upright.
Licence my roving hands, and let them go
Before, behind, between, above, below.
O, my America, my Newfoundland,
My kingdom, safest when with one man mann'd,
My mine of precious stones, my empery;
How am I blest in thus discovering thee!
To enter in these bonds, is to be free;

> Then, where my hand is set, my soul shall be.
> Full nakedness! All joys are due to thee;
> As souls unbodied, bodies unclothed must be
> To taste whole joys. Gems which you women use
> Are like Atlanta's ball cast in men's views;
> That, when a fool's eye lighteth on a gem,
> His earthly soul might court that, not them.
> Like pictures, or like books' gay coverings made
> For laymen, are all women thus array'd.
> Themselves are only mystic books, which we
> –Whom their imputed grace will dignify–
> Must see reveal'd. Then, since that I may know,
> As liberally as to thy midwife show
> Thyself; cast all, yea, this white linen hence;
> There is no penance due to innocence:
> To teach thee, I am naked first; why then,
> What needst thou have more covering than a man?

Cleopatra boasts that when Antony slept she 'put my tires and mantles on him, whilst / I wore his sword Phillipian' (2.5.21–3), celebrating a gender and power inversion through her cross-dressing, and his consequent emasculation in women's clothes and without his phallic sword. Caesar's anger at Antony is expressed simultaneously in gendered, nationalist and imperial terms, when he attacks his celebration of power in Alexandria through pomp. Caesar constructs Cleopatra's spatial imperial power over the North African and Middle Eastern lands (lower Cyprus, Syria, Lydia, 3.6.10) as an affront to 'Rome' (1) and in conversation with Octavia attacks Antony that 'he hath given his empire / to a whore' (3.6.66–7). Antony is the vehicle through which the gendered spatial economics of imperial ideology is figured: his military and sexual defeat (foreshadowed in that cross-dressing story) confirms the correct version of Roman imperial history in the necessary defeat of Cleopatra's sexual and geographic power.

However, what of Cleopatra's counter-account and the play's closure? How does Shakespeare ask us to view this military defeat? First, Cleopatra's women re-configure Antony's account of their power relationship when Antony rails that Cleopatra's wiles have tricked him: Mardian's 'my mistress loved thee, and her fortunes mingled / With thine entirely' (4.14.24–5) posits an equality of power between the masculine and feminine. When Antony believes Cleopatra has already killed herself, the epitaph he offers her opposes Roman conquests of land to Cleopatra's actions who, in refusing submission to Caesar, retains agency over her own destiny, body, and land: '[I] / condemn myself to lack / The courage of a woman; less noble mind / Than she which, by her death, our Caesar tells / "I am conqueror of myself"' (4.14.60–3). His own justification for suicide is framed in gendered and spatial terms, when he describes his military defeat as sexual penetration (75) figuring himself as feminised rape victim to Caesar's masculine subjection, a Caesar who would ride in triumph through the streets (75–6). Conquest and victory are spatial and spatially resisted through discourse and dramaturgy.

The final scene is staged in Cleopatra's secluded monument, a phallic symbol of public space appropriated as female, where she is finally defeated by the Roman army. Her initial abasement once they have stormed her monument is framed in conventional gendered terms but the semantics of her response to Caesar's assertion of power are ambiguous:

CLEOPATRA   Sole sir o'th' world,
  I cannot project mine own cause so well
  To make it clear, but do confess I have
  Been laden with like frailties which before
  Have often shamed our sex.
CAESAR   Cleopatra, know
  We will extenuate rather than enforce.
  If you apply yourself to our intents,
  Which towards you are most gentle, you shall find
  A benefit in this change; but if you seek
  To lay on me a cruelty by taking
  Antony's course, you shall bereave yourself
  Of my good purposes, and put your children
  To that destruction which I'll guard them from
  If thereon you rely. I'll take my leave.
CLEOPATRA
  And may through all the world! 'Tis yours, and we,
  Your scutcheons and your signs of conquest, shall
  Hang in what place you please. Here, my good lord.

(5.2.119–35)

By emphasizing herself and her people as objects of war booty ('we your scutcheons and your signs of conquest' (34)) within a gendered discourse in a land for which she has been metonymized, Cleopatra critiques and makes explicit the power dynamics of space, colonization and gender. The 2016 Stratford Ontario production (Arich) used casting to emphasize this duality: by casting black actors for the Egyptian characters, the powerful articulation of an anti-colonialist production was explicit in the performance of suicide as resistance.

Cleopatra's conversations with her women re-create the monument as a safe female space in which alternatives to Roman notions of colonization and power are articulated. Cleopatra convinces her women that being paraded and mocked as captives in Rome ('Thou, an Egyptian puppet shall be shown / In Rome as well as I' (207–8)) is untenable. Cleopatra's claim 'To fool their preparation and to conquer / Their most absurd intents' (5.2.224–6) celebrates suicide as political resistance. Her demands to perform death in role ('show me, my women, like a queen' (226)) posit an alternative ending, appropriating the term and ideology of conquest in terms of personal agency and symbolic meanings: Egypt lives on in fiction as a symbol of female power and resistance. The play's spatial and gendered politics ask audiences to challenge how individuals and states represent power as necessarily gendered or hierarchical.

One of Shakespeare's late plays, *Pericles* (1609) stages two scenes in a brothel: one in which Marina is sold into the brothel and one in which she persuades her first client to repent of illicit sexual behaviour (4.2, 4.6). When Marina appears, men bargain over her as a commodity ('this piece' 40), confirm the quality ('You say she's a virgin?', 37–8; 'there's no farther necessity of qualities', 44) and finally agree 'her price' (46). Bawd's exultant assessment of her continues this explicit objectification of the female body as defined by her market(place) value:

> Bolt, take you the marks of her, the colour of her hair, complexion, height, her age, with warrant of her virginity, and cry, 'He that will give most shall have her first.' Such a maidenhead were no cheap thing, if men were as they have been.
>
> (4.2.51–5)

Bawd and Bolt's insistence that sexuality itself can be performed (appear to act for love, appear fearful, weep) and marketed for profit is posited against Marina's staged body, her appeal to God (81), and her subsequent silence. Her virginal appearance embodies a visual emblem of the cost of sex as business reinforced by Bawd's older (female) body. The brothel's setting, the

Sexual Excess: Space, Sex and Gender

space occupied by these men and women, helps crystalize these notions of femininity as objectified.

The second scene in the brothel illuminates a shift in agency and control over space. Lysimachus's arrival ('how now a dozen of virginities?', 4.5.27–8) begins the trade between him and Boult ('never plucked yet, I can assure you', 48) for Marina's virginity. Bawd enumerates the reasons for Marina to acquiesce: 'I would have you note, this is an honourable man… he's the governor of this country, and a man whom I am bound to' (54–9). Marina's responses deconstruct his key words: 'If he govern the country, you are bound to him indeed; but how honourable he is in that, I know not' (60–1). Her linguistic strategies, which Bawd denigrates as "virginal fencing' (62) draw attention to Lysimachus's political status and codes of honour, which clash with this male embodied self in a brothel. Marina's forthright questioning of both the language of power and place draws attention to a female viewpoint on the trade in sex and power. As the couple are left alone, Marina continues to challenge this language:

LYSIMACHUS
Now, pretty one, how long have you been at this trade?
MARINA
What trade, sir?
LYSIMACHUS
Why, I cannot name't but I shall offend.
MARINA
I cannot be offended with my trade. Please you to name it.
LYSIMACHUS
How long have you been of this profession?
MARINA
E'er since I can remember.
LYSIMACHUS
Did you go to't so young? Were you a gamester at five or at seven?
MARINA
Earlier too, sir, if now I be one.
LYSIMACHUS
Why, the house you dwell in proclaims you to be a creature of sale.
MARINA
Do you know this house to be a place of such resort, and will come into't? I hear say you're of honourable parts, and are the governor of this place … [MARINA *weeps*]

(4.5.72–87)

The debate focuses on the meanings of words, rather than on the possible sex. Marina's refusal to understand Lysimachus's meanings ('gamester' 'principal', 'house', 'sale') offers female knowledge and agency as 'other', witty, and alternate to men's versions of truth. When she weeps, he interprets this as a performance, demanding obedience to his political power ('come…come, come', 102).

Marina transitions from silent weeping, emblematically typical of womanhood, to active political advocacy of ethical behaviour, based on public meanings of key words ('authority', 'honour' and 'justice' (105, 108, 113)):

> MARINA
> My Lord, I entreat you but to hear me
> If as you say you are the governor,
> Let not authority which teaches you
> To govern others be the means
> To make you misgovern much yourself.
> If you were born to honour, show it now;
> If put upon you, make the judgment good
> That thought you worthy of it.
> LYSIMACHUS   How's this?
> How's this? Some more; be sage.
> MARINA   What reason's in
> Your justice, who hath power over all,
> To undo any? If you take from me
> Mine honour, you are like him that makes
> A gap into forbidden ground, whom after
> Too many enter, and you are guilty
> Of all their evils. My life is yet unspotted,
> My chastity unstained even in thought.
> Then if your violence deface this building,
> The workmanship of heaven, made up for good,
> And not for exercise of sin's intemperance,
> You kill your honour, abuse your justice,
> And impoverish me.
> LYSIMACHUS   Why this house
> Wherein thou liv'st is a receptacle
> Of all men's sins, and nurse of wickedness.
> How canst thou then be otherwise than naught
> That liv'st in it?

Sexual Excess: Space, Sex and Gender

MARINA   My yet good Lord
If there be fire before me, must I fly
There straight and burn myself? Suppose this house –
Which too many feel such houses are –
Should be the doctor's patrimony and
The surgeon's feeding, follows it that I
Must needs infect myself to give them maintenance?

(4.5.103–34)

Marina's rhetoric of the supplicant to her lord uses conventional patriarchal concepts of femininity as land ('forbidden ground' (115)) and a building, connoting her body as occupied space, and enacts a defence against rape, based on those traditionalist images. Through actively evoking and performing the iconography of chastity as unsullied land or property, Marina finds personal salvation. Lysimachus's initial belief that place and status define identity ('this house… How canst thou then be otherwise than naught / That liv'st in it?' (123–7)) is challenged and debunked by female speech and interpretation. There are two contradictory narrative impulses here. First, the story reinforces and confirms patriarchal notions that female chastity is essential to female identity and the patriarchal masculine prerogative, proved through Marina's self-characterization as untouched land and her conversion of Lysimachus. Its converse is that excessive female sexuality (represented by the Bawd) leads to political chaos and corruption. However, more positively, ideological assumptions about identity, sexuality and place are flawed: Marina might be in a bawdy house but she is not a prostitute and a woman might be on the streets, but that does not make her a shrew or a whore. Such a perception offers up a radical notion of gender, identity and space.

Conclusions

1. Some plays (*Macbeth*, *Henry VI*) figure sexuality as a monstrous threat to political stability and authority (see Chapters 2, 6 and 9); however, this threat may be contained both through plot resolutions in hetero-patriarchal marriages and by figuring chaste female sexuality confined indoors and subject to male authority in comedies.
2. In the Tragedies and the Roman plays, the overt silencing of women's voices and containment of their bodies to the private realm

through the plot's action ensures conformity between body, space, sexuality and voice (see Chapter 8).

3. Spaces and streets where women perform their voices and emotions during the action stage and challenge early modern ideological notions that a woman's sexuality is defined only by her presence in a particular space. *Twelfth Night*'s settings might suggest a woman can only walk the streets alone when cross-dressed, but also intimates that domestic spaces are masculine as well as feminine.

4. Scenic and narrative structure show how Shakespeare used dramaturgy to problematize conventional ideology, using scenic juxtapositions to ask us to judge one set of characters and spaces against another, one ideology against another.

5. Female agency within both the private and public realms remains explicit and an explicit challenge to voiced opinions about masculine power over space and bodies.

6. Plots show that political anxieties can be translated into sexual and gender anxieties, played out through alternate settings, where space can connote different versions of power and identity. Early modern political discourse in its specific articulation of patriarchy as divine, royal and paternal explicitly links the domestic sexual spaces and power relationships to those of broader political structures and hierarchies and vice versa.

Further Work

1. Look at scenic structures in relation to setting and plot, and consider the ways in which setting might be gendered (for example, in *Henry IV*, *Pericles* and *Macbeth*).
2. Look at the bedroom scene in Cymbeline (2.2): how is female sexuality positioned vis-à-vis setting and viewing?
3. Think about how setting and virginity in *The Tempest* intersect to generate political and gendered meanings.

Further Reading

Laura Gowing, 'The Freedom of the Streets: Women and Social Space 1540-1640', in Mark Jenner (ed.), *Londinopolis: Essays in the Cultural and Social History of Early Modern London* (Manchester University Press, 2000), 130-53. **Seminal discussion of assumptions about femininity and space in early modern London, and of data showing women had access to liminal and working spaces in the city.**

Jean E. Howard, *Theatre of a City: The Places of London Comedy* (University of Pennsylvania Press, 2007). **Brilliant discussion of synergies between London and the drama in dramaturgy, language, setting and characters.**

Natasha Korda, *Shakespeare's Domestic Economies* (University of Pennsylvania Press, 2002). **Challenge to some feminist versions of the containment of women – argues that female agency inside and outside domestic settings plays out the agency of women in the early modern economy.**

Stephen Mullaney, *The Place of the Stage: License, Play and Power in Renaissance England* (Chicago University Press, 1988). **Classic articulation of the intersection between location, stage and ideology.**

Catherine Richardson, *Shakespeare and Material Culture* (Oxford University Press, 2011). **Ground-breaking discussion of the ways in which material culture and space is invoked and carries meaning in the plays.**

CHAPTER 8
ANXIOUS MASCULINITY
Key Texts: *Love's Labour's Lost, Othello, Cymbeline, The Winter's Tale*

Our contemporary concern with anxiety as a condition acknowledges its combined psychological and physical sensations, but this conjunction of the emotional and physical is equally early modern. This chapter shows how masculinity is predicated on physiological beliefs about male and female bodies and behaviour and how Shakespeare's plays engage with and challenge such notions through plot, characterization and genre. Many of Shakespeare's plays foreground, problematize and play with ideas about masculinity, manliness and identity. We shall look at how commonalities about anxious masculinity recur and are tested through plot, character and dramaturgy (see also Chapters 2 and 6).

Early modern medicine argued that the human body consisted of four humours: blood (hot and moist), phlegm (cold and moist), yellow bile (hot and dry), and black bile (cold and dry), which in different combinations within an individual's body produced personality types of the sanguine, the phlegmatic, the choleric and the melancholic, respectively. Each personality 'type' expressed certain attitudes and emotions through behaviour and psychology (see also Chapter 5). Mental health existed along a continuum of bodily humoral production, and the easing of symptoms through exercise, eating and bloodletting all aimed to re-balance the body's equilibrium. Robert Burton's *Anatomy of Melancholy* (1621) debated these conceptions of body and feeling, giving explicit voice to a notion of 'anxiety' (Resource 8.a).

> **Resource 8.a: Robert Burton, *Anatomy of Melancholy* (1621)**
>
> Love's Melancholy [is].... full of feare, anxietie, paine and griefe, doubt, care, suspition, peevishnesse, and bitternesse.... Most part a louers life is full of anxietie, feare and griefe, complaints & sighes, suspitious cares & discontents, except at such times that he hath ... pleasant gales, or sudden alterations, as if his mistris smile upon him, give him a good looke, or kisse, or that some comfortable message be brought him.
>
> (p. 602)

Anxiety is located in the melancholic humour and emotions of uncertainty associated with being in love. More broadly he locates anxiety in social interaction, theology and human experience (Resource 8.b).

Resource 8.b: Robert Burton, *Anatomy of Melancholy* (1621)

The generall cause, a continuate cause, an inseparable accident to all men, is discontent, care, misery; were there no other particular affliction (which who is free from?) to molest a man in this life, the very cogitation of that common misery, were enough to macerate him, and make him aweary of his life: to thinke that he can never be secure, but still in danger, sorrow, griefe, and persecution. For to begin at the first houre of his birth, as *Pliny* doth elegantly describe it, *he is borne naked, and fals a whining at the very first, he is swadled and bound up like a prisoner, and cannot helpe himselfe, and so he continues to his liues end.* No estate, age, sexe, can secure himselfe from this common misery. *A man that is borne of a woman, is of short continuance, and full of trouble, Iob 14.1. & vers. 22. and while his flesh is upon him, he shall be sorrowfull, and while his soule is in him, it shall mourne.*

(p. 144)

The combination of humoral models of identity, the theological belief in the post-lapsarian wretchedness of mankind, and emergent urban proto-capitalist economic competition all placed a burden on psychic and physical identity. Robert Cawdry gives voice to this sense of burden as integral to men's identity:

a worldly man having infinite Cares, cogitations, and anxieties hanging upon his minde, as waights upon the Clocke, can never have rest or quiet day or night, but is enforced to beate his braines when other men sleepe, for the compassing of those trifles wherwith he is encombred.

(*A Treasurie or Storehouse of Similes*, 1600, p. 60)

Love's Labour's Lost (1595) plays out a common comic plot: the male hero who reluctantly and against his better judgement falls in love. The play self-consciously draws attention to the discourses of love and fictional

Anxious Masculinity

plot devices to validate structures of desire. The dominant mode of erotic discourse, Petrarchanism (using conventional sexual tropes and anatomizing a woman's beauty), is challenged by female characterization: self-professedly invulnerable men become physiologically vulnerable. Berowne delineates this neatly via juxtaposing his past self with his current infatuation ('I, forsooth, in love! I, that have been love's whip' (3.1.169)):

> What? I love, I sue, I seek a wife?
> A woman that is like a German clock,
> Still a-repairing, ever out of frame
> And never going aright, being a watch,
> But being watched that it may still go right!
> Nay, to be perjured, which is worst of all;
> And among three to love the worst of all,
> A whitely wanton with a velvet brow,
> With two pitch-balls stuck in her face for eyes;
> Ay, and by heaven, one that will do the deed
> Though Argus were her eunuch and her guard.
> And I to sigh for her, to watch for her.
>   (3.1.184–95)

Berowne's emotions run ahead of his prejudices about erotic love. This speech simultaneously articulates chauvinisms assuming that men are trapped into love, alongside his new feelings, paradigmatic of masculine anxiety over how to reconcile sexual and public identity. The segue between his notion of his self ('What? I love, I sue, I seek a wife?' (184)) and his characterization of all women ('A woman that is like a German clock, / Still a-repairing, ever out of frame' (185–6)) posits a mismatch between the self of the speaker and the mechanically imagined woman as non-human other. Berowne's clock metaphor connotes the intersection between *explicit* male surveillance of female behaviour and *implicit* anxiety involved in that watching: 'never going aright, being a watch, / But being watched that it may still go right' (187–8). Berowne's imagination conjures other watchers ('among three'), suggesting public surveillance is essential to being in love, and implying both that love always engages with an absolute 'other' and that betrayal always seems inevitable (see also Chapter 1). This essential, universalizing view of woman as other, corrupt and in need of male control originates in the dual construction of woman as responsible for the Fall and as physiologically lesser than man (Resource 8.c).

> **Resource 8.c: Matthew Griffith, *Bethel* (1633)**
>
> The Apostle proves not man's superiority merely from his priority: but from such a priority that makes Adam the end and Eve serving to that end as a helper ...
> Of corruption; Eve was first deformed and so brought that into the world which brought the whole world into bondage.
>
> (p. 324)

Contemporary critical discussions of anxious masculinity are informed as much by changing political and social interests in masculinity as psychoanalytic, political, sexual or social identities. Freud partially framed his model of psychic masculine identity (the Oedipus complex) by a reading of Shakespeare's *Hamlet*, arguing that masculine identity was formed by the anxiety generated in a young boy by the loss of the maternal breast, simultaneously creating erotic desire for completion with the mother and a sense of competition with other men, particularly the father (Freud, 1900). In the Freudian model, anxious masculinity becomes integral to adult male sexual identity, fusing erotic desire for women with competition with men, an analysis impacting critical approaches, often through the lens of post-structuralism and Lacan (Adelman, 1992; Breitenberg, 1996; Enterline, 1995; Kahn, 1981). Problematically, however, this approach universalizes and privileges masculine identity across history and culture, as well as assuming desire is heteronormative. Materialist (sometimes explicitly Marxist) accounts of masculinity, by contrast, focus on early modern accounts of identity, desire and physicality within a political environment (Belsey, 1985; Dollimore and Sinfield, 1994; Greenblatt, 1988), situating men's lived, material experience with some psychoanalytic theory, acknowledging loss as integral to psychic identity (Breitenberg, 1996; Howard, 2007; Smith, 2000). Feminist, queer and post-colonial critics and performers, using postmodern recalibrations of gender and sexuality as constructed, fluid and performative, have questioned previous critical assumptions about a binary gender/sexuality system in the early modern period and in drama in particular (Masten, 2016; Smith, 2000; Stanivukovic, 2017; Traub, 1992). This approach is reparative, engaging the literary canon in debates meaningful to contemporary viewers, using resources and sources in texts written 450 years ago that speak anew to us when anxiety, gender and sexual identities are being challenged by alt-right perceptions of the 'normal'

(Cartelli, 2019). Accounts of affect and emotion as central to notions of the performing body and character in the early modern period have turned away from materialist notions of patriarchy (Gallagher, 1987; Meek and Sullivan, 2015), suggesting anxious masculinity as a felt and known experience, not just an expression of power. Finally, theoretical and performative interest in the post-anthropocene posits anxiety as a state of being human in a nearly post-human world, displacing gender and sexuality into a broader notion of precarity (Dionne and Kapadia, 2016).

Love's Labour's Lost's plot shows masculine identity constructed through two competing, mutually constitutive oppositions. First, there is one between masculinity and femininity – where erotic engagement complicates and questions masculine autonomy, both through what is lost and what such erotic engagement requires in surveillance of the beloved. The second is a continuous competition between men and their differing versions of what 'honour' might mean; for example, Berowne implies honourable masculinity does not submit to the discourse of love ('I post [run] from love', 4.3.185). Masculine self-identity is further complicated by Berowne's speech at the finale, extending this anxiety to the physiological: 'Your beauty, ladies, / Hath much deformed us, fashioning our humours / Even to the opposed end' (5.2.750–2). Female beauty changes male humoral identity: femininity *per se* threatens masculinity's physiological definition (see also Chapters 4 and 6). Anxieties about bodily changes (whether of becoming effeminized by being in love, or growing horns by being cuckolded) thread their way through expressions of male identity.

In the play's closing moments, Berowne offers salvation for masculine identity:

> We to ourselves prove false
> By being once false, forever to be true
> To those that make us both – fair ladies, you.
> And even that falsehood, in itself a sin,
> Thus purifies itself and turns to grace.
>
> (5.2.767–70)

The promise that love may be redemptive is a crucial supplement that displays the psychic disequilibrium that is masculine identity under early modern patriarchal political and familial discourse. Within the Catholic Church, the dichotomy between Eve as agent of the Fall and Mary as agent of salvation was central to representations of women. Within the Protestant

Elizabethan and Jacobean church, salvation was figured through Christ and the Bible rather than through Mary, but traces of such imagery persist as narrative solutions to the negative energies of masculine anxiety through a number of Shakespeare's plays (see also Chapter 9).

> **Resource 8.d: T. E., *The Law's Resolution of Women's Rights* (1632)**
>
> See here, the reason of that which I touched on before, that women have no voice in parliament. They make no laws, consent to none, they abrogate none. All of them are understood either married or to be married, and their desires are subject to their husband.
>
> (p. 6)

The play's ending comments on narrative as a construction of normativity:

> BEROWNE
>   Our wooing doth not end like an old play:
>   Jack hath not Jill. These ladies' courtesy
>   Might well have made our sport a comedy.
> KING
>   Come, sir, it wants a twelvemonth and a day,
>   And then 'twill end.
> BEROWNE   That's too long for a play.
>
> (5.2.862–6)

The closing rhyming couplet paradoxically emphasizes a formal *lack* of closure suggesting comedy on stage cannot contain (in time or space) the complexities of male sport or desire. By questioning the code of comedic closures, the play equally questions the codes of masculinity that drive such genres: male conduct as legitimately sportive and heteronormative marriage as a happy end-point to anxious masculinity (see also Chapters 3 and 4). The plot operates at two levels. First, it offers a possible closure to the marriage plot in a year's time, re-establishing a normative (if self-conscious) consummation to erotic engagement. Conversely, it questions, through linguistic play and women's setting of conditions, the very conventions of erotic love and gendered identities that the promised closure appears to offer.

Resource 8.e: Stefano Guazzo, *The Court of Good Counsell* (1607)

THE greatest joy, and sweetest comfort, that a man may have in this worlde, is a louing, kinde, and honest wife: Contrariwise, there is no greater plague, nor torment to his minde then to be matched with an untoward, wicked, and dishonest Woman. Therefore let him that intendeth to marry, and tye himselfe to that honorable state of life: (being the first bargaine of thrift, and the first step to good husbandry) take all the best Counsell he can in the world in the choyce of a Wife, yet scarce sufficient enough: for being once done it can never be recall'd, but eyther lamented too soone or repented too late. ….

A woman should take heede that she give not men occasion to thinke hardly of her, either by her Deedes, Wordes, Lookes, or Apparell.

(fo. B1ʳ, D3)

Othello plots masculine identity as both competitive with other men (hence inherently anxious) and embedded in the surveillance and control of women (hence exteriorally anxious). But the play also challenges these models of masculinity: through genre (as a tragedy, the actions of both Iago and Othello are tested and fail); through notions of race; and through female characterization and conversations. Iago's soliloquy to the audience at the end of the opening act marks out his explicit intentions and implicit anxieties:

>… I hate the Moor
>And it is thought abroad that 'twixt my sheets
>He's done my office. I know not if 't be true,
>But I for mere suspicion in that kind
>Will do as if for surety. He holds me well,
>The better shall my purpose work on him.
>Cassio's a proper man: let me see now,
>To get his place, and to plume up my will
>In double knavery. How? How? let's see:
>After some time to abuse Othello's ear
>That he is too familiar with his wife.
>He hath a person and a smooth dispose

To be suspected, framed to make women false.
The Moor is of a free and open nature
That thinks men honest that but seem to be so,
And will as tenderly be led by th' nose
As asses are.

(1.3.385–401)

Iago's self-representation as a plain-spoken man is rhetorically and performatively formulated. Alone on stage, he delivers this speech at the boundaries of the stage/audience interaction, playing out key attributes of anxious masculinity. Iago implicitly attributes his own competitive relationship with Othello as driven by the belief and fear of his own wife's perceived sexual betrayal (385–6). The fear of cuckoldry (which he goes on to incite in Othello) dominates many debates about masculine identity in the period (Resource 8.f). This sense of sexual rivalry drives Iago's plot to discredit and discomfort Othello; the mere suspicion of sexual misconduct 'will do as if for surety' (390). Proof and knowledge lie simultaneously in the masculine construction of femininity and in man's anxiety about their control of their wives. Further, Iago's sense of self is articulated through his thwarted ambition to gain a lieutenantship and hence masculine competition with both Cassio *and* Othello. Additionally, his ironic 'Cassio's a proper man' (391) posits Cassio simultaneously as a man publicly respected and sexually pleasing ('a smooth dispose / To be suspected, framed to make women false' (396–7)). Iago announces and uses popular views of masculinity: a handsome man of high status is simultaneously a reputable model of male identity and a threat to other men. Finally, Iago believes that Othello should be inducted into the worldly codes of political masculinity ('a free and open nature / That thinks men honest that but seem so' (398–9)). Male competition, a fear of cuckoldry, political status, and rivalry delineate a complex system of social and patriarchal identity (Resource 8.f).

Resource 8.f: Robert Tofte, *The Blazon of Jealousy* (1615)

IEALOVSIE springeth from the Propertie or Right that wee have, when we (enjoying our Lady or Mistresse) would have her soly and wholy unto our selves; without being able (by any meanes) to suffer or endure, that another man should have any part or interest in her, anyway, or at any time.

(p. 19)

Anxious Masculinity

Iago's role as tutor in masculine knowledge and behaviour continues in his lengthy discussion with Othello in 3.3. He lectures Othello on women's nature, status, and relationship to man:

> Good name in man and woman, dear my lord,
> Is the immediate jewel of their souls:
> Who steals my purse steals trash – 'tis something-nothing,
> 'Twas mine, 'tis his, and has been slave to thousands –
> But he that filches from me my good name
> Robs me of that which not enriches him
> And makes me poor indeed.
>
> (3.3.157–63)

Linking this to a key component of masculine pride and identity, he claims:

> O beware, my lord, of jealousy!
> It is the green-eyed monster, which doth mock
> The meat it feeds on. That cuckold lives in bliss
> Who, certain of his fate, loves not his wronger,
> But O, what damned minutes tells he o'er
> Who dotes yet doubts, suspects yet strongly loves!
>
> (3.3.166–72)

For Iago, jealousy is the emotion most near the surface in a married man (Resource 8.f). Fear of cuckoldry was based on the misogynist notion that all women would betray men because of their inheritance from Eve and their natural humours which, being moist and hot, generated excess sexual desires (Matthews-Grieco, 2018; Resource 8.g). This model of physiology and historical guilt underlay not only the period's misogyny, but the psyche of masculinity itself.

Othello's initial defence against Iago's philosophical discussion of jealousy proffers a better version of suspicion-less masculinity:

> ...Think'st thou I'd make a life of jealousy
> To follow still the changes of the moon
> With fresh suspicions? No: to be once in doubt
> Is once to be resolved. Exchange me for a goat
> When I shall turn the business of my soul
> To such exsufflicate and blown surmises,

> Matching thy inference. 'Tis not to make me jealous
> To say my wife is fair, feeds well, loves company,
> Is free of speech, sings, plays and dances well:
> Where virtue is, these are more virtuous.
> Nor from mine own weak merits will I draw
> The smallest fear or doubt of her revolt,
> For she had eyes and chose me. No, Iago,
> I'll see before I doubt, when I doubt, prove,
> And on the proof there is no more but this:
> Away at once with love or jealousy!
>
> (3.3.180–95)

His robust defence rejects Iago's insinuations ('blown surmises' (185)), arguing that women's external behaviour should not be 'read' as guilt and masculine identity should not be predicated on mistrust and jealousy. The play's tragedy pivots on this scene in which an initially high-minded view of masculine sufficiency ('not from mine own weak merits will I draw / The smallest fear or doubt of her revolt' (189–90)) is so rapidly set aside. Action, proverbial knowledge and plot allow the populism of Iago's views on femininity and masculinity to stand as truths. Iago's cultural truisms about woman's natural deceptiveness ('their best conscience / Is not to leave't undone, but keep't unknown' (206–7)) become enacted truths: 'She did deceive her father, marrying you, / And when she seemed to shake, and fear your looks, / She loved them most' (209–10). Othello's answer seals the endpoint of masculine anxiety about women's fidelity in masculine homosocial bonding: 'I am bound to thee for ever' (3.3.217).

Resource 8.g: Robert Burton, *The Anatomy of Melancholy* (1621)

The worldly cares, miseries, discontents, that accompany marriage, I pray you learne of them that have experience, for I have none, many married men exclaime at the miseries of it, and raile at wives downe right; but I never tried.

    An *Irish* Sea is not so turbulent & raging as a litigious wife, *better dwell with a Dragon or a Lion, then keepe house with a wife. Ecclus. 25.18. better dwell in a wildernesse. Pro. 21.1. no wickednesse like to her, Ecclus. 25.21. She makes a sorry heart, an heavy countenance, and a wounded mind, weake hands, and feeble knees, vers. 5…*

> ... in sober sadnesse marriage is a bondage, a thraldome, an yoke, an hinderance to all good enterprises, a rocke on which many are saved; many impinge and are cast away.
>
> (p. 648)

The swift descent from a model of masculine autonomy based on trust between man and wife to the common dramatic stereotype of a man fearful of cuckoldry occurs within twenty lines. Othello plays out the anxiety of a married man who characterizes women's sexual desire as an unknown force, a witchcraft, uncontrollable, and always ready to betray the male subject (Resource 8.g). Shakespeare locates this testing of masculine sexual, political and homosocial anxieties in the centre of the play: Othello's acquiescence to populist notions of masculinity becomes his and Desdemona's downfall.

The subsequent scene (3.4) structures Shakespeare's dramatization of male anxiety, positioning it within an interpretative frame. The scene falls performatively into four parts. The first is a conversation between the clown, Desdemona and Emilia about helping Cassio with his suit to re-enter Othello's good graces. The second sees Othello's indirect accusations of Desdemona's infidelity, including the business of the handkerchief. The third, has Iago ushering in Cassio to importune Desdemona publicly. The fourth part shows Cassio demanding Bianca copy the embroidery on the handkerchief and leave him to his public duties so he will not seem 'womaned' (3.4.195).

The scene sets out battle lines between genders, knowledge and appearance. The audience's pre-knowledge that Othello is wrong in his assumptions helps create a critical distance about the motivation of masculine anxiety. Dramatic irony is a critical lens through which the dramaturge enables performers and viewers to critique masculine jealousy. Here is their initial conversation.

OTHELLO
Give me your hand. This hand is moist, my lady.
DESDEMONA
It yet hath felt no age, nor known no sorrow.
OTHELLO
This argues fruitfulness and liberal heart:
Hot, hot, and moist. This hand of yours requires
A sequester from liberty, fasting and prayer,
Much castigation, exercise devout,

> For here's a young and sweating devil, here,
> That commonly rebels. 'Tis a good hand,
> A frank one.
>
> (3.4.36–44)

Othello interprets all physical signs through the frame Iago has established: femininity as betrayal and masculinity as suspicious and sceptical interrogator of female sexuality. The humoral nature of femininity (hot and moist) *requires* the sequestration (40) of women because they will 'naturally' rebel. Othello's account of the handkerchief's origins posit cross-cultural continuities about gendered and sexual anxieties. When Othello narrates the history ('That handkerchief… an Egyptian to my mother give' (57–8)) as a gift from his dying mother (a 'charmer' (59)) to pass on to his future wife, which 'To lose… or give… away were such perdition / As nothing else could match' (69–70), he sets up the stage property as a magical and metonymic talisman:

> 'Tis true, there's magic in the web of it.
> A sibyl that had numbered in the world
> The sun to course two hundred compasses,
> In her prophetic fury sewed the work;
> The worms were hallowed that did breed the silk,
> And it was dyed in mummy, which the skilful
> Conserved of maidens' hearts.
>
> (3.4.71–8)

The handkerchief is a physical metonym for Desdemona's body and Othello's 'ownership' of it. However, the story behind its possession tells of maternal power over both sons and husbands, a magical history in which women subdue men ('twould make her amiable and subdue my father', 61). Othello's tale ostensibly of masculine ownership, subtextually reveals his anxiety that female sexuality is manipulative, self-interested, and built on the death of chastity ('mummy / … conserved of maidens' hearts' (77–8)).

The subsequent rough exchange in which Othello repeatedly demands 'the handkerchief!' (93, 94, 98) is countered by Desdemona's continual insistence that he forgive Cassio. Desdemona's distress displays a naivety about masculinity the audience can admire, since she continues to insist that politics (not prejudices about female sexuality) drives his actions ('Something sure of state / Either from Venice, or some unhatched practice /

Made demonstrable here in Cyprus to him, / Hath puddled his clear spirit' (141–3)). Imogen Stubbs as Desdemona (Nunn, RSC, 1989), with her classic visual appearance of a young innocent English woman, managed this rather well. By contrast, Emilia's world-weary claim of the twinning of masculinity and jealousy foreshadows the coming tragedy:

> 'Tis not a year or two shows us a man.
> They are all but stomachs, and we all but food:
> They eat us hungerly, and when they are full
> They belch us.
>
> (3.4.104–6)

Emilia's words close this scene: 'They are not ever jealous for the cause, / But jealous for they're jealous. It is a monster / Begot upon itself, born on itself' (59–64). This voiced finale ensures that female perspectives on anxious masculinity act as critical counterpoints to its very expression. Masculinity is produced as predicated on the control of a 'dangerous' femininity. Emilia's words echo other early modern women's voices in poetry and pamphlets written by women in the period (Resource 8.h).

Resource 8.h: Rachel Speght, *A Mouzell for Melastomus* (1616)

We shall finde the offence of *Adam* and *Eve* almost to paralell: For as an ambitious desire of being made like unto God, was the motive which caused her to eate, so likewise was it his; as may plainely appeare by that *Ironica, Behold, man is become as one of vs:* Not that hee was so indeed; but heereby his desire to attaine a greater perfection then God had given him, was reproved. Woman sinned, it is true, by her infidelitie in not beleeving the Word of God, but giving credite to Sathans faire promises, that *shee should not die;* but so did the man too.

(p. 4)

Act 4, Scene 3 is located in the play's only female-only space, when Emilia and Desdemona debate sexuality, prepare for bed and Desdemona sings 'the willow song'. Shakespeare transposes this ballad from a male voice on betrayed love[1] with Desdemona appropriating the male lover's defence ('If I court moe women you'll couch with moe men' (56)).

---

[1] See commentary note in the Arden Third Series edition, ed. E.A.J. Honigman.

Shakespeare and Gender

By giving the woman an explicit voice in the narrative and implying marital sexual relationships should be based on mutual trust, Desdemona enacts a different story about masculine anxiety. Emilia's subsequent discussion anatomizes masculinity:

> ... I do think it is their husbands' faults
> If wives do fall: say that they slack their duties,
> And pour our treasures into foreign laps,
> Or else break out in peevish jealousies,
> Throwing restraint upon us; or say they strike us,
> Or scant our former having in despite;
> Why, we have galls, and though we have some grace,
> Yet have we some revenge. Let husbands know
> Their wives have sense like them: they see and smell
> And have their palates both for sweet and sour,
> As husbands have. What is it that they do
> When they change us for others? Is it sport?
> I think it is: and doth affection breed it?
> I think it doth: is't frailty that thus errs?
> It is so too: and have not we affections,
> Desires for sport, and frailty, as men have?
> Then let them use us well: else let them know,
> The ills we do, their ills instruct us so.
>
> (4.3.85–102)

Emilia exposes the double sexual standard of male jealousy as constructed as a norm of masculine identity and an assumption of feminine frailty and how this ideology justifies male acting-out. Her solution is to speak female desire as legitimate: the casting of Zoe Wanamaker as Emilia in Trevor Nunn's 1989–90 RSC production enabled her off-stage and on-stage personality to produce a convincing weighty counterpart to male constructions of feminine failure.

The play's climax symbolically focuses on the marital bed: a symbol of union, sexuality, birth and death. Visually, this scene is where Othello's black body is most contrasted with Desdemona's white one, given the white sheets she has asked for (see particularly the Orson Welles film, 1952). His colour becomes embedded in the notions of masculinity that follow: his opening speech exemplifies his belief in his masculine prerogative over his wife's body as the righteous 'cause' of his jealousy and the paradox of contradictory masculinity. Desdemona is virgin and whore: the ideal woman is in fact a silent, dead one.

The bed as stage property locates and brilliantly symbolizes this very paradox: chaste marriage bed, or hotbed of lust? Willard White's film performance (Nunn, 1990) trod a fine line in suggesting both these functions simultaneously and sensitively. We believe in Othello's version of Desdemona as both beloved and betrayer, because White's anguish and self-belief were enacted as credible.

Othello's final speech recognizes the split male self created by the binary construction of femininity:

> I have done the state some service, and they know't:
> No more of that. I pray you, in your letters,
> When you shall these unlucky deeds relate,
> Speak of me as I am. Nothing extenuate,
> Nor set down aught in malice. Then must you speak
> Of one that loved not wisely, but too well;
> Of one not easily jealous, but, being wrought,
> Perplexed in the extreme; of one whose hand,
> Like the base Indian, threw a pearl away
> Richer than all his tribe; of one whose subdued eyes,
> Albeit unused to the melting mood,
> Drops tears as fast as the Arabian trees
> Their medicinable gum. Set you down this,
> And say besides that in Aleppo once,
> Where a malignant and a turbanned Turk
> Beat a Venetian and traduced the state,
> I took by th' throat the circumcised dog
> And smote him – thus!   [*He stabs himself.*]
>
> (5.2.337–54)

Although Othello's self-characterization begins with his political status (336), he quickly rejects this public persona, asking those listening to 'speak of me as I am' (340); the truth can be spoken when all else is lost. Othello constructs his own funeral oration as a lesson to other men ('Nothing extenuate' (340)): for a man in love, jealousy can be 'wrought' (340) – by others and himself. Self-reflectively meditating on masculinity as a cause of this fall, Othello splits masculine identity into multiple actions and identities ('you speak of one .... / of one ... / ...of one' (342–4)). Thus he patterns out both his own psychological breakdown and the way divergent racial identities have formed and undone him. He is, variously: a man manipulated by other men; a man who others himself as a 'base Indian' for mis-reading his wife's behaviour; a man who is both a Turk (251) (connoting his foreignness, Islamic religion and colour) and a Venetian (252), conflicted between two cultures and two religions. Switching within two lines between both identities ('I took by the throat the circumcised dog / And smote him thus' (353–4)), his final 'I' is a verbally explicitly Venetian and Christian expulsion of the extreme jealousy of his othered (Muslim or Indian) masculinity. Here, jealous and anxious masculinity is something to acknowledge and expel – albeit by displacing such emotions onto the Other: a precarious state competing all the time between different versions of oneself.

Two later plays re-examine masculine constructions of feminine sexuality and masculine anxiety, presenting counter-conclusions to *Othello*'s tragic suggestion that masculine anxiety is inevitable and deadly. *Cymbeline*'s Iachimo (like Iago) is intent on playing on contemporary prejudices to prove to Posthumus that his wife is unfaithful. Iachimo's initial play for Posthumus occurs in a scene where men talk competitively, claiming their own women are 'less attemptable' (1.4.59) than women from other countries. Femininity is defined as 'owned' by men and, in counter-distinction to 'othered' women, masculinity is defined by that ownership and by the implied possibility of sexual conquests with those othered women. Iachimo manoeuvres Posthumus into betting against his wife's infidelity through a series of wily rhetorical hooks taunting his assumptions about her honour and faithfulness. Here is the conclusion to their negotiation:

> IACHIMO .... If I bring you no sufficient testimony that I have enjoy'd the dearest bodily part of your mistress, my ten thousand ducats are yours, so is your diamond too: if I come off, and leave her in such honour as you have trust in, she your jewel, this your jewel, and my gold are yours: provided I have your commendation for my more free entertainment.
>
> POSTHUMUS
> I embrace these conditions, let us have articles betwixt us. Only, thus far you shall answer: if you

make your voyage upon her, and give me directly
to understand you have prevail'd, I am no further
your enemy; she is not worth our debate. If she
remain unseduc'd, you not making it appear otherwise,
for your ill opinion, and th' assault you have
made to her chastity, you shall answer me with your
sword.

IACHIMO
Your hand, a covenant: we will have these things
set down by lawful counsel, and straight away for
Britain, lest the bargain should catch cold and
starve. I will fetch my gold, and have our two
wagers recorded.

POSTHUMUS
Agreed.

(1.4.145–67)

Although Posthumus initially defends his wife by making a distinction between inanimate objects and his wife (a ring is not a worthy match against an honourable woman), his discourse slips into acknowledging Iachimo's discursive frame: drawn into Iachimo's wager Posthumus indirectly exchanges his wife's body. If Iachimo can 'get ground of your fair mistress' (100) he will earn the ring, symbolic of Posthumus's marital union and, metonymically, his wife's body.

Iachimo makes the nature of the bargain as explicit as possible: he aims to enjoy 'the dearest bodily part' (146) and proof will determine payment. This scene patterns out masculine competition for women: beginning in disagreement about women and ending on the men agreeing on a bet about a woman's sexuality. Indeed, their 'covenant' (162) at the end is literally an agreement 'between men' (Sedgwick, 1985) and in law ('bargain' (162–3)). Peace and masculine agreement is predicated on the betrayal of women ('I am no further your enemy' (156–7)). Worse, the plot suggests that female virtue will actively sow dissent and competitive wagers between men. Masculinity is defined simultaneously by an assumption of female un-chastity – for it is this that unites men in their maleness – and mutual bonding achieved through competitive play for women.

Iachimo wins his bet by sneaking into Innogen's bedchamber hidden in a trunk (2.2) in a masterpiece of dramaturgical scenic organization, anatomizing the ways the male gaze possesses women's bodies. Iachimo writes down her body's identifying marks, moving around Innogen and her room while she sleeps to ensure his research will, in combination with the bracelet stolen from her arm, convince Posthumus that such visual knowledge is equivalent to carnal knowledge. Iachimo's subsequent account to Posthumus (2.4) effects the 'madding' at which Iachimo had aimed (2.2.37), but the plot enables the audience a privileged view of how the male gaze and masculine competition for women has produced this destructive outcome. The finale, which reaffirms Innogen's chastity (after an apparent death) echoes other Shakespearean plays (*Much Ado About Nothing, All's Well That Ends Well, Pericles* and *The Winter's Tale*) which suggest that the only solution to masculine anxiety about female chastity is salvation through a symbolically cleansing female re-birth. However, there is an alternative way to read this closure. Iachimo's observation that Innogen had been reading the tale of Tereus and Philomel (2.2.46) indirectly signals a story in which male rape and violence against a woman is countered by feminine recalibration of alternative modes of representation.[2] Although Philomel's tongue is removed, she still manages to weave her story to tell the truth about her rape. Because we already know this is a set-up, through symbolic connotations of setting (bedroom) and referents (such as the Philomel story) this scene establishes an explicitly female and critical point of view outside the action on stage.

The Winter's Tale examines how masculine anxiety plays out after marriage. Here, masculine competition for women, alongside the male characters' insistence of women as sexually voracious, can drive a man mad. The play acts as a psychological study of such madness and as a narrative road-map for possible alternative masculinities. Leontes' speeches in the first act are exemplary case studies of the jealous man's inner anguish (Resource 8.b) when he watches his wife's interaction with another man. Shakespeare intensifies the symbolic representational impact of this state of being by making the man his best friend and playing out the essence of masculine anxiety as simultaneously a fear about female sexuality and male competitive loss in the masculine marketplace of status. Leontes' first soliloquy ('Too hot, too hot! / To mingle friendship far is mingling bloods. / I have *tremor cordis* on me. My heart dances' (1.2.108–10)) posits physical discomfort alongside a watchful paranoia about his wife's gestures and an anxious consciousness of his son's paternity ('Art thou my boy?' (119)).

---

[2] Philomela was raped by Tereus, her brother-in-law, who cut out her tongue to try to ensure she could not testify against him. She uses her skill as a weaver to bear witness through visual representation and bring him to justice (Ovid, *Metamorphosis* VI, 519–62).

> ... Yet they say we are
> Almost as like as eggs – women say so,
> That will say anything. But were they false
> As o'erdyed blacks, as wind, as waters, false
> As dice are to be wished by one that fixes
> No bourn 'twixt his and mine, yet were it true
> To say this boy were like me. Come, sir page,
> Look on me with your welkin eye. Sweet villain,
> Most dearest, my collop! Can thy dam? May't be
> Affection? – Thy intention stabs the centre,
> Thou dost make possible things not so held,
> Communicat'st with dreams – how can this be? –
> With what's unreal thou coactive art,
> And fellow'st nothing. Then 'tis very credent
> Thou mayst co-join with something, and thou dost,
> And that beyond commission, and I find it,
> And that to the infection of my brains
> And hard'ning of my brows.
>   (1.2.129–46)

The observation of his wife's public behaviour generates immediate thoughts about legitimate paternity, not only of his son, but of the unborn child in Hermione's womb. Leontes continually reassures himself that Mamillius looks enough like him to credibly believe in his paternity and his wife's fidelity ('were they false as o'erdyed blacks ...yet were it true to say this boy were like me' (131–4)). How can a father know whether his children are his? Leontes' pain is that the answer is that you cannot know for certain. With his pregnant wife on stage visibly enacting the possibilities of such uncertainty, Leontes breaks down, cataloguing the embodied experience of jealousy. The fear of cuckoldry produces psychological ('the infection of my brains' (145)) and physical effects ('tremor cordis', 'hard'ning of my brows' (110, 146)). The notion that horns would grow on the forehead of a cuckolded man as an external sign of female betrayal was a popular and extraordinary trope for male cuckoldry, representing men's feared physical and public shame if betrayed by a woman as one of bodily and bestial transformation (Figure 8.1).

Shakespeare has found the language of emotional breakdown in the psychological anxiety generated by an ideology of competitive masculinity in the abrupt rhetorical questions breaking up the logical grammatical

Figure 8.1 Seventeenth-century ballad, *The Hen-Peck'd Frigate* (with kind permission of the National Library of Scotland).

sense (138, 139, 140). Antony Sher (Doran, 1998, RSC) plays his jealousy as logical because emergent from an internalized cultural masculinity that forces him to 'read' his wife's behaviour: Sher's physical movements, delivery and facial anguish shows the pain emerging from both this observation of his wife and his own internal thoughts. Some productions show that Hermione's behaviour suggests residual doubts to the audience about her loyalty (Donnellan, 1999, Cheek by Jowl; Doran, 1998, RSC) but subsequent speeches by Hermione, courtiers, and Paulina re-position our attention to how masculine anxiety generates these suspicions in the first place.

Leontes' second soliloquy intermixes self-conscious shamed articulation of bodily and psychic transformation with a more general account of masculine anxiety.

> Inch-thick, knee-deep, o'er head and ears a forked one!
> Go play, boy, play. Thy mother plays, and I
> Play too; but so disgraced a part, whose issue
> Will hiss me to my grave. Contempt and clamour
> Will be my knell. Go play, boy, play. There have been,
> Or I am much deceived, cuckolds ere now,
> And many a man there is even at this present,
> Now, while I speak this, holds his wife by th'arm,
> That little thinks she has been sluiced in's absence,
> And his pond fished by his next neighbour, by
> Sir Smile, his neighbour. Nay, there's comfort in't,
> Whiles other men have gates, and those gates opened,
> As mine, against their will. Should all despair
> That have revolted wives, the tenth of mankind
> Would hang themselves. Physic for't there's none:
> It is a bawdy planet, that will strike
> Where 'tis predominant; and 'tis powerful, think it,
> From east, west, north and south; be it concluded,
> No barricado for a belly. Know't,
> It will let in and out the enemy
> With bag and baggage. Many thousand on's
> Have the disease and feel't not. How now, boy?
>
> (1.2.185–206)

Leontes paradoxically takes comfort both in the universality of his condition ('many a man there is even at this present' (191)) and the inevitability of women's sexual betrayal ('those gates opened / As mine against their will' (196–7)). The supposedly universal nature of women ('it is a bawdy planet', 'no barricado for a belly' (200, 203)) means that men are not to blame or able to change women or themselves ('physic for it there is none' (199)). This hollowed-out, misogynist and misanthropic argument promises a tragic denouement. When Leontes confronts Hermione, removing Mamillius and sequestering her, the male courtiers' responses continue to follow the false logic of masculine anxiety. Even Antigonus's defence of Hermione subscribes to a narration of the violent punishing of women if they are unchaste: 'If it prove / She's otherwise, I'll keep my stables where / I lodge my wife;' 'every dram of woman's flesh, is false / If she be' (2.1.133–5). Antigonus's hypotheticals (if … if) reveal masculine cultural assumptions about suitable punishments for women if they betray men. His threat to 'geld' his three daughters' (147) if Hermione is false reiterates mutual male assumptions: husbands and fathers must control female sexuality to ensure psychic health, economic security (both social and familial) and inheritance.

But Shakespeare uses plot and character to swerve away from the potential tragic denouement of the self-destruction of a masculine subject and the threatened violence against women. Leontes' accusation that Hermione 'had a bastard by Polixenes' (3.2.81) is juxtaposed instead by a different conceptual frame by Hermione's 'You speak a language that I understand not. / My life stands in the level of your dreams' (78–9). The fear of cuckoldry and the accompanying psychic paranoia comes from a hermeneutic system that Hermione suggests is all-male and a foreign tongue to women. Her subsequent speech acts as an experiential counterpoint, articulating the human cost of such masculine anxiety:

> Sir, spare your threats.
> The bug which you would fright me with I seek.
> To me can life be no commodity;
> The crown and comfort of my life, your favour,
> I do give lost, for I do feel it gone
> But know not how it went. My second joy,
> And first fruits of my body, from his presence
> I am barred, like one infectious. My third comfort
> Starred most unluckily, is from my breast,
> The innocent milk in it most innocent mouth,
> Haled out to murder; myself on every post
> Proclaimed a strumpet; with immodest hatred

Anxious Masculinity

> The childbed privilege denied, which 'longs
> To women of all fashion; lastly, hurried
> Here, to this place, i'th' open air, before
> I have got strength of limit. Now, my liege,
> Tell me what blessings I have here alive,
> That I should fear to die. Therefore proceed.
> But yet hear this – mistake me not – no life,
> I prize it not a straw, but for mine honour,
> Which I would free – if I shall be condemned
> Upon surmises, all proofs sleeping else
> But what your jealousies awake, I tell you
> 'Tis rigour, and not law.
>
> (3.2.89–112)

Hermione's three 'comforts' (his love, her son and her baby (92, 96)) have all been stolen. Her reputation is destroyed and despite coming directly from her childbirth bed, she is publicly on trial. Nevertheless, she asserts her right to clear her name and exposes Leontes' jealousy as the sole 'proof' (110) of guilt. By opposing 'law' (112) to 'rigour' (112) (tyranny) Hermione offers women a way to challenge the paranoia instilled by anxious masculinity. Judgement of the 'integrity' (25) of her fidelity arrives from the Oracle, a proxy for a higher law. The plot punishes Leontes for his jealousy and his refusal to adhere to that law, with the loss of son, daughter and wife ('For being transported by my jealousies' (3.2.155–6): Hermione's losses will be discussed in Chapter 9). Paulina's perception of Leontes ('Thy tyranny / Together working with thy jealousies / Fancies too weak for boys, too green and idle / For girls of nine' (3.2.176–80)) interprets jealousy as a childish and unmanly emotion, implying instead masculinity is the ability to out-grow such febrile passions. Their epitaphs will be emblematic comments on his jealousy: 'the causes of their death [shall] appear, / Unto our shame perpetual' (3.2.233–4).

The magical plot resolution that Hermione is alive, that daughter and wife can return to Leontes after sixteen years is conditional on Paulina's demand that he first swear never to marry but by her 'leave' (5.1.70). The classic closure of a play on marriage is re-calibrated to emphasize the agency of such marriage as female (see also Chapter 1). Leontes' future is subject to Paulina's good will (although he attempts to arrange a marriage for her in return): this apparently redemptive resolution is figured through the characters, actions and speeches of three women in the final moments, arguably suggesting that once 'cured' from jealousy and after an appropriate time of seclusion, adult male masculinity can be purged of anxiety and made anew.

Conclusions

1. Many of these plays use plot to enact the cultural anxiety of the cuckoldry threat, an enactment which contains that anxiety by punishing women (through imprisonment, restrictions of marriage, or death). The teleology of this narrative arc is conservative and regressive, appearing to confirm both the necessity of female containment and the innate anxiety of masculine identity as ineluctable.
2. However, these plays also anatomize anxious masculinity through characterization, action and genre: scenic structure and dramatic irony position the audience as critics of extreme exempla of masculinity.
3. Even an early play like *Love's Labour's Lost* provides alternative models of narrative closure than marriage and heteronormative confinement and these posit some alternative responses to male sexual anxiety and jealousy.
4. The plays draw attention to sexual, socioeconomic and status factors as sources of masculine anxieties. Proto-capitalism and patriarchy, humoral and religious models of masculine competition and bodily identity forge a complex and damaged masculinity that is anatomized by the play's fictions.
5. Physical transformation and psychic pain are attendant upon the articulation of masculine anxiety, making its embodiment on stage and performance both tangible and emotive.
6. Dead women – or apparently dead women who are resurrected – recur in many plots as an apparent solution to masculine fears about sexual betrayal, functioning doubly as confirmation of the effectiveness of masculine anxiety to contain women, and as symbols of the extremity of that ideology. Resurrected women similarly function as symbolic of a purified sexuality and the possibility that femininity can redeem a corrupted masculinity.

7. Female voices and perspectives speak from 'outside' the masculine frame of reference against a language they 'understand not' (*The Winter's Tale*, 3.2), providing an alternative to the apparent inevitability of masculine anxiety as totalitarian ideology.

Further Work

Much Ado About Nothing and *All's Well That Ends Well*

1. How does the plot function of female death and the fifth act 'resurrection' play out?
2. Look at speeches by Benedict in *Much Ado* and Bertram in *All's Well*: where and why do we find reiterations of masculine cuckoldry and political anxieties in their characterizations?
3. In what ways have modern performances looked at anxious masculinity in these plays?
4. How and where do women's voices act as counterpoint to these (see also Chapter 1)?

Two Noble Kinsmen

Look at how the romance plot narrates masculine competition as both martial and sexual: comment on the intersection of genres as a way of interrogating identity and masculinity.

Pericles

In what ways does the reappearance of Perdita and her mother reinforce the view that resurrected women 'save' men? Are there aspects of the play which problematize this?

Macbeth

1. How and where does Lady Macbeth use notions of anxious masculinity as a rhetorical strategy to force a notion of action on Macbeth?

2. In what ways do rigid notions of gender actively engender the Macbeths' eventual psychological fragility?
3. How does Lady Macbeth's 'unsex me here' speech (1.5.41–54) and their conversation prior to the murder of Duncan (1.6) figure masculinity as a weapon used against men and women in constructing and justifying identity and action?

Further Reading

Christian Billing, *Masculinity, Corporality and the English Stage 1580–1635* (Ashgate, 2008). **Debates the distinctiveness of a male body and male physical experiences to theatrical representation and affect.**

Mark Breitenberg, *Anxious Masculinity in Early Modern England* (Cambridge University Press, 1996). **Classic study of notions of masculine anxiety through prism of Lacan's notion of desire for and of the phallus.**

Coppélia Kahn, *Mans' Estate: Masculine Identity in Shakespeare* (University of California Press, 1981). **Ground-breaking debate about masculine identity in Shakespeare's plays through prism of second-wave feminism and object-relations psychoanalysis.**

Coppélia Kahn, *Roman Shakespeare: Warriors, Wounds and Women* (Routledge, 1991). **Kahn's second monograph on the subject focuses on the Roman history plays as sites of debate about certain types of martial masculinity.**

Bruce Smith, *Shakespeare and Masculinity* (Oxford University Press, 2000). **Considers political, bodily, chivalric and cultural notions of early modern masculinity.**

Valerie Traub, *Desire and Anxiety: Circulations of Sexuality in Shakespearean Drama* (Routledge, 1992). **Foundational study on hetero- and homoerotic desire(s) as constitutive of gender anxieties.**

Robin Headlam Wells, *Shakespeare on Masculinity* (Cambridge University Press, 2000). **Argues that Shakespeare's plays challenge notions of an idealized heroic martial masculinity.**

CHAPTER 9
MATERNAL BODIES: FEMALE POWERS
Key Texts: *Henry VI, All's Well That Ends Well, The Winter's Tale*

Boys playing female parts on the early modern stage mostly played young women whose emotions, experiences and even physique were arguably close to their own. However, they also had to play older women and women who were mothers or pregnant, bodily experiences far removed from the consciousness and understanding of a young male actor. The question 'where are the mothers in Shakespeare?' (Rose, 1991) requires a nuanced understanding not just of the symbolic, political and social construction of maternity in Shakespeare's time but of the material conditions of the theatre and resistances to those constructions and theatrical constraints. The higher number of mature women and maternal roles in the plays after 1600 (including Gertrude, Lady Macbeth and Cleopatra) may have been consequent upon a number of material factors: greater confidence amongst maturing actors and/or the specific skills of an individual male actor (Maguire and Smith, 2012); the political context in which an ageing infertile queen gave way to a married royal couple with very public pregnancies and miscarriages (Barroll, 2001); and an increasingly vocal audience that included women (Howard, 2007).

The Elizabethan Church's *Homilies* acted as royally authorized sermons on key political, religious and ideological practices. The *Homily on the State of Matrimony* (first published in 1562/3) delineates the dominant Protestant model of a wife's status as simultaneously and paradoxically subordinate and equal to man: subject to male authority, but authoritative within the domestic sphere, over servants, children and household (see Resource 3.b). This ideology, combined with the version of 'mother Eve' who had engendered the Fall through her sin, a female monarch (whose political power was often sexualized; Berry, 1994), and a physiological belief that mothers were 'leaky bodies' (Paster, 1993) meant that married mothers carried a number of contradictory symbolic resonances.

Shakespeare's first staged plays were likely to have been the *Henry VI* trilogy (*c.* 1592), probably collaboratively written with Marlowe and others (Cox and Rasmussen, 2001). The focus on masculine political infighting, its place in English history and debates about appropriate political succession are compelling. Two women act as plot-pivots: Joan of Arc and Queen Margaret of Anjou (married to Henry VI, mother to Prince Edward) who both take active political and martial roles, one for the French defence of territory and one for the continuity of the English succession. Both women either represent themselves, or are slandered by others, as demonic and both claim either 'the childbed privilege' (*Winter's Tale*, 3.2.101) or maternity as justification for action and survival. When Joan is captured and sentenced by the English army, she cries:

> Will nothing turn your unrelenting hearts?
> Then, Joan, discover thine infirmity,
> That warranteth by law to be thy privilege.
> I am with child, ye bloody homicides:
> Murder not then the fruit within my womb.
>
> (*1 Henry VI*, 5.4.59–63)

Her plea acts as stage-double for the play's gender politics; the female body is simultaneously sacred and crudely sexualized. As a body possibly bearing a child, her life might be saved: but as a body bearing a child, and unmarried, she is a sinner. The Englishmen's responses 'read' her performance of maternity sceptically: the Earl of Warwick and Richard subsequently compete in heaping insults on her. Shakespeare's introduction of a possibly pregnant body on stage – his own addition to the Chronicle versions inherited from the historians Holinshed and Hall – presents a number of key ideas. The audience has watched her as a military and political actor, engaging equally with men. In 5.3, Joan appears invoking thunder and fiends, where her representation as a performing witch focalizes her body as a site of demonized femininity. A witch's body was said to be the location for proofs of their demonic identity: warts, supernumerary nipples, moles and other bodily marks were 'read' as evidence of possession (Resource 9.a). The audience experiences this 'proof' in her performance of witchcraft and maternity, invited to read Joan's previous appearances retrospectively as part of her wily witchcraft against the English. When she claims pregnancy, the play contrasts the female body (simultaneously witch and potential child-bearer) as a 'naturally' deceptive foil to the masculine military and political success(ion) which the history play asserts. Anti-French sentiment is intensified by Joan's execution as a lying witch ('break thou to pieces and consume with ashes / Thou foul accursed minister of hell!' (5.5.94–5)). By

Maternal Bodies: Female Powers

positioning the female body as doubly 'other', physically and politically, female power appears dangerous to English masculinity. The play's narrative structure, then, reinforces an ideological political and physical opposition between a dangerous physical femininity and a (necessarily) dominant militaristic masculine (English) political state (see also Chapter 2).

Resource 9.a: *A detection of damnable driftes, practised by three witches arraigned at Chelmsforde in Essex, at the laste assizes there holden* (1579)

She also confesseth, that she knowes one Mother Osborne, a Widowe in the same toune to be a witche, and that she hath a marke in the ende of one of her fingers like a pitt, and an other marke uppon the outside of her right legge, whiche she thinketh to bee pluckt out by her Spirit: and that one Mother Waterhouse her owne sister (long since executed for Witchcrafte) had the selfsame markes, whiche she termeth nippes.

(fo.Av^{r-v})

Margaret of Anjou's characterization acts as counterweight and commentary to Joan's. Margaret attacks her husband because he wants to disinherit their son:

Who can be patient in such extremes?
Ah, wretched man! would I had died a maid
And never seen thee, never borne thee son,
Seeing thou hast proved so unnatural a father
Hath he deserved to lose his birthright thus?
Hadst thou but loved him half so well as I,
Or felt that pain which I did for him once,
Or nourish'd him as I did with my blood,
Thou wouldst have left thy dearest heart-blood there,
Rather than have that savage duke thine heir
And disinherited thine only son.

(*3 Henry VI*, 1.1.215–25)

Margaret's defence of her son uses explicit reminders of her maternal body ('borne thee', 'felt that pain' 'nourish'd him ... with my blood' (217, 221, 222)) in opposition to his 'unnatural' (218) father. The physical action of giving birth becomes validation of her own identity and her son's political rights, based on an implicit theory of the maternal as 'natural' and legitimate. The semantics of 'birthright' allow her to appropriate the conventional, legal term for patriarchal inheritance, linking it instead directly to the biological connection between a mother and her child, their legal and political rights and a mother's right to be engaged in that. This maternal intervention into a debate about rightful political (and inheritable) succession goes to the heart of the debate across Shakespeare's History plays about who has the right to rule: the most powerful, the most politically effective, the most royal, or the most manly (see also Chapter 2).

She continues:

> Had I been there, which am a silly woman,
> The soldiers should have toss'd me on their pikes
> Before I would have granted to that act.
> But thou preferr'st thy life before thine honour:
> And seeing thou dost, I here divorce myself
> Both from thy table, Henry, and thy bed,
> Until that act of parliament be repeal'd
> Whereby my son is disinherited.
>
> (1.1.243–50)

Having authorized herself through both her maternal body and her role as (political) nurturer of her son, she posits herself as the agent of divorce, honour and political and military action ('our army is ready; come we'll after them', 256). She has appropriated the discourse of maternity as power and protectiveness and inserted it into the political realm.

As a military leader she subsequently engages in stand-offs with male military leaders, when she demands:

> Where are your mess of sons to back you now?
> The wanton Edward, and the lusty George?
> And where's that valiant crook-back prodigy,
> Dicky your boy, that with his grumbling voice
> Was wont to cheer his dad in mutinies?
> Or with the rest where is your darling, Rutland?
> Look York, I stained this napkin with the blood
> That valiant Clifford with his rapier's point
> Made issue from the bosom of the boy.
>
> (1.4.73–81)

Maternal Bodies: Female Powers

Margaret's language moves between the mockery of belittling the adult masculinity of her opponents ('Dicky your boy ... to cheer his dad' (76–7)) and asserting her own martial active success ('I stain'd this napkin with the blood' (79)). At times she conjoins these two registers: ('with this rapier's point / Made issue from the bosom of the boy' (80–1)), troping her troops' military agency as both birth-producing and death-giving ('issue' (81)). She goes on to draw attention to her status as performer and power-broker in calling for a crown to mock-coronate Richard of York ('I .... do mock thee thus' (1.4.90)), a self-consciousness about the rhetorical performance of physical and cultural power. She uses tone and semantics to make her political power credible as a wife to a monarch and mother to the rightful heir, marshalling legalistic language to question the rebels' breaking of oaths of allegiance to a sitting monarch (1.4.100, 105), and the political succession. Richard's lengthy, misogynistic answer (1.4.97–146) demonizes her as the 'She-wolf of France .... How ill-beseeming is it in thy sex / To triumph, like an Amazonian trull' (111–14):

> Thou art as opposite to every good
> As the Antipodes are unto us,
> Or as the south to the septentrion.
> O tiger's heart wrapt in a woman's hide!
> How couldst thou drain the life-blood of the child,
> To bid the father wipe his eyes withal,
> And yet be seen to bear a woman's face?
> Women are soft, mild, pitiful and flexible;
> Thou stern, obdurate, flinty, rough, remorseless.
>
> (1.4.134–42)

Richard's rhetoric displaces the debate about the law and succession onto other cultural assumptions about how a woman should or should not act ('She-wolf of France', 'Amazonian trull' (111, 115)). He castigates her bloodline as inferior, poor and other: 'as opposite to every good / As the Antipodes to us' (134–5). He implies she is unwomanly ('And yet be seen to wear a woman's face?', 140), reinforced by listings of supposedly ideal feminine characteristics ('soft, mild, pitiful, flexible' (41)), which contrast with hers ('stern, obdurate, flinty, rough, remorseless' (42)). Richard downplays maternal femininity, demonizing her through discursive, ideologically conservative, misogyny. Yet, amidst the violent narrative and linguistic symbolism, the female body as a valiant survivor and counter-narrative to masculinist political histories resonates.

In the final act Margaret rallies her troops – a performance magnificently and powerfully articulated by Sophie Okenedo in the BBC *Hollow Crown* tetralogy in 2013–14 (Figure 9.1) – allying her own voice, actions and body to masculine leadership: 'Great lords, wise men ne'er sit and wail their loss, / … And, though unskilful, why not Ned and I / For once allow'd the skilful pilot's charge? / We will not from the helm to sit and weep' (5.4.1.19–21). Moments later she draws attention to the opposition between words and her (performing) female (weeping) body:

> Lords, knights, and gentlemen, what I should say
> My tears gainsay; for every word I speak,
> Ye see, I drink the water of mine eyes.
> Therefore, no more but this: Henry, your sovereign,
> Is prisoner to the foe; his state usurp'd,
> His realm a slaughter-house, his subjects slain,
> His statutes cancell'd and his treasure spent;
> And yonder is the wolf that makes this spoil.
> You fight in justice: then, in God's name, lords,
> Be valiant and give signal to the fight.
>
> (5.4.73–84)

Although she begins by referencing herself and her body through the first person pronoun ('my tears gainsay' (74)), she shifts the subject to Henry, reiterating his legal status and power ('his state … his realm … his subjects … his statutes .. his treasure' (77–9)). Her body speaks on behalf of her husband. Her attack on her son's murderers is an embodied, emotive exposure ('no no my heart will burst … so that my heart may burst' (5.5.59–60)). Her claim that their childlessness renders them remorseless ('you have no children, butchers' (63)) fleshes out an embodied maternal view of the impact and motivation of civil war as un-civil, un-familial, reinforced by the soon-to-be-Richard III's self-characterization as a monstrous birth, 'the midwife wondered and the women cried … I am myself alone' (5.6.74, 83).

The plot creates a narrative arc in which civil war and political disruption are gendered through maternal bodies in a number of contradictory ways. First, femininity is used as an insult against men seen to be un-martial or politically ineffective. Second, however, female bodies as performed on stage enact martial and political power in the absence of ineffective men. Third, in such appropriation of conventionally male roles, both women (Joan and Margaret) lose, first via demonization as witches or amazons and, second, via

Maternal Bodies: Female Powers

Figure 9.1 Sophie Okenedo as Margaret of Anjou in *The Hollow Crown: Henry VI Part 2* (Dominic Cook, BBC, 2016).

military defeat. However, emotional resonances amongst the audience draw us to Margaret's perspective as mother and public political figure; language, plot and visual physical enactment of female imprisonment simultaneously create the female body as dangerous and powerful, demonic and yet a possible agent of salvation (see Figure 9.1). But this remains an ambiguous negotiation of female agency: although Margaret is a tragic victim, she can be read as a symbol of ineffective political governance, as Richard himself suggests.

How can contemporary critical and theoretical debates about maternity and the female body help focus analyses of the plays? One of the most influential interpretative models is the psychoanalytic: as we saw in Chapter 8, Freud's model of the mother as an eroticized figure who threatens masculinity (the 'castration complex'; Freud, 1900) still informs critical and performative versions of *Hamlet* in particular; Zeffirelli's direction and casting of Glenn Close as Gertrude (1990) is a good example of the longevity of this interpretative tradition. Feminist challenges to Freud's model reframed identity by rejecting this demonization of the female body: feminist object-relations psychoanalytic theory argues instead that the male child's identity is formed through separation from the primacy of the maternal body, acknowledging such physical separation as the source of notions of difference and of woman as 'other' in masculine notions of the 'self'. The female child, recognizing her sameness to her mother, defines her identity as physically and bodily connected to others (see Adelman, 1992). Performative interpretations acknowledging this counter-Freudian tradition include the 2017 *All's Well That Ends Well* (Caroline Byrne, Sam Wanamaker Playhouse), in which the female characters explicitly shared commonalities based on maternal experience, in contradistinction to hyper-masculinized young men. One drawback of psychoanalytic approaches is the assumption that gender identity is formed through supposedly universal natural biological functions existing for all humans, no matter the time or place.

Materialist readings of maternity and maternal bodies have been influenced by the work of De Beauvoir and Foucault, arguing that motherhood (like other identities) is constructed and ideological, and that conventions of the maternal body and assumptions about motherhood as a universal condition of femininity are policed ideologically throughout society, education and popular culture. This theoretical and political engagement with motherhood has situated the discourses of motherhood as necessity and conformity within the political, medical and historical situation of early modern patriarchal ideologies and practices (Crawford and Mendleson, 2000; Moncrief and McPherson, 2007). Doran's 1999 *Winter's Tale* (RSC) reflected this historicized version of both maternity and masculinity through the visual sympathetic lighting and the warmly maternal yet sexy characterization of Hermione by Alexandra Gilbreath.

Feminist articulations of the importance of embodiment have emphasized the experiential nature of the female body: identical to her mother, menstruating, birthing, menopausal, more commonly subject to violent sexual assault, experienced as economically and spatially different to that of men. A woman's body will bear the marks of both biology and life experiences. These anthropological and sociological interventions have nuanced an object-relations acknowledgement of the specificity of female bodily experiences with historicized and place-based knowledge (Bordo, 2003; Grosz, 1995). Theories of embodiment as constitutive and contingent have influenced queer, non-white, post-colonial and trans engagements with Shakespeare (Traub, 2016b) and discussions about cross-casting by theatre companies like Cheek by Jowl, Propeller (their all-male *Winter's Tale*, for example) and Shakespeare's Globe's original practices productions under Mark Rylance. Given Shakespeare's female characters are written for adolescent or possibly even what today we might define as trans actors (Wells, 2009), his stage and plays should instead suggest embodiment be conceived as acting a knowledge at one moment in time and space (Grosz, 2017) or that the creative reimagining of female bodies in different formations through performance can open up what we understand by female bodies in time and space (Haraway, 2003, 2016). Casting and directing – for example using race-blind casting, or enabling men, women and trans actors to be cross-cast – can play a huge part in opening up such debates.

Judith Butler's theory of performed identity can inform notions of the maternal body as constructed and socially and politically performed: a body that can be deconstructed and appropriated as needed (Orgel, 1996; Shapiro, 1996). Maternity as performed on stage has been most explicitly reconfigured through non-female bodies in all-male productions or male casting of mothers, albeit rarely (for example, Pohlmeier's production of Q1 *Hamlet* (Two Gents, 2008) and Edward Hall's *Winter's Tale* (Propeller, 2012)). Such casting should theoretically queer maternity but, for example, the Two Gents' gestural interpretation of maternity (Gertrude's palm gesture at her face) was a conventional emblematic gesture signifying shame, reinforcing maternity as 'other' through re-inscribing masculinist notions of female abjection. Future productions might see the casting of older women or trans actors to explore how performed and biological gender intersect in character articulation on stage.

When Claudio in *Measure for Measure* explains that Juliet's physically visible pregnancy proves a crime of extramarital sex, four key points about pregnancy are highlighted. First, Juliet's pregnant body is visibly displayed ('character too gross is writ on Juliet' (1.2.144)) and paraded across the stage as a shaming act. Second, men talk about women's bodies over women's silence, an objectification that demonizes and others her voice and body. Third, a pregnant body as shameful evidence of unlawful sexuality triggers the plot for a play about both male and female sexuality. Fourth, pregnancy is an outward bodily sign of sexual activity for women when such activity for men is invisible. This visibility and 'legibility' of women's bodies and sexuality within early modern patriarchal culture is one that traverses a number of discourses: medical, conduct literature and law (Resource 9.b).

All's Well That Ends Well addresses these notions from a woman's perspective through a female central protagonist with agency over her own body: Helena, in reward for her medical healing of the King, demands Bertram as her prize (see Chapter 3). Helena's solution to Bertram's riddling rejection is the bed-trick, which culminates in the finale at the King of France's court with her appearing visibly pregnant alongside Diana and the widow to provide witnessed proof that she has met Bertram's supposedly impossible conditions. Diana acknowledges the reparative female response to Bertram's original riddling language, with a version of female discourse ('my riddle'):

DIANA
> ... He knows himself my bed he hath defiled;
> And at that time he got his wife with child:
> Dead though she be, she feels her young one kick:
> So there's my riddle: one that's dead is quick:
> And now behold the meaning.

Enter HELENA *and the* WIDOW

KING OF FRANCE   Is there no exorcist
> Beguiles the truer office of mine eyes?
> Is't real that I see?

HELENA   No, my good lord;
> 'Tis but the shadow of a wife you see,
> The name and not the thing.

BERTRAM   Both, both. O, pardon!

HELENA
> O my good lord, when I was like this maid,
> I found you wondrous kind. There is your ring;
> And, look you, here's your letter; this it says:
> *When from my finger you can get this ring*
> *And are by me with child*, etc. This is done:
> Will you be mine, now you are doubly won?

BERTRAM
> If she, my liege, can make me know this clearly,
> I'll love her dearly, ever, ever dearly

HELENA
> If it appear not plain and prove untrue,
> Deadly divorce step between me and you!

(5.3.298–316)

Diana's language frames their actions as a reparative female riddle, but Helena uses legal and performatively demonstrative language ('there is your ring ... here's your letter' (308–9)). She claims five proofs to legitimate her status as Bertram's legal wife: her literal appearance back from apparent death; her possession of his ring; her visible pregnancy ('she feels her young one kick' (300)); Diana and the Widow's testimony; and the citation of Bertram's previous letter as an enforceable contract. Helena frames her physical embodiment ('this is done' is gestural (311)) as alive and pregnant within the cited symbols of marriage (ring and contract), testified to by, and in front of, witnesses. Helena reconstructs and engineers an early modern marriage ceremony and the equivalent of an early modern legal court in which women could bring cases of slander (Gowing, 1999). Helena uses her (pregnant) body as an emblem of her marital rights in a private relationship, within the court of public opinion and in the world of social and political status. This public forum is how adolescent masculinity (represented by Bertram) comes to adult knowledge ('can make me know this clearly' (313)). Caroline Byrne's 2017 production characterized Bertram (Will Merrick) as a self-regarding, self-obsessed man, one of the lads defining himself in contradistinction to adult women. The play's resolution has always posed this question – can this boy-man reconcile himself to the real body of a woman? Both Byrne's version and Dove's 2011 production (Shakespeare's Globe) tried to finesse the issue by presenting the baby already born, with Bertram cooing over his offspring as a delighted new father, whereas the original text gives him only two and a half lines promising repentance (5.3.307, 313–14).

The state of pregnancy was a mysterious condition in the early modern period – how can we know the signs when the body itself is often unknowable and traitorous (Resource 9.b)? The pregnant body is a visual physical and emblematic symbol of the tensions of early modern fatherhood and masculinity as much as the embodiment of an essential femininity. Helena has used that symbolism to attain her own legitimacy and prove herself legal agent of her own destiny. Perhaps it is the active female agency, located in female bodies, and its challenges to conventional early modern patriarchy that have led critics to label this as a 'problem' play.

Resource 9.b: Jacques Guillemeau, *Child-birth or the Happy Deliverie of Women* (1612)

The signes to know whether a woman be with childe, or no.
A Chirurgion must bee very circumspect, in determining whether a woman be conceiued, or no; because many have prejudiced their knowledge, and discretion, by judging rashly hereof. For there is nothing more ridiculous, then to assure a woman that shee is with childe; and afterward, that her naturall sicknesse, or store of water should come from her: and instead of a childe, some windie matter should break from her, and so her belly fall, and grow flat againe: which hath hapned unto many men, that have beene well esteemed, both for their learning, and experience.

(p. 2)

Shakespeare and Gender

The Winter's Tale can be read as a disquisition on anxious masculinity (see Chapter 8). However, it is equally a play about motherhood, the maternal body, the aged woman's body and redemption through female power(s). Act 2 opens with mother, son and attendants:

> 1 LADY   Hark ye,
> The queen, your mother, rounds apace. We shall
> Present our services to a fine new prince
> One of these days, and then you'd wanton with us
> If we would have you.
> 2 LADY   She is spread of late
> Into a goodly bulk: good time encounter her!
> HERMIONE
> What wisdom stirs amongst you? Come, sir, now
> I am for you again. Pray you sit by us,
> And tell's a tale.
> MAMILLIUS   Merry or sad shall't be?
> HERMIONE
> As merry as you will.
> MAMILLIUS
> A sad tale's best for winter. I have one
> Of sprites and goblins.
> HERMIONE   Let's have that, good sir.
> Come on, sit down, come on, and do your best
> To fright me with your sprites. You're powerful at it.
> MAMILLIUS
> There was a man –
> HERMIONE   Nay, come sit down; then on.
> MAMILLIUS
> Dwelt by a churchyard – I will tell it softly,
> Yon crickets shall not hear it.
> HERMIONE   Come on then,
> And give't me in mine ear.
>
> (2.1.15–32)

The intimacy between mother and son acts as an iconic memento throughout the subsequent tragic narrative. Mamillius's very name echoes his bodily connection to his mother (mam/mama/mammary). His precocious knowledge about the world and his open speech suggest a physical and intellectual freedom which acts as a counterpoint to the claustrophobic male court. His physical attachment to his mother enrages Leontes and motivates his banishment from Hermione in the next part of the scene (arguably a confrontation between a Freudian and an object-relations psychic model of identity). This quiet moment is all the more resonant because of the audience's anticipation of Leontes' building anger and the suppressed violence witnessed in Act 1 (see Chapter 8). The all-women social space in which children are nurtured and loved opens in what feels momentarily like safety: although they tell scary fairy stories it is with laughter; a child patterns out women's faces with their hands; child and women receive and offer kisses and play; Mamillius sits on their laps and whispers in their ears. Hermione's words help the actor perform a pregnant body: pushing Mamillius away she quickly returns after moving around ('come sir now / I am for you again' (21–2)). The comments that 'she rounds apace' and 'is spread of late / Into a goodly bulk' (16, 19–20) enable actor and director to use dialogue to frame stage action. Hermione's 'What wisdom stirs amongst you?' (21) posits this female-dominated space as a place of serious knowledge and gossip: of childbirth, motherhood, children and ancient tales. This feminized space and knowledge – emblematically signalled through the pregnant body on stage – is literally invaded and destroyed by Leontes. The validation of a female realm of knowledge through maternity and motherhood gathered strength during the early modern period, reflected in published and manuscript writings by women on motherhood and household topics, which acknowledged voice, audience and space of female knowledge (see Resource 9.c and Chapter 1).

Resource 9.c: Elizabeth Grymeston, *Miscellenea. Meditations. Memoratives* (1604)

To her louing sonne *Bernye Grymeston*.
MY dearest sonne, there is nothing so strong as the force of love; there is no love so forcible as the love of an affectionate mother to hir naturall childe: there is no mother can either more affectionately shew hir nature, or more naturally manifest hir affection, than in advising hir children out of hir owne experience, to eschue euill, and encline them to do that which is good; ... I resolved to break the barren soile of my fruitlesse braine, to dictate something for thy direction; the rather for that as I am now a dead woman among the living.

(fo.A3^r)

Act 2's narrative structure offers further feminized perspectives on the action: 2.1 displays the relationship between mother and son, and its destruction by a father and husband; 2.2 sees Paulina's discussion with the midwife Emilia about the premature birth of Hermione's daughter; and 2.3 the encounter between Paulina and Leontes in the masculine world of the court in which Leontes violently rejects his daughter. Although the birthing scene is sandwiched between scenes of paternal denial, all scenes show women arguing back and asserting alternative versions of events and knowledge.

In that third scene (discussed in Chapter 1), Paulina's language remains simultaneously respectful ('loyal servant') and rooted in her status as a woman of knowledge ('physician ... obedient counsellor' (2.3.54–5)). By contrast, Leontes uses misogynist insults to attack her knowledge and status by attacking her husband directly as well as her: 'Thou dotard; thou art woman-tired, unroosted' (2.3.73). However, Paulina controls the stage space. She puts the child down, she tells Antigonus not to touch her or the child. Leontes' accusations of her as a witch, a bawd, Dame Partlet, and 'crone' (66, 67, 75, 76), his insults against his courtiers' manliness and his order to remove her are all violent whirlwinds surrounding Paulina and baby on stage. Visually, we are drawn to that still centre: a female body, protected by an older woman, around which the anxiety of masculine knowledge rails. Paulina's final argument, which focuses on the child's bodily identity, suggests paternal imprinting is visible:

> It is yours,
> And might we lay th'old proverb to your charge,
> So like you, 'tis the worse. Behold, my lords,
> Although the print be little, the whole matter
> And copy of the father – eye, nose, lip,
> The trick of's frown, his forehead, nay, the valley,
> The pretty dimples of his chin and cheek, his smiles,
> The very mould and frame of hand, nail, finger.
> And thou, good goddess Nature, which hast made it
> So like to him that got it.
>
> (2.3.94–103)

Paulina's argument to prove paternity assumes visible paternal printing on (and ownership of) the body of the female child: 'the whole

Maternal Bodies: Female Powers

matter / And copy of the father' (97–8). Leontes, however, apprehends that a man cannot *know* paternity. Female and male knowledge is thus contrasted, although Paulina tries to imply it is about both trust and visible physical attributes.

Resource 9.d: *Mrs Thimelby, On the Death of Her Only Child* (late 1630s)

Deare Infant 'twas thy mother's fault
So soone inclos'd thee in a vault
And father's good, that in such hast
Has my sweet child in heaven plac'd.
I'le weep the first as my offence,
Then joy that he made recompence:
Yet must confesse my frailty such
My joy by grief's exceeded much:
Though I, in reason, know thy blisse
Can not be wish'd more than it is,
Yet this selfe love orerules me so;
I'de have thee here, or with thee goe.
But since that now neyther can be,
A virtue of necessitie
I yet may make, now all my pelf
Content for thee, though not myself.

Hermione explicitly draws attention to the bodily state of the postpartum woman and her appearance when she enters for the trial scene in 3.2. The maternal body, which would usually have been nursed and nurtured amongst female friends for up to six weeks, appears in a public court lactating ('from my breast, / The innocent milk in it most innocent mouth, / Haled out to murder' (3.2.97–9)), bleeding and exhausted ('the childbed privilege denied, which 'longs / To women of all fashion, lastly hurried / Here, to this place, i'th' open air, before / I have got strength of limit' (3.2.101–4)). Her words tell the actor to perform maternity as physical endurance (whatever the actor's gender) and as universal to all mothers, no matter their class ('women of all fashion' (102)). The female body we see and hear on stage is

Figure 9.2 Alexandra Gilbreath as Hermione, *The Winter's Tale* (Gregory Doran, Royal Shakespeare Company, 1998). Photo by Bob Collier © RSC.

on trial and emblematizes the cost of early modern patriarchal notions of gender and power. This emotional cost is present in Mrs Thimbleby's poem on the death of her child (Resource 9.d) and the physical and emotional cost in Alexandra Galbraith's representation of Hermione in Doran's 1998 RSC production (Figure 9.2).

Resource 9.e: Aemilia Lanyer, *Salve Deus Rex Judeorum* (1611)

To the Queenes most Excellent Majestie.
Renowned Empresse, and great Britaines Queene,
Most gratious Mother of succeeding Kings;
Vouchsafe to view that which is seldome seene,
A Womans writing of divinest things:
Reade it faire Queene, though it defective be,
Your Excellence can grace both It and Mee.

*

And since all Arts at first from Nature came,
That goodly Creature, Mother of Perfection,
Whom *Ioues* almighty hand at first did frame,

Taking both her and hers in his protection:
Why should not She now grace my barren Muse,
And in a Woman all defects excuse.

(fo.a3ʳ ff)

Aemilia Lanyer's female-centred dedications to, and content of, her poem *Salve Deus Rex Judeorum* (1611, Resource 9.e) celebrates female knowledge as embodied in the stories and voices of women. Anne of Denmark (James I's wife) was the dedicatee of Lanyer's poem and her pregnancies were publicly discussed, both as gossip and as matter for reassurance about peaceful political succession. When James was on his way to England for his coronation, he had insisted his son be removed from his mother. Anne's fury and subsequent travel to retrieve him had (reportedly) caused her to miscarry. Her portrait (Figure 9.3) emblematizes her pregnant body alongside a crown and a dog (symbolic of her status and faithfulness). Publicly, the pregnant body was a symbol of male primogeniture and succession figured through the female body but, at the same time, the unknowability of the female body appeared threatening. Did such representations confine that body to patriarchal prescriptions or suggest alternative subaltern female identities?

The play's overall narrative structure radically plays out ideas about maternity. For example, Acts 1 and 2 exist in counterpoint, the first displaying a hyper-masculinized world, the second a more feminized one. Act 3 functions as the public clash between those worlds in the trial and its aftermath, the loss of both children and apparent death of Hermione, an ostensibly tragic elucidation of the cost of a patriarchal denial of maternal power(s). The plot device of a sixteen-year gap, a daughter rediscovered and a political future re-figured through the marriage of Polixenes and Leontes' children, offers a non-tragic outcome by changing the narrative away from jealous masculinity. The popular Jacobean reception of the Italian Guarinis's *Faithful Shepherd* (1602) and his preface's suggestion that tragicomedy's 'happy reversal' and 'comic order' proffer dramatic ways of resolving tragic conflicts undoubtedly influenced Shakespeare's thinking about genre. The critical tradition surrounding the late plays has located closing reunions as redemptive and inclusive: however, maternal embodiment within tragicomedy can complicate and deepen such interpretations.

Figure 9.3 Unknown artist, portrait probably depicting Anne of Denmark (*c.* 1605). Private collection, image produced by auction house Dorotheum.

In the finale, Paulina unveils the life-like statue of Hermione (sixteen-years dead), offering to enable the statue to 'take you by the hand' (5.3.89). As stage manager and director, she instructs/authorizes Hermione:

> PAULINA   Music, awake her; strike!   (*Music*)
> [*to* HERMIONE] 'Tis time; descend; be stone no more; approach.
> Strike all that look upon with marvel. Come,
> I'll fill your grave up. Stir – nay, come away;

Maternal Bodies: Female Powers

> Bequeath to death your numbness, for from him
> Dear life redeems you. You perceive she stirs.
>   HERMIONE *steps down.*
> Start not. Her actions shall be holy as
> You hear my spell is lawful. [*to* LEONTES] Do not shun her
> Until you see her die again, for then
> You kill her double. Nay, present your hand.
> When she was young, you wooed her; now in age,
> Is she become the suitor?
> LEONTES   O, she's warm!
> If this be magic, let it be an art
> Lawful as eating.
> POLIXENES   She embraces him.
> CAMILLO
> She hangs about his neck;
> If she pertain to life, let her speak too!
>   (5.3.98–113)

Paulina's incantatory opening words to the statue evoke sacral and magical rhythms, while the content connotes the resurrection of Christ, early modern notions of witchcraft and the process of birth itself. Paulina's role is therefore divine and demonic (her actions 'holy as ... my spell is lawful' (104–5)): she directs both actors on stage ('present your hand / When she was young you wooed her; now in age / Is she become the suitor?' (108–10)). Yet, these directions appear to restore patriarchal reverential order. While Hermione does not speak to Leontes, courtiers comment on the reunion, particularly on Hermione's body ('she hangs about his neck' (112)), a physical performance of what seems to be wifely subjection. Paulina's magical intervention and the rediscovery of a lost daughter and a lost queen suggest a narrative arc in which women act as sacral (and quite silent) symbols of the restoration of patriarchal values. The women have returned respectively to father and husband and Paulina directs Leontes in the appropriate gestural modes of hetero-patriarchal behaviour (see also Chapter 1).

However, this reading is problematized both by Paulina as female agent of this reconciliation, and by the closure:

> PAULINA   That she is living,
> Were it but told you, should be hooted at
> Like an old tale. But it appears she lives,

> Though yet she speak not. Mark a little while.
> [*to* PERDITA] Please you to interpose, fair madam. Kneel,
> And pray your mother's blessing. [*to* HERMIONE] Turn, good lady,
> Our Perdita is found.
> HERMIONE   You gods, look down,
> And from your sacred vials pour your graces
> Upon my daughter's head! Tell me, mine own,
> Where hast thou been preserved? Where lived? How found
> Thy father's court? For thou shalt hear that I,
> Knowing by Paulina that the oracle
> Gave hope thou wast in being, have preserved
> Myself to see the issue.
> PAULINA   There's time enough for that,
>
> (5.3.115–28)

Hermione speaks directly only to her daughter and not to her husband. As she becomes fully human, with language as well as movement, she transforms from the abject passive body into the active mother. Her motivation in staying alive was 'to see the issue' (128). This wording explicitly echoes the oracle's judgement in Act 3 ('the king himself will live without an issue if that which is lost be not found' (3.2.132–3)). Hermione's voice therefore links the supra-authority of a divine judgement with her own actions and with her reunion with her daughter, eliminating male agency. This conversation is between three women (although Perdita speaks very briefly) and the relationship between mother and daughter provides the emotional closure, not that between either father and daughter or husband and wife. Matriarchal rather than patriarchal values are promised – a symbolic closure which echoes the pastoral and fructive imagery surrounding Perdita's language and characterization in Act 4. Perdita's plea to the goddess Proserpina (4.4.106) explicitly evokes the story of Ceres and Proserpina. The female goddess of fertility who rescued her daughter from the underworld (where Pluto, the king of hell, had dragged her) for six months of the year is a symbolic female narrative of seasonal cyclicity, of alternate winter and summer in which female power and agency triumph. This resonant female-centred narrative echoes through the plot (and title) of *The Winter's Tale*. Women are characterized as active agents to the cyclical rhythms of non-linear time (reversing death through their connection to birth). They pattern out a radical re-reading and re-performing of female powers and potential. Blanche Macintyre's 2018 production (Shakespeare's Globe) drew on this kind of interpretation in Hermione's regally pregnant body as symbolic of a beneficient earthly maternity.

Maternal Bodies: Female Powers

However, this momentary pause on female-centric experience is partially countered by the play's final speech, and Leontes' insertion back into the women-only reconciliation. Leontes' closing words cannot tell us how the characters on stage respond: many productions have focused on the notion of reconciliation as confirmed between Hermione and Leontes, as in Doran's 1998 RSC production. However, other productions, such as Donnellan's in 1999 (Maly Theatre), show Leontes as an uneasy third party in the family reunion. Donnellan's production used white lighting and make-up to emphasize the physical ravages of the terrible events which Leontes' anxious masculinity had evoked, and the women stood together against Leontes in the finale. This dissonance is arguably present in his final long speech of twenty uninterrupted lines (135–55) spoken in complicity with Polixenes ('by us a pair of kings' (146)). He begins by engineering a husband for Paulina, and then turns to Hermione:

> What? Look upon my brother. Both your pardons,
> That e'er I put between your holy looks
> My ill suspicion. This your son-in-law,
> And son unto the king, whom heavens directing,
> Is troth-plight to your daughter. Good Paulina,
> Lead us from hence, where we may leisurely
> Each one demand and answer to his part
> Performed in this wide gap of time since first
> We were dissevered. Hastily lead away.
> *Exeunt.*
>
> (5.3.147–55)

Leontes' insistence that he will find a husband for Paulina, physically manoeuvring Camillo and Paulina on stage ('Come Camillo take her by the hand' (143)) shows that Paulina's body becomes subject to the King as an object exchanged 'between men', although his 'lead us from hence' (152) potentially suggests a kind of equality as Paulina takes the lead off the stage. His direct contract with Polixenes (146) confirms the dynastic political union between their children as patriarchally satisfying. The empowering of female agency and the maternal and ageing female body through plot and characterization in Paulina, Hermione and Perdita, are framed by a very conventional ending. The dissonance of these two endings (that framed by women, and that framed by men) was explicitly brought to the fore in MacIntyre's 2018 production (Shakespeare's Globe) in the groupings of characters on stage. But how is

Leontes' own speech and character framed here? Is it an awkward ending given all that has gone before? Does the play suggest that maternal love and the maternal experience are a distinctive counter-narrative to the early modern patriarchal imperative? Or is that agency merely swallowed up by the reassertion of political and husbandly authority? Perhaps these are questions that have different answers in each individual production, even performance, or in each particular reading.

> **Resource 9.f: Constantia Mundi, *To the Right Worshipful lady her Most Dear Mother, the Lady Prudentia Mundi* from, *The Worming of a Mad Dogge* (1617)**
>
> As, first, your paines in bearing me was such
> A benefit beyond requitall that 'twere much
> To thinke what pangs of sorrows you sustain'd
> In child-birth, when mine infancy obtain'd
> The vitall drawing-in of ayre, so your love,
> Mingled with care, hath shewen it selfe above
> The ordinary course of nature: seeing you still
> Are in perpetuall labour with me, even untill
> The second birth of education perfect me:
> You travaill still, though Churched oft you be.
>
> (pp. 1–2)

Conclusions

1. The narrative arc of history plays situate female bodies as simultaneously problematic threats to national stability and central to the continuity of that stability, since only women's bodies can bear children. The necessity of controlling women's bodies in the interests of maintaining patriarchal legitimacy is repeatedly figured in the history plays' stories. Yet equally, these plays recognize masculine aggression and violence as the cause of civil war and civil discord: so emblematically 'pure' female bodies may offer salvation and security against such civil war (Katherine in *Henry V*, for example). The complex discourses surrounding Margaret of Anjou in the *Henry VI* plays (heroine and demonized mother) offer powerful legitimate spheres of action for a mother when defending her children.

Maternal Bodies: Female Powers

2. When pregnant mothers' bodies appear on stage, they are often emblematized to signal ideas about female sexuality and agency. In *Measure for Measure*, for example, Julietta's body symbolizes the city's sinfulness; in *All's Well That Ends Well*, Helena's pregnant body emblematizes her successful intervention in Bertram's riddle of masculine control; and in *The Winter's Tale* Hermione's pregnant and then maternal body pattern out first the threat of Leontes' suspicions and second, Hermione's fructive power as an alternative narrative to that of anxious masculinity (see Resources 9.f and 9.g)

Resource 9.g: Aemilia Lanyer, *Salve Deus Rex Judeorum* (1611)

Till now your indiscretion sets us free,
And makes our former fault much lesse appeare;
Our Mother *Eve*, who tasted of the Tree,
Giving to *Adam* what shee held most deare,
Was simply good, and had no powre to see,
The after-comming harme did not appeare:
The subtile Serpent that our Sex betraide,
Before our fall so sure a plot had laide.

(fo.D1^r)

3. Mothers in the tragedies (*Hamlet, Coriolanus, Macbeth*, for example) are often associated with corruption of masculine virtue and with a dangerous and invasive sexuality. In the history plays and comedies discussed in this chapter, such notions of dangerous maternity are mocked as male fantasies through the action, and seen as part-causation of a hero's fall. In comedy and tragi-comedy Shakespeare moves beyond the narrative teleology of masculine tragedy and offers up alternative models of maternal agency – creating female worlds in which women give alternative versions of femininity and maternity (see Resource 9.e and Chapter 6).

4. In the late plays, female bodies attain a sacral quality: Miranda in *The Tempest*, the re-born Hermione in *The Winter's Tale*, the re-born Innogen in *Cymbeline*. Women symbolize the promise of a new life. Unusually, *The Winter's Tale* offers such re-birth of a

maternal body, rather than that of an innocent virgin: the (ageing) female body is given agency, within a patriarchal symbolic economy.
5. Women's voices and perspectives on identity, children, birthing and nature begin to be validated through plot and characterization as necessary to a new world, and the salvation of men. The plays discussed in this chapter offer a critique of the notion of Shakespeare as a 'patriarchal bard' (McCluskie, 1989).

Further Work

1. Look at maternity in *Hamlet*, *Coriolanus* and *Macbeth*. How do characterization and maternal agency drive and inform plot and notions of tragedy?
2. How does Miranda's characterization in *The Tempest* denote ideas about women as islands and consequent notions of political identity? How does the emblematic revelation of her and Ferdinand playing chess reinforce or complicate these notions? How does Sycorax (Caliban's absent, dead mother) haunt the play's narrative? If we assume she is black (since she came from Algiers), albeit 'blue-eyed' (1.2.269), how and why does black maternity act as a choral undercurrent to Prospero's (white) patriarchal empire?
3. *Henry VIII* closes on the birth of the future Elizabeth I (appearing on stage as a baby for her christening). How does this female (never-to-be-maternal) body haunt many of Shakespeare's plays and the way critics read them?

Further Reading

Janet Adelman, *Suffocating Mothers: Fantasises of Maternal Origin from 'Hamlet' to 'The Tempest'* (Routledge, 1992). **Still influential and insightful study of the plays in the light of feminist object-relations psychoanalytic theory.**
Patricia Crawford, *Blood, Bodies and Families in Early Modern England* (Routledge, 2004). **Materialist and contextual account of maternal experiences in the period.**
Gail Kern Paster, *The Body Embarrassed: Drama and the Disciplines of Shame in Early Modern England* (Cornell University Press, 1993). **Foundational account**

of how humoral theories of the body impacted notions of femininity, maternal bodies, and masculine attitudes to femininity.

Chris Laoutaris, *Shakespearean Maternities: Crises of Conception in Early Modern England* (Edinburgh University Press, 2008). **Ground-breaking investigation of images of maternity and conception, from magical to medical and their location in the plays.**

Fiona McNeil, *Poor Women in Shakespeare* (Cambridge University Press, 2007). **Account of how marginal women in the plays act as ciphers to and commentaries on broader notions of femininity and maternity.**

Kathryn McPherson and Kathryn Moncrieff, *Performing Maternity in Early Modern England* (Routledge, 2016). **Series of essays on representing and performing maternity in plays, journals and conduct literature.**

BIBLIOGRAPHY

Arden Third Series play editions quoted, unless otherwise specified:

All's Well That Ends Well, ed. Suzanne Gossett and Helen Wilcox (2018)
As You Like It, ed. Juliet Dusinberre (2006)
The Comedy of Errors, ed. Kent Cartwright (2016)
Cymbeline, ed. Valerie Wayne (2017)
Hamlet, eds Ann Thompson and Neil Taylor (2016)
King Henry IV Part 1, ed. David Scott Kastan (2002)
King Henry IV Part 2, ed. James C. Bulman (2016)
King Henry V, ed. T. W. Craik (1999)
King Henry VI Part 1, ed. Edward Burns (2000)
King Henry VI Part 2, ed. Ronald Knowles (1999)
King Henry VI Part 3, eds John D. Cox and Eric Rasmussen (2001)
King Lear, ed. R. A. Foakes (1997)
Measure for Measure (Second Series), ed. J. W. Lever (1967)
The Merchant of Venice, ed. John Drakakis (2011)
Much Ado About Nothing, ed. Claire McEachern (2016)
Othello, eds Ayanna Thompson and E. A. J. Honigmann (2016)
Pericles, ed. Suzanne Gossett (2004)
Richard II, ed. Charles R. Forker (2002)
Richard III, ed. James R. Siemon (2009)
The Taming of the Shrew, ed. Barbara Hodgdon (2010)
The Tempest, eds Alden T. Vaughan and Virginia Mason Vaughan (2011)
Twelfth Night, ed. Kier Elam (2014)
Two Noble Kinsmen, ed. Lois Potter (2015)
The Winter's Tale, ed. John Pitcher (2010)

Productions

All's Well That Ends Well
John Dove, Shakespeare's Globe, 2011
Caroline Byrne, Sam Wanamaker, 2017

As You Like It
Declan Donnellan, Cheek by Jowl, 1991–4, 2014
Kenneth Branagh, 2006, UK/USA

Michelle Terry, Shakespeare's Globe, 2018, 2019
Kimberley Sykes, RSC, 2019

The Comedy of Errors
Blanche McIntyre, Shakespeare's Globe, 2014

Hamlet
Franco Zeffirelli, 1990, USA
Kenneth Branagh, 1996, UK/USA
Michael Almereyda, 2000, USA
Gregory Doran, RSC, 2008
(Q1) Arne Pohlmeier, Two Gents Productions, 2008
Lindsey Turner, The Barbican, 2015

Henry VI
Dominic Cook, *The Hollow Crown*, BBC, 2016

King Lear
Trevor Nunn, RSC, 2007
Richard Eyre, 2018, UK/USA

Measure for Measure
Yuri Butusov, Shakespeare's Globe, 2012
Gregory Doran, RSC, 2019

The Merry Wives of Windsor
Fiona Laird, RSC, 2018

Much Ado About Nothing
Kenneth Branagh, 1993, UK/USA
Gregory Doran, RSC, 2002
Marianne Elliott, RSC 2006
Joss Whedon, 2012, USA
Mark Rylance, The Old Vic, 2013

Othello
Orson Welles, 1952, USA
Trevor Nunn, RSC, 1989
Trevor Nunn, 1990, UK
Oliver Parker, 1995, UK/USA

Richard II
Deborah Warner, National Theatre, 1995
Gregory Doran, RSC, 2013
Adjoa Andoh with Lynette Lynton, Wanamaker Playhouse, 2019

Bibliography

The Taming of the Shrew
Michael Bogdanov, RSC, 1978
Bill Alexander, RSC, 1992
Phyllida Lloyd, Shakespeare's Globe, 2003
Toby Frow, Shakespeare's Globe, 2012
10 Things I Hate About You, Gil Junger, 1999, USA

Twelfth Night
Trevor Nunn, 1996, UK
Tim Supple, 2003, UK
Gregory Doran, RSC, 2009
Simon Godwin, National Theatre, 2016
Christopher Luscombe, RSC, 2017–18

The Two Noble Kinsmen
Blanche McIntyre, RSC, 2016

The Winter's Tale
Declan Donnellan, Cheek by Jowl, 1999
Gregory Doran, RSC, 1998–1999
Edward Hall, Propeller, 2012
Blanche MacIntyre, Shakespeare's Globe, 2018

Primary Texts

Anon. (1681) *The Valarous Acts performed at GAUNT,/By the brave Bonny Lass Mary Ambree*. London: J. Wright.
Anon. (1579) *A detection of damnable driftes, practised by three witches arraigned at Chelmsforde*. London: Edward White.
Anon. (1640) *The cruell shrow: or, The patient mans woe Declaring the misery, and the great paine, by his unquiet wife he doth dayly sustaine*. London: M Parsons.
Bentley, Thomas. (1582) *A Monument to Matrons conteining seven severall lamps of virginitie, or distinct treatises*. London: H. Denham.
Bright, Thomas. (1586) *A Treatise on Melancholie*. London: Thomas Vautrollier.
Burton, Robert. (1621) *Anatomy of Melancholy*. Oxford: John Lichfield.
Cawdry, Robert. (1600) *A Treasurie or Storehouse of Similes*. London: Thomas Creede.
Church of England. (1559) *Certayne sermons appoynted by the Quenes Maiestie*. London: Richard Jugge and John Cawood.
Cleaver, Robert. (1615) *A briefe explanation of the whole booke of the Prouerbs of Salomon*. London: Felix Kyngston.
Crooke, Helkiah. (1615) *Microcosmographia: a description of the body of man*. London: William Jaggard.
Dod, John and Cleaver, Robert. (1598, 1630) *A Godly Form of Household Government*. London: Elliot's Court Press.

Bibliography

Elizabeth I. (1588) Speech at Tilbury. BL, BL Harley 6798, f.87.
Foxe, John. (1563) *Actes and Monumentes*. London: John Day.
Gentillet, Innocent. (1602) *A discourse upon the meanes of well governing*, trans. Simon Patericke. London: Adam Islip.
Gosson, Stephen. (1579) *The Schoole of Abuse*. London: Thomas Woodcock.
Griffith, Matthew. (1633) *Bethel or, A forme for families in which all sorts, of both sexes, are so squared, and framed by the Word of God*. London: Richard Badger.
Grymeston, Elizabeth. (1604) *Miscellenea. Meditations. Memoratives*. London: Melch. Bradwood.
Guarini, Battista. (1602) *Il Pastor Fido; or the Faithfull Shepherd*. London: Thomas Creed.
Guazzo, Stefano. (1607) *The Court of Good Counsell*. London: Ralph Blower.
Guillemeau, Jacques. (1612) *Child-birth or the Happy Deliverie of Women*. London: A Hatfield.
Jorden, Edward. (1603) *A Brief Discourse of the Disease of the Suffocation of the Mother*. London: John Windet.
Lanyer, Aemilia. (1611) *Salve Deus Rex Judeorum*. London: Valentine Simmes.
Marston, John. (1602) *Antonio and Mellida*. London: Richard Bradock.
Mundi, Constantia. (1617) *The Worming of a Mad Dogge*. London: Laurence Hayes.
Norden, John. (1600) *Vicissitudo Rerum*. London: Simon Stafford.
Plowden, Edmund. ([1588] 1761) *The Commentaries, or Reports of Edward Plowden*, trans. Francis Hargrave. London: In Ædibus Richardi Tottelli.
Smith, Henry. (1591) *A Preparative to Marriage*. London: R. Field.
Speght, Rachel. (1616) *A Mouzell for Melastomus*. London: Nicholas Oakes.
Stuart, James. (1598 and 1603) *The True Law of Free Monarchies*. Edinburgh and London: Robert Waldegrave.
Stubbes, Philip. (1583) *The Anatomy of Abuses*. London: Richard Jones.
T. E. (1632) *The Law's Resolution of Women's Rights; or the lawes provision for women*. London: I. Moore.
Tilley, Morris Palmer. (1950) *A Dictionary of the Proverbs in the Sixteenth and Seventeenth Centuries*. Ann Arbor: University of Michigan Press.
Tofte, Robert. (1615) *The Blazon of Jealousy*. London: Thomas Snodham.

Secondary Texts

Adelman, Janet. (1992) *Suffocating Mothers: Fantasises of Maternal Origin in Shakespeare's Plays*. London: Routledge.
Alexander, Catherine M.S. and Wells, Stanley. (eds) (2000) *Shakespeare and Race*. Cambridge: Cambridge University Press.
Althusser, Louis. (2014) *On The Reproduction of Capitalism: Ideology and ideological State Apparatuses*. London: Verso Books. (First published in 1970.)
Arikha, Noga. (2007) *Passions and Tempers: A History of the Humours*. New York: Harper Collins.

Bibliography

Armstrong, Nancy. (1987) *Desire and Domestic Fiction: A Political History of the Novel*. Oxford: Oxford University Press.
Aughterson, Kate. (ed.) (1995) *Renaissance Woman: An Anthology of Sources and Documents*. London: Routledge.
Axton, Marie. (1977) *The Queen's Two Bodies: Drama and the Elizabethan Succession*. London: Royal Historical Society.
Bakhtin, M. M. [1968] 1984) *Rabelais and His World*, trans. Helene Iswolsky. Bloomington: Indiana University Press.
Baldwin, T. W. (1944) *William Shakspere's Small Latine and Lesse Greeke*. Chicago: University of Illinois Press.
Barber, C. L. (2011) *Shakespeare's Festive Comedy: A Study of Dramatic Form and its Relation to Social Custom*. Princeton: Princeton University Press.
Barroll, Leeds. (2001) *Anna of Denmark: Queen of England, A Cultural Biography*. University of Pennsylvania Press.
Belsey, Catherine. (1985) *The Subject of Tragedy: Identity and Difference in Renaissance Drama*. London: Routledge.
Belsey, Catherine. (2007) *Why Shakespeare?* London: Palgrave.
Berry, Phillipa. (1994) *Of Chastity and Power: Elizabethan Literature and the Unmarried Queen*. London: Routledge.
Berry, Phillipa. (1999) *Shakespeare's Feminine Endings*. London: Routledge.
Billing, Christian. (2008) *Masculinity, Corporality and the English Stage 1580-1635*. Farnham: Ashgate.
Blakemore Evans, G. (1988) *Elizabethan-Jacobean Drama: The Theatre in its Time*. London: A & C Black.
Blakemore, Colin and Jennett, Sheila. (eds) (2001) *The Oxford Companion to the Body*. Oxford: Oxford University Press.
Blocksidge, M. (2005) *Shakespeare in Education*. London: Continuum.
Bloom, Gina. (2007) *Voice in Motion: Staging Gender, Shaping Sound in Early Modern England*. Philadelphia: University of Pennsylvania Press.
Boone, Alan. (1989) *Tradition Counter Tradition: Love and the Form of Fiction*. Chicago: University of Chicago Press.
Bordo, Susan. (2003) *Unbearable Weight: Feminism, Western Culture and the Body*, 2nd edn. Berkeley: University of California Press.
Breitenberg, Mark. (1996) *Anxious Masculinity in Early Modern England*. Cambridge: Cambridge University Press.
Brook, Peter. (1968) *The Empty Space*. Harmondsworth: Penguin.
Bruster, Douglas. (1995) 'The Jailor's Daughter and the Politics of Madwomen's Language', *Shakespeare Quarterly*, 46: 277–300.
Browne, Kath and Lim, Jason. (eds) (2009). *Geographies of Sexualities: Theories, Practices and Politics*. London: Routledge.
Butler, Judith. (1992) *Gender Trouble*. London: Routledge.
Butler, Judith. (1993) *Bodies That Matter: Gender and the Discursive Limits of Sex*. London: Routledge.
Calaresu, Melissa and Van den Heuvel, Danielle. (eds) (2018) *Food Hawkers: Selling in the Streets from Antiquity to the Present*. London: Routledge.

Bibliography

Callaghan, Dympna. (2002) *Shakespeare Without Women: Representing Gender and Race on the Renaissance Stage*. London: Routledge.

Callaghan, Dympna. (ed.) (2016) *A Feminist Companion to Shakespeare*, 2nd edn. London: Blackwell.

Carlson, Marvin A. (2001) *The Haunted Stage: The Theatre as Memory Machine*. Ann Arbor: University of Michigan Press.

Carlson, Susan. (2006) 'Politicizing Harley Granville Barker: Suffragists and Shakespeare', *New Theatre Quarterly* 22(2): 122–140.

Cartelli, Thomas. (2019) *Re-Enacting Shakespeare in the Shakespeare Aftermath: The Intermedial Turn and Turn to Embodiment*. London: Palgrave.

Chamberlain, Prudence. (2017) *The Feminist Fourth Wave: Affective Temporality*. London and New York: Palgrave.

Chess, Simone. (2016) *Male to Female Cross-Dressing in Early Modern Literature*. London: Routledge.

Cochrane, Kira. (2013) *All the Rebel Women: The Rise of Fourth Wave Feminism*. London: Guardian Books.

Cox, John D. and Rasmussen, Eric. (2001) *King Henry VI Part 3* (3rd edn). London: Arden Shakespeare.

Crawford, Patricia. (2004) *Blood, Bodies and Families in Early Modern England*. London: Routledge.

Crawford, Patricia and Mendleson, Sara. (2000) *Women in Early Modern England 1550-1720*. Oxford: Oxford University Press.

Crenshaw, Kimberlé, et al. (eds) (1995) *Critical Race Theory*. New York: New Press.

Crystal, David. (2005) *Pronouncing Shakespeare*. Cambridge: Cambridge University Press.

Daileader, Cecilia R. (2005) *Racism, Misogyny, and the 'Othello' Myth: Inter-racial Couples from Shakespeare to Spike Lee*. Cambridge: Cambridge University Press.

Danson, Laurence. (2000) *Shakespeare's Dramatic Genres*. Oxford: Oxford University Press.

Dawson, Lesel. (2008) *Lovesickness and Gender in Early Modern English Literature*. Oxford: Oxford University Press.

de Certeau, Michel. (1984) *The Practice of Everyday Life*. Los Angeles: University of California Press.

de Sousa, Geraldo. (1999) *Shakespeare's Cross-Cultural Encounters*. London: Palgrave Macmillan.

Dionne, Craig and Kapadia, Patricia. (2016). *Native Shakespeares: Indigenous Appropriations on a Global Stage*. London: Routledge.

Dolan, Brian. (2001) 'The Great Chain of Being' in Blakemore, Colin and Jennett, Sheila (eds) *The Oxford Companion to the Body*, Oxford: Oxford University Press, 324.

Dolan, Frances. (2008) *Marriage and Violence: The Early Modern Legacy*. Philadelphia: University of Pennsylvania Press.

Dollimore, Jonathon and Sinfield, Alan. (1994) *Political Shakespeare: New Essays in Cultural Materialism*, 2nd edn. Manchester: Manchester University Press.

Dreyer, Diane Elizabeth. (1986) *Defiance and Domination: Fathers and Daughters in Shakespeare*. Lexington: University Press of Kentucky.

Bibliography

Dugaw, Dianne. (1989) *Warrior Women and Popular Balladry, 1650–1850.* Chicago: University of Chicago Press.

Duncan, Sophie. (2016) *Shakespeare's Women and the Fin-de-Siecle.* Oxford: Oxford University Press.

Egan, Gabriel. (2006) *Green Shakespeare: From Ecopolitics to Ecocriticsm.* London: Routledge.

Enke, Anne. (ed.) (2012) *Transfeminist Perspectives in and beyond Transgender and Gender Studies.* Philadelphia, PA: Temple University Press.

Enterline, Lynn. (1995) *The Tears of Narcissus: Melancholia and Masculinity in Early Modern Writing.* New York: Stanford University Press.

Finlay, Roger. (1981) *Population and Metropolis: The Demography of London 1580–1650.* Cambridge: Cambridge University Press.

Ford Davies, Oliver. (2017) *Shakespeare's Fathers and Daughters.* London: The Arden Shakespeare.

Forker, Charles R. (2002) 'Introduction', in Forker, Charles R. (ed.) *Richard II*, 3rd rev edn. London: The Arden Shakespeare.

Fortier, Mark. (2016) *Theory/Theatre: An Introduction.* London: Routledge.

Freud, Sigmund. (1900) *The Interpretation of Dreams.* New York: Basic Books.

Gallagher, Catherine. (1987) *The Making of the Modern Body.* Los Angeles: University of California Press.

Gamboa, Brett. (2018) *Shakespeare's Double Plays: Dramatic Economy on the Early Modern Stage.* Cambridge: Cambridge University Press.

Garber, Marjorie. (1992) *Vested Interests: Cross Dressing and Cultural Anxiety.* London: Routledge.

Gay, Penny. (1994) *As She Likes It: Shakespeare's Unruly Women.* London: Routledge.

Gordon, Andrew and Klein, Bernard. (eds) (2001) *Literature, Mapping, and the Politics of Space in Early Modern Britain.* Cambridge: Cambridge University Press.

Gosbee, Mark. (2001) 'Body Politic' in Blakemore, Colin and Jennett, Sheila (eds) *The Oxford Companion to the Body.* Oxford: Oxford University Press, 109.

Gowing, Laura. (1999) *Domestic Dangers: Women, Words and Sex in Early Modern London.* Oxford: Oxford University Press.

Gowing, Laura. (2000) 'The Freedom of the Streets: women and social space 1540-1640', in Jenner, Mark (ed.) *Londinopolis: Essays in the Cultural and Social History of Early Modern London.* Manchester: Manchester University Press, 130–53.

Grant Ferguson, Ailsa. (2019) *The Shakespeare Hut: A Story of Memory, Performance, and Identity.* London: Bloomsbury.

Greenblatt, Stephen. (1988) *Shakespearean Negotiations: The Circulation of Social Energy in Renaissance England.* Oxford: Oxford University Press.

Grosz, Elizabeth. (1995) *Space, Time and Perversion: Essays on the Politics of Bodies.* London: Routledge.

Grosz, Elizabeth. (2017) *The Incorporeal: Ontology, Ethics and the Limits of Materiality.* New York: Columbia University Press.

Hall, Kim. (1995) *Things of Darkness: Economies of Race and Gender in Early Modern England.* Ithaca: Cornell University Press.

Bibliography

Haraway, Donna. (2003) *The Companion Species Manifesto: Dogs, People, and Significant Otherness*. Chicago: Prickly Paradigm Press.

Haraway, Donna. (2016) *Staying with the Trouble: Making Kin in the Chthulucene*. Durham: Duke University Press.

Higginbotham, Derrick. (2014) 'The Construction of a King: Waste, Effeminacy and Queerness in Shakespeare's *Richard II*', *Shakespeare in Southern Africa*, 26: 59–73.

Howard, Jean E. and Rackin, Phyllis. (1997) *Engendering a Nation: A Feminist Account of Shakespeare's English Histories*. London/New York: Routledge.

Howard, Jean E. (2007) *Theatre of a City: The Places of London Comedy*. University of Pennsylvania Press.

Jardine, Lisa. (1983) *Still Harping on Daughters: Women and Drama in the Age of Shakespeare*. Brighton: Harvester.

Jardine, Lisa. (1992) 'Twins and Travesties: Gender, Dependency, and Sexual Availability in *Twelfth Night*' in Zimmerman, Susan, ed. *Erotic Politics: Desire on the Renaissance Stage*. London: Routledge, 27–38.

Kahn, Coppélia. (1981) *Man's Estate: Masculine Identity in Shakespeare*. Berkeley: University of California Press.

Kahn, Coppélia. (1991) *Roman Shakespeare: Warriors, Wounds and Women*. London: Routledge.

Kantorowicz, Ernst H. (1957) *The King's Two Bodies: A Study in Medieval Theology*. Princeton: Princeton University Press.

Kean, Danuta. (2018) 'Margot Robbie is Rethinking Shakespeare's Women. It's About Time', *The Guardian*, 27 March.

Kirwan, Peter. (2014) 'Review of Shakespeare's *Richard II* (dir. Gregory Doran, RSC), 29 October 2013', *Shakespeare*, 10(2): 197–200.

Korda, Natasha. (2002) *Shakespeare's Domestic Economies*. Philadelphia: University of Pennsylvania Press.

Korda, Natasha. (2011) *Labor's Lost: Women's Work and the Early Modern Stage*. Philadelphia: University of Pennsylvania Press.

Kristeva, Julia. ([1975] 1981) 'Women's Time', trans. Alice Jardine and Harry Blake, *Signs*, 7 (1, Autumn): 13–35.

Ladurie, Emmanuel le Roy. (1981) *Carnival in Romans: A People's Uprising at Romans 1579–80*. Harmondsworth: Penguin.

Lamming, George. (1960, 1984) *The Pleasures of Exile*. New York: Basic Books.

Laoutaris, Chris. (2008) *Shakespearean Maternities: Crises of Conception in Early Modern England*. Edinburgh: Edinburgh University Press.

LaRoche, Rebecca and Munroe, Jennifer. (2017) *Shakespeare and Ecofeminist Theory*. London: Bloomsbury.

Laroque, Francois. ([1988] 1991) *Shakespeare's Festive World: Elizabethan Seasonal Entertainments and the Professional Stage* trans. Janet Lloyd. Cambridge: Cambridge University Press.

Lefebvre, Henri. (1974) *The Production of Space*. Oxford: Blackwell.

Levine, Laura. (1994) *Men in Women's Clothes: Anti-Theatricality and Effeminization 1579–1652*. Cambridge: Cambridge University Press.

Bibliography

Long, Kathleen. (ed.) (2016) *Gender and Scientific Discourse in Early Modern Culture*. London: Routledge.
Loomba, Ania. (1998) *Shakespeare, Race and Colonialism*. Oxford: Oxford University Press.
Loomba, Ania and Sanchez, Melissa. (2016) *Rethinking Feminism in Early Modern Studies*. London: Routledge.
McNeil, Fiona. (2007) *Poor Women in Shakespeare*. Cambridge: Cambridge University Press.
Massey, Doreen. (1994) *Space, Place and Gender*. London: Polity.
Masten, Jeffrey. (2016) *Queer Philologies: Sex, Language and Affect in Shakespeare's Time*. Philadelphia: University of Pennsylvania Press.
Matthews-Grieco, Sara. (2018) *Cuckoldry, Impotence and Adultery in Europe*. London: Routledge.
McCluskie, Kathleen. (1989) 'The Patriarchal Bard: Feminist Criticism and Shakespeare: *King Lear* and *Measure for Measure*', in Dollimore, Jonathon and Sinfield, Alan (eds), *Political Shakespeare: New Essays in Cultural Materialism*. Manchester: Manchester University Press.
McPherson, Kathryn and Moncrieff, Kathryn. (2016) *Performing Maternity in Early Modern England*. New York: Routledge.
Maguire, Laurie and Smith, Emma. (2012) *Thirty Great Myths about Shakespeare*. Oxford: Wiley Blackwell.
Meek, Richard, and Sullivan, Erin. (2015) *The Renaissance of Emotion: Understanding Affect in Shakespeare and his Contemporaries*. Manchester: Manchester University Press.
Moncrief, Kathryn and McPherson, Kathryn. (2007) *Performing Maternity in Early Modern England*. Aldershot: Ashgate.
Moss, Pamela. (ed.) (2007) *Feminisms in Geography: Rethinking Space, Place and Knowledge*. Lanham: Rowman & Littlefield.
Mullaney, Steven. (1988) *The Place of the Stage: License, Play and Power in Renaissance England*. Ann Arbor: Michigan University Press.
Neely, Carol Thomas. (2004) *Distracted Subjects: Madness and Gender in Shakespeare and Early Modern Culture*. Ithaca: Cornell University Press.
Neely, Carol Thomas, Greene, Gayle and Lenz, Ruth. (eds) (1980) *The Woman's Part: Feminist Criticism of Shakespeare*. Urbana: University of Illinois Press.
Newman, Karen. (1991) *Fashioning Femininity and English Renaissance Drama*. Chicago: Chicago University Press.
Novy Marianne. (2019) *Shakespeare and Feminist Theory*. London: Bloomsbury, the Arden Shakespeare.
Orgel, Steven. (1996) *Impersonations: The Performance of Gender in Shakespeare's England*. Cambridge: Cambridge University Press University Press.
Paster, Gail Kern. (1993) *The Body Embarrassed: Drama and the Disciplines of Shame in Early Modern England*. Ithaca: Cornell University Press.
Rackin, Phyllis. (2005) *Shakespeare and Women*. Oxford: Oxford University Press.
Rackin, Phyllis. (2016) 'Misogyny Is Everywhere' in Callaghan, Dympna (ed.) *A Feminist Companion to Shakespeare* (2nd edn). London: Blackwell, 60–74.

Bibliography

Richardson, Catherine. (2011) *Shakespeare and Material Culture*. Oxford: Oxford University Press.

Rivers, Nicola. (2017) *Postfeminism(s) and The Arrival of the Fourth Wave: Turning Tides*. London: Palgrave.

Rose, Mary Beth. (1988) *The Expense of Spirit: Love and Sexuality in English Renaissance Drama*. Ithaca: Cornell University Press.

Rose, Mary Beth. (1991) 'Where Are the Mothers in Shakespeare? Options for Gender Representation in the English Renaissance'. *Shakespeare Quarterly* 42(3): 291–314.

Rubin, Gayle. (1975) 'The Traffic in Women: Notes on the "Political Economy" of Sex', in Reiter, Rainer (ed.), *Towards an Anthropology of Women*. Monthly Review Press, 157–210.

Schafer, Elizabeth. (2000) *Ms-Directing Shakespeare: Women Direct Shakespeare*. London: Palgrave, 2000.

Schulte, Regina. (ed.) (2006) *The Body of the Queen: Gender and Rule in the Courtly World, 1500-2000*. New York: Berghahn Books.

Schwartz, Kathryn. (2011) *What You Will: Gender, Contract and Shakespearean Social Space*. Philadelphia: University of Pennsylvania Press.

Scott, Joan W. (1986) 'Gender: A Useful Category of Historical Analysis', *The American Historical Review*, 91 (5): 1053–75.

Scott, Joan W. (2010) 'Gender: Still a Useful Category of Analysis?', *Diogenes*, 57 (1): 7–14.

Sedgwick, Eve Kosofsky. (1985) *Between Men: English Literature and Male Homosocial Desire*. New York: Columbia University Press.

Sedgwick, Eve Kosofsky. (1994) *Tendencies*. New York: Routledge.

Shapiro, Michael. (1996) *Gender in Play on the Shakespearean Stage: Boy Heroines and Female Pages*. Ann Arbor: University of Michigan Press.

Shepard, Alexandra. (2006) *Meanings of Manhood in Early Modern England*. Oxford: Clarendon Press.

Showalter, Elaine. (1985) 'Representing Ophelia: Women, Madness and the Responsibilities of Feminist Criticism', in Parker, Patricia and Hartman, Geoffrey (eds), *Shakespeare and the Question of Theory*. London: Routledge, 77–94.

Sinfield, Alan. (1992) *Faultlines: Cultural Materialism and the Politics of Dissident Reading*. Oakland, CA: University of California Press.

Singh, Jyotsna. (2017) *Shakespeare and Postcolonial Theory*. London: Bloomsbury Arden Shakespeare.

Smith, Bruce. (1995) *Homosexual Desire in Shakespeare's England: A Cultural Poetics*. Chicago: University of Chicago Press.

Smith, Bruce. (2000) *Shakespeare and Masculinity*. Oxford: Oxford University Press.

Smith, Emma. (2004) *Shakespeare's Histories*. Oxford: Blackwell.

Stanivukovic, Goran V. (ed.) (2017) *Queer Shakespeare: Desire and Sexuality*. London: Bloomsbury.

Tennenhouse, Leonard. (1986) *Power on Display: The Politics of Shakespeare's Genres*. London: Routledge.

Thompson, Ann and Taylor, Neil. (eds) (2016) *Hamlet*, rev. edn. London: The Arden Shakespeare.

Bibliography

Tillyard, E.M.W. (1943) *The Elizabethan World Picture*. London: Chatto & Windus.
Traub, Valerie. (1991) 'Desire and the Difference It Makes' in Wayne, Valerie (ed.), *The Matter of Difference*. Ithaca: Cornell University Press, 81–114.
Traub, Valerie. (1992) *Desire and Anxiety: Circulations of Sexuality in Shakespearean Drama*. London: Routledge.
Traub, Valerie. (2010) *The Renaissance of Lesbianism in Early Modern England*. Cambridge: Cambridge University Press.
Traub, Valerie. (2016a) *The Oxford Handbook of Shakespeare and Embodiment: Gender, Sexuality and Race*. Oxford: Oxford University Press.
Traub, Valerie. (2016b) *Thinking Sex with the Early Moderns*. University of Pennsylvania Press.
Wayne, Valerie. (1991) *The Matter of Difference: Materialist Feminist Criticism of Shakespeare*. Cornell University Press.
Weimann, Robert. (1978) *Shakesepeare and the Popular Tradition in the Theatre*. Baltimore: Johns Hopkins University Press.
Wells, Robin Headlam. (2000) *Shakespeare on Masculinity*. Cambridge: Cambridge University Press.
Wells, Stanley. (2009) '"Boys should be Girls": Shakespeare's Female Roles and Boy Players', *New Theatre Quarterly* 25 (2): 172–7.
Woodbridge, Linda. (1984) *Women and the English Renaissance: Literature and the Nature of Womankind 1540-1620*. Chicago: University of Illinois Press.
Yachnin, Paul. (2017) *Making Publics in Shakespeare's Playhouse*. Manchester: Manchester University Press.
Young, Iris Marion. (1984) 'Pregnant Embodiment: Subjectivity and Alienation'. *Journal of Medicine and Philosophy* 9 (1): 45–62.
Young, Iris Marion. (2005) *On Female Body Experience: 'Throwing Like a Girl' and Other Essays*. Oxford: Oxford University Press.
Zimmerman, Susan. (1992) *Erotic Politics: Desire on the Renaissance Stage*. London: Routledge.

INDEX

Adam and Eve 23, 159, 208, 217, 253
all-female Shakespeare productions 55–6, 61, 63, 85, 150
All's Well That Ends Well 13, 15, 88, 90–4, 222, 239–41, 252
   dir. Byrne 93, 97, 238, 241
   dir. Dove 241
Anatomy of Melancholy, The 131, 205, 206, 214
Andoh, Adjoa 5, 13, 60–3, 65–72, 257
androgyny 54, 55, 56, 123, 146
Antony and Cleopatra 15, 159, 179, 191–8, 231
   dir. Arich 198
anthropocentrism 170–3, 177
Arden of Faversham 74
As You Like It 13, 104–12, 119–20
   dir. Branagh 107
   dir. Donellan 106
   dir. Terry 105
Astell, Mary 4
audience 61–71, 73–4, 115, 231
   audience complicity 94, 157, 212, 233
   audience understanding 7, 13, 80, 85, 92, 142–4, 166
   direct address to 80, 82, 87, 90, 111
   early modern audience 43
   positioning 95–6, 119–20, 176, 186–7, 222, 228
   suspension of disbelief of 110
   within plays 128, 137–41, 150

Bakhtin, Mikhail 165
bed trick 91–3
Bible 24–5, 105, 181, 159, 208–10, 217, 253
birth 15–16, 49–51, 59, 160, 227, 233, 235–55
blazon 8–12, 19–20, 57, 90, 120, 147, 175
body 82, 123–31, 167, 216, 221, 254; *see also* body politic; humours; maternity
   actor(s)' bodies 3, 102, 111, 209
   black body 218
   disabled body 58–61, 64
   female body 8, 19, 51–2, 90–4, 101, 167, 182, 185, 194, 197–202, 232–9
   gendered body 6
   humoral body 205
   male body 7, 39–41
   monarch's body 45–7
   pregnant body 226, 232–6, 239–54
   unchaste body 30
   witch's body 232–3, 237
body politic 12–13, 39–64, 154, 163
boy actors 13, 15, 97–103, 107–13, 119–20
   boy actors' voices 146
Branagh, Kenneth 27–8, 107, 137, 141
breast 8, 10–11, 208, 226–7, 245
Brexit 1, 60, 62, 65, 174
Bright, Thomas 129–35, 142, 148–9
Burton, Robert *see Anatomy of Melancholy*
Butler, Judith 104, 239

carnivalesque 14, 24–5, 29, 105–6, 113, 119–20, 164–6, 176; *see also* festivity
casting 53, 55, 60, 85, 168
   all-female casting 85
   all-male casting 106, 238
   celebrity casting 89, 218, 237
   cross-casting 4, 55, 61, 85, 113, 186, 238–9
   doubling 80
   gender-blind casting 55, 124–6, 151
   politics of 14, 37, 174–5
   'race-blind' casting 61
   race-positive casting 198
characterization 4, 53, 90–5, 205–11, 228–9, 254
chastity 8–11, 19–20, 36, 51–2, 147, 200–1, 222; *see also* body
   as dangerous 216
   as ideal femininity 87–9, 95, 147, 170–1
Cheek by Jowl 106, 107, 225, 238
children 41, 57, 143, 236; *see also* patriarchy
   and fathers 159, 169–70, 191, 223, 231
   as heirs 251
   and mothers 79, 243–4, 252–4

Index

city comedies 182
colonialism 4–5, 65–72, 186, 192–8, 208
Comedy of Errors, The 15, 74, 182–6
    dir. McIntyre 185
comic plots 74–5
Coriolanus 253, 254
costume 70, 100, 120
Croll, Dona 62
cross-dressing 5, 13–14, 95, 97–121
crying 49–50, 58, 118–19, 198–200, 236
Cymbeline 121, 202, 220–222, 253

disability 58–60
divine right of kings 41–5, 57–8, 63, 159, 190
Dod, John and Cleaver, Robert 25, 29, 36, 162–6, 181–2
Donmar Trilogy 61

ecocriticism/eco-theory 170, 173, 177
Elizabeth I 42, 52, 101, 104, 118–19, 254
empire 61, 65, 69, 72, 194, 196, 254
Essex Rising 42
Eve 23, 208, 209, 213, 217, 253
Eyre, Richard 14, 156, 167, 174–5

folk-tales 92, 239, 243
fatherhood 154, 159, 163, 169, 170, 175, 241; *see also* maternity; patriarchy
female sexuality 15, 95, 188–91, 202, 252; *see also* body; sexuality
    policing of 139
    threats of 186
    valuation of 180
femininity 47–9, 106–7, 125–6, 214; *see also* body; masculinity; maternity
    as biological 203, 209, 216–17, 235, 238
    constructed 84, 95, 212
    and effeminacy 53, 236
    as land 201, 203
    as passivity 78, 81
    performative 113
    as redemptive 228
    unconventional femininity 87, 253
    as witchcraft 185, 232–3
feminist theory 2–5
festivity 20–4, 31, 37, 94, 96, 175–6, 188; *see also* carnivalesque
Fletcher, John 14, 131, 142–9
Foxe, John 33
Freud, Sigmund 208, 237, 238, 243

gaze 119
    female 25, 92
    homo-erotic gaze 99
    lesbian gaze 113, 116
    male 11, 19, 90, 147, 221–2
gender fluidity 119–20
gender 1–5, 67–71, 179–82, 232; *see also* casting; femininity; masculinity
    conformity 79, 84, 87–8, 94–6, 238–9
    and emotions 49, 135, 149, 168
    gendered metaphors 139
    insults 32
    and land 51, 202
    as performance 74, 85, 123–6, 208
    reversal of gender roles in plots 29
    transgressions 63–4, 97–121, 148, 177, 196
gender-blind 150
Gentillet 42–3
Gilbreath, Alexandra 238
Gosson, Stephen 179–80
great chain of being 45
greensickness 145, 151
Grymestone, Elizabeth 243

Hamlet 12, 14, 35, 45, 49, 73, 124, 127–51, 155, 171, 176, 208, 237, 239, 253–4
Henry IV Part 1 13, 51–2, 56
Henry V 13, 39, 49–50, 55–8, 64
Henry VI 15, 231–7
    dir. Cooke 236
Henry VIII 254
heteronormativity 5, 113–15; *see also* queer identities
    desire 99
    as 'norm' 53, 75
    through performance 113, 118–19, 210
    through plotting 13, 85, 89–90, 94–5, 99, 119
heterosexuality 13, 74–5, 93, 106, 107, 111, 112; *see also* heteronormativity; lesbian; queer
History plays 13, 230, 252, 253
Homily on the State of Matrimony 79–80
Homilies 79, 231
homoeroticism 13–14, 102–3, 107; *see also* boy actors
Hopkins, Antony 167, 174–5
humours 3, 22, 50, 120, 205, 209, 223
hysteria 26, 131, 142, 168

Index

James I 3, 190–1, 247
Jonson, Ben 97, 182
Jorden, Edward 131, 142, 148–9

Kanuta, Dean 1
King Lear 12, 14, 27, 151, 153–76
Kristeva, Julia 16

Lanyer, Aemilia 4, 23, 30, 246–7, 253
Leonard, Robert Sean 27
lesbian 113, 116
Lindsay, Nigel 54
Linton, Lynette 13, 60, 73, 75
Lloyd, Phyllida 56, 61, 85
Love's Labour's Lost 206–10, 228
lovesickness 14, 22, 132, 141–5, 149, 151

Macbeth 28, 35, 103, 107, 147–8, 151, 193, 201, 202, 229, 231, 253–4
madness 12, 26, 51, 127–51, 168, 172, 222
mapping *see* maps
maps 14, 51, 98–9, 153–4, 180, 186
marriage 13, 74–96, 119–20, 228; *see also* heteronormativity; marriage plot
  arranged by men 194–5
  celebrations 14
  as comic closure 37, 190, 227, 247
  as constraint 17
  as cure 148–9, 210
  feminizing of 222, 227, 240–1
  men's attitude to 37, 214
  mock-marriage 108
  queering of 14, 105
marriage plot 74–96
Marston, John 98–9, 182
  Antonio and Mellida 98–9
masculinity 2, 114, 120, 166, 205–30, 237; *see also* femininity; patriarchy
  adolescent 241
  attacks on 235
  as constructed 74–5, 95
  contemporary 89
  ideal 64
  and male friendship 93
  opposed to femininity 55, 78, 81, 86–7, 186, 192, 194, 233
  performed 100, 105, 107, 182
  theories of 208–9
maternity 15, 168, 231–54; *see also* fatherhood
matrilineage 173

McKellen, Ian 174
Measure for Measure 14, 15, 92, 122–6, 187–91, 238, 252
  dir. Elliot 89
  dir. Rylance 89
  dir. Sykes 122–6
  dir. Wheedon 89
Mehta, Prima 68–9
melancholy 127–51
Mendes, Sam 136–7
Merchant of Venice, The 35, 99–103
Merry Wives of Windsor, The 119, 121
metatheatricality 29, 80, 127, 128
Middleton, Thomas 97, 182
misogyny 1, 36, 88, 99
metonymy 23, 27, 49, 189, 198, 216, 221
mortality 19, 45, 50, 56
mothers 176, 231, 239; *see also* fatherhood; patriarchy
motherhood 231–56; *see also* fatherhood; maternity
  black motherhood 254
Much Ado About Nothing 12–13, 17–37, 58, 85–90, 94–6, 155–6, 160, 170, 222, 219

narratives 94–5; *see also* marriage plot
National Theatre 61
Norden, John 40–1
Nunn, Trevor 113, 115–16, 174, 188, 217–19

Okenedo, Sophie 236–7
original practices 55
Othello 15, 211–20
  dir. Nunn 217, 218, 219
  dir. Welles 218
Ove, Indra 61–2
Ovid 222

Patericke, Simon 42–3
pathetic fallacy 170
patriarchy 14, 29, 61, 62, 153–77, 228, 241; *see also* fatherhood; heteronormativity; homilies; James 1; maternity
patrilineage 14, 53, 153–5, 164, 171–2
penis 7; *see also* bodies; vagina
performativity 1, 5, 84
Pericles 15, 198–202, 222
Phelps, Lucy 14, 110, 122–6, 189–90
Philomela 222

269

Index

pregnancy 15, 16, 47–50, 59, 232–3, 237–41, 252–3; *see also* bodies; fatherhood; maternity; mothers
prostitution 52
Pugh, Florence 174
puns 7, 20, 49, 91, 140–1, 155

queer identities 99, 106–11, 208, 238, 239
queer readings 106–11, 115; *see also* heteronormativity; lesbian

Richard II 40–72
Richard III 58–60, 63–4
Romeo and Juliet 177
Rowling, J. K. 17
Royal Shakespeare Company 122
    As You Like It 122–6
    King Lear 164, 174
    Measure for Measure 14, 189
    Merry Wives of Windsor 120
    Much Ado About Nothing 89
    Othello 217, 218
    Richard II 15, 54
    Taming of the Shrew, The 4, 80–1, 85
    Twelfth Night 113, 115
    Two Noble Kinsmen, The 149
    Winter's Tale, The 225, 238, 246, 251
Royal Shakespeare Theatre; *see* Royal Shakespeare Company

Sam Wanamaker Playhouse 13, 60–2, 75, 93, 238
sexuality 2–5, 179–203; *see also* heteronormativity; maternity; queer identities
    and female agency 252–3
    female sexuality 95, 97, 180, 216, 220–2, 226–8
    links to gender 208
    and space 186–98
Shakespeare's Globe 65–72, 80, 85, 105, 150, 185, 190, 238, 241, 250–1
Sher, Anthony 225
Sidney, Philip 19–20
singing *see* song
Slade, Marie 56
Smith, Zadie 10
song 14, 70
    in *As You Like It* 111, 114
    in *Hamlet* 127, 131, 136–41, 150
    in *Much Ado About Nothing* 86–7, 95

    in *Othello* 147, 217
    in *Two Noble Kinsmen* 145–7
sonnets 5–11, 20, 47, 49, 118, 120, 147
    Sonnet 20 5–7, 47, 49, 118, 120
    Sonnet 130 8–11, 22
space 179–203
    female space(s) 49, 56, 96, 217, 243–4
    geographical space 52
    in *King Lear* 169
    stage space 13, 62, 67–9, 123, 139, 150, 210
    urban space 15, 179–203
Speght, Rachel 4, 31, 37, 217
Spenser, Edmund 8–11
Stubbes, Philip 103
Stubbs, Imogen 116, 217
suffrage, women's 4, 103
Suzman, Janet 5

Taming of the Shrew, The 1, 4, 13, 73–84, 96
    dir. Alexander 80
    dir. Bogdanov 4, 81, 85
    dir. Frow 80
    dir. Lloyd 85
Tempest, The 5, 14, 153, 171–2, 202, 253, 254
    dir. Miller 5
Ten Things I Hate About You 85
Tennant, David 54–5, 141
Terry, Ellen 103
Terry, Michelle 75, 105, 150
Thompson, Emma 28, 167, 174–5
tongue 19, 22, 28–34, 147, 149, 222
toxic masculinity 53
trans 7, 70, 113, 120, 237–9; *see also* feminist theory; queer identities
truth to power 30, 33, 35
Twelfth Night 13, 15, 112–19, 187–8
    dir. Godwin 113
    dir. Nunn 113
    dir. Supple 113
Two Noble Kinsmen, The 14, 127, 131, 142–50, 229
Two Gentlemen of Verona 100

vagina 7, 47, 49, 141, 155, 190

Walter, Harriet 46
Warner, Deborah 61
Watson, Emily 174
waves of feminism *see* feminist theory

Index

weeping *see* crying
Windrush scandal 60, 62, 72
Winter's Tale, The 12, 15, 16, 17, 30–5, 222–8, 242–52, 253
   dir. Donellan 225, 241
   dir. Doran 225, 238, 246, 251
   dir Hall 239
   dir. McIntyre 250, 251

witchcraft 60, 63, 148, 185–6, 215, 232–3, 249
Wollstonecraft, Mary 3, 4
womb 47–52, 166–8
   in *1 Henry VI* 232
   as metaphor for 'hysteria' 131, 148, 168
   as metonym for 'woman' 159–60, 168
Woolf, Virginia 11

www.ingramcontent.com/pod-product-compliance
Lightning Source LLC
Chambersburg PA
CBHW060946230426
43665CB00015B/2077